Plagiarism, Intellectual Property and the Teaching of L2 Writing

NEW PERSPECTIVES ON LANGUAGE AND EDUCATION

Series Editor: Professor Viv Edwards, *University of Reading, Reading Great Britain*
Series Advisor: Professor Allan Luke, *Queensland University of Technology, Brisbane, Australia*

Two decades of research and development in language and literacy education have yielded a broad, multidisciplinary focus. Yet education systems face constant economic and technological change, with attendant issues of identity and power, community and culture. This series will feature critical and interpretive, disciplinary and multidisciplinary perspectives on teaching and learning, language and literacy in new times.

Full details of all the books in this series and of all our other publications can be found on http://www.multilingual-matters.com, or by writing to Multilingual Matters, St Nicholas House, 31-34 High Street, Bristol BS1 2AW, UK.

Plagiarism, Intellectual Property and the Teaching of L2 Writing

Joel Bloch

MULTILINGUAL MATTERS
Bristol • Buffalo • Toronto

This book is dedicated to Milton and Ida Bloch.

Library of Congress Cataloging in Publication Data
A catalog record for this book is available from the Library of Congress.
Bloch, Joel.
Plagiarism, Intellectual Property and the Teaching of L2 Writing/Joel Bloch.
New Perspectives on Language and Education: 24
Includes bibliographical references and index.
1. English language–Study and teaching–Foreign speakers–Moral and ethical aspects.
2. Plagiarism. 3. English teachers–Professional ethics.
I. Title.
PE1128.A2B54 2012
808.02'5–dc23 2011048972

British Library Cataloguing in Publication Data
A catalogue entry for this book is available from the British Library.

ISBN-13: 978-1-84769-652-6 (hbk)
ISBN-13: 978-1-84769-651-9 (pbk)

Multilingual Matters
UK: St Nicholas House, 31-34 High Street, Bristol BS1 2AW, UK.
USA: UTP, 2250 Military Road, Tonawanda, NY 14150, USA.
Canada: UTP, 5201 Dufferin Street, North York, Ontario M3H 5T8, Canada.

The policy of Multilingual Matters/Channel View Publications is to use papers that are natural, renewable and recyclable products, made from wood grown in sustainable forests. In the manufacturing process of our books, and to further support our policy, preference is given to printers that have FSC and PEFC Chain of Custody certification. The FSC and/ or PEFC logos will appear on those books where full certification has been granted to the printer concerned.

Typeset by Datapage International Limited.
Printed and bound in Great Britain by Short Run Press Ltd.

Contents

Acknowledgments

I would like to thank Anna Roderick and the staff at Multilingual Matters, the Center for the Study of Teaching and Writing at The Ohio State University for their financial support, and Lan, Hannah and Moonlight for their moral support.

1 The Problem of Plagiarism

Art comes not out of the void, but chaos
Mary Shelley

The great French filmmaker René Clair was once asked whether Charlie Chaplin had plagiarized one of his films, *A Nous la Liberte*, in the making of *Modern Times*. Clair responded that if Chaplin had plagiarized him, he would have been honored. As Clair's response indicates, the definition of what is considered plagiarism and its effect on the creative process can be vague, inconsistent, confusing and highly contested. For writing teachers, the problem of plagiarism has emerged as one of the central pedagogical issues while, at the same time, presenting a unique opportunity for instruction.

Plagiarism refers to the inappropriate use of what is called intellectual property. In the United States, intellectual property is defined as creative acts that have been placed in a fixed medium. Intellectual property differs from physical property in that, with often complex restrictions, it can be borrowed, distributed and utilized without seeking the permission of the owner, something that would be a clear violation of the law in regard to physical property. Intellectual property is often given a fixed limit of protection, which is rarely true for physical property. Ideas, on the other hand, are not considered intellectual property unless they are placed in a fixed medium. Boyle (1996) argues that this concern for separating the idea and its expression is deeply rooted in concepts related to free speech: that the ability to express an idea should not be hampered by claims of ownership.

The use of intellectual property, both inside and outside the classroom, is governed by a myriad of often highly contested legal and ethical rules. Today, there has been much concern about violations of these rules, what are sometimes termed as the 'plagiarism epidemic' or the 'piracy' epidemic (Lessing, 2004, 2006). As will be discussed in more detail later, there is no general agreement as to whether such epidemics exist and, if they do, how they should be dealt with. Nevertheless, a variety of high-profile plagiarism scandals have permeated the news throughout the world. A study at an American university estimated that 18% of students plagiarize at some time, which increases to 31% for students scoring in the lower 25th percentile of the Student Aptitude Test (SAT), which many students need to take in order to enter university (Dee & Jacob, 2010). A poll at Cambridge University in Britain found that 49% of students admitted to cheating while only 5% admitted to having been caught (Sugden, 2008).

Surveys across universities often report similar estimates of presence of plagiarism; however, these estimates are not always matched by the number of students formally accused of plagiarism. In a survey of undergraduates in online courses in the United Kingdom, Selwyn (2008) found that more than 60% reported some instances of plagiarism. In the 2009–2010 school year, the Ohio State University, which has about 60,000 students, received 174 complaints of plagiarism (Coleman & Curry, 2010). The relatively low number may have resulted from the difficulty in identifying plagiarism or from the reluctance of instructors to involve themselves in the consequences of sending students to the academic misconduct committee (Curry, personal communication). The internet has often been cited as one of the key causes of this upsurge (see Howard, 2007). In a recent survey of teenagers in the United States, 36% reported using the internet for plagiarizing ('The Ethics', 2008).

This concern has not been limited to the West. Reports of cheating at Chinese college entrance exams have been widespread (Wong, 2009). A UNESCO publication entitled 'Corrupt Schools, Corrupt Universities: What Can Be Done?' (Hallak & Poisson, 2007) argues that plagiarism, as well as similar forms of academic corruption, is a worldwide phenomenon that involves people from a wide variety of backgrounds, including students, academics, journalists and politicians.

The growth of such reports has coincided with the growing Westernization of academic life throughout the world, particularly in areas such as publishing (Lillis & Curry, 2010), which has sometimes led to an importation of Western-style rhetoric regarding plagiarism. Often the rhetoric attached to plagiarism in non-Western cultures is also attached to the discussion of intellectual property. In many developing countries, there has been a pragmatic dimension to the concern over plagiarism, often viewing plagiarism as a threat to the credibility of the research rather than as a threat to academic integrity. A survey of the Higher Education Commission in Pakistan, for example, found that the fear of plagiarism has greatly hampered research at universities across Pakistan (Lodhi, 2010).

How plagiarism should be defined and dealt with has long been a controversial matter in L2 writing pedagogy (see Abasi *et al.*, 2006; Abasi & Graves, 2008; Bloch, 2001, 2008b; Deckert, 1993; Fox, 1994; Matalene, 1985; Ouelette, 2008; Pecorari, 2001, 2003, 2008; Pennycook, 1996; Sapp, 2004; Scollon, 1995, 1999; Shi, 2004, 2006; Stanley, 2002; Sunderland-Smith,

2008). The problems that L2 writers have with plagiarism have often been ascribed to a variety of possible reasons, some of them highly contradictory: a lack of understanding of the use of intellectual property (Deckert, 1993), a lack of knowledge about plagiarism (Pecorari, 2008), cultural differences in concepts of authorship (Fox, 1994; Scollon, 1995) and the consequences of particular cultural and historical developments (Bloch, 2001, 2008a; Pennycook, 1996; Scollon, 1995).

The Debate over Plagiarism

The lack of a consensus has led to highly charged, and often emotional, debates over the nature of plagiarism and the appropriate responses to it. Despite attempts by many institutions throughout the world, defining and codifying a universal definition of plagiarism has remained a highly contentious topic in discussions of almost every form of writing.

The debate has touched some of the most prestigious institutions and individuals in the world. Well-respected newspapers like the *New York Times* and the *Washington Post* have been shaken by controversies over plagiarism by its reporters. One of the most famous cases of plagiarism is that of US Vice-President Joe Biden, who copied from the British politician Neil Kinnock, a charge that Biden attributes to a 'lapse' (Greenberg, 2008). Recent cases have ensnared politicians in Germany (Weber-Wulff, 2011), the United States, Great Britain and Korea, where the Minister of Education was accused of plagiarizing a former student's paper and a famous pop singer was accused of copying a hit song. In Iran, a group of researchers responded to the charges, pointing out that much of the fraud has been perpetrated by politicians, who rely on academic credentials for professional advancement (Ardalan *et al.,* 2009).

Extensive publicity has been given to the plagiarized dissertation of Karl-Theodor zu Guttenberg, Germany's defense minister (Schuetze, 2011), which led to an online search for other instances in plagiarism among leading German individuals, which were then published on the *VroniPlag Wiki* (http://de.vroniplag.wikia.com). New technologies have created new forms of plagiarism and new kinds of excuses. Technology writer Chris Anderson was found to have copied a number of passages from Wikipedia without attribution, a charge he attributed to a 'screw-up' that could have resulted from the ease of cutting and pasting (Jaquith, 2009), a problem often seen in the work of the most inexperienced writers.

University faculty are often accused of plagiarism since they have many opportunities to indulge in plagiarism through their work with graduate students or as peer reviewers for journals and grant agencies since often there is little fear of punitive action. Senior faculty can plagiarize junior faculty. Grant or journal readers can plagiarize submitters. The number of graduate students plagiarized by their professors has been identified as a major problem in research work internationally (Haas, 2009). More and more academic journals are employing some form of plagiarism detection software, such as CrossCheck, to deal with plagiarism as the pressures to publish grow (Rampell, 2007), although such use may involve a different set of relationships than those found in a classroom.

Historians, for example, have had to reexamine their standards of what constitutes plagiarism after the accusations of plagiarism leveled against highly regarded historians such as Stephen Ambrose and Doris Kearns Godwin, who were both accused of not appropriately citing their sources. The field of medicine, in particular, has had a number of cases that have raised concerns about plagiarism. Scientific journals such as *The International Journal of Cardiology, Foot and Ankle Surgery* and the publications of the Royal School of Nursing have published articles about plagiarism and ethical guidelines in their field. Here again, the problem is worldwide.

Accusations of plagiarism in many fields have shown the inconsistency in how plagiarism is viewed. Some journalists have had their careers ruined by such accusation while others have received only a symbolic slap on the wrist. Many of our greatest artists – Woody Guthrie, Bertolt Brecht, Vladimir Nabokov and Bob Dylan – have all been accused of plagiarism at one time, yet their reputation as artists has never diminished. Such accusations are not new. As LaFollette (1992) pointed out, even Leonardo Da Vinci was accused of plagiarism. While plagiarism often arouses a great amount of anger, it has its humorous side as well. The humor website Cracked.com published an article called '5 Great Men Who Built Their Careers on Plagiarism' that spread widely on the internet.

The possibility of large financial settlements has led to a number of well-known authors being taken to court because of accusations of plagiarism, sometimes for specious reasons. Stephanie Myers, the author of a popular series of novels about vampires, was sued for plagiarizing plot devices, but the case was dismissed and the plaintive was admonished for bringing a frivolous suit. Authors, too, have sued those they feel have plagiarized their works. Before his death, J.D. Salinger sued another author for appropriating his most famous character, Holden Caulfield, for a sequel to *Catcher in the Rye*. J.K. Rowling sued one of her biggest fans for publishing a compendium of events in her Harry Potter series. She, in turn, was sued by the publisher of a little known book called *Willy the Wizard*, who claimed that:

> [b]oth Willy and Harry, the featured wizards in the respective works, are required to deduce the exact nature of the central task in the competition, . . . Both Willy and Harry uncover the nature of this central task covertly in a bathroom. (Sloan, 2010: para 6)

There is, in fact, no one more immersed in the world of copying and remixing than Rowling, with her work surrounded by large numbers of fan fiction on the one side and numerous derivative versions in various foreign languages (e.g. *Harry Potter and the Chinese Porcelain Doll*) on the other (Boon, 2010). The intense emotions surrounding plagiarism have often made it an ideal motive for murder plots in novels and television mysteries. The true case of the controversy over who owned the concept for Facebook was a major plotline in a highly popular movie called *The Social Network*. Facebook and other 'cloud' services, such as Dropbox where information can be stored, are themselves centers of controversy over their rights to use materials that have been uploaded in their sites.

In all these cases, the definition of plagiarism was not readily apparent even to serious scholars since what appears to be plagiarism to one person may be an act of creativity to another. One of the most controversial areas has been found in memoirs, where a number of writers have been accused of falsifying events (Bawarshi & Reiff, 2008). There are also situations where plagiarism may be acceptable. Business managers may want their team members to plagiarize each other's goals to show they are on the same page. Lawyers may want their briefs plagiarized by judges as a vindication of their arguments (see Volokh, 2011). A law student may need to be concerned with plagiarism because he or she is being judged on his or her ability to think, but, for a lawyer, plagiarizing may be a more efficient and cheaper way to serve a client than starting from the scratch (Peterson & Gregor, 2011). Employers who own the intellectual property created by their employees under the principle of 'work for hire' can then 'plagiarize' their work.

Questions have similarly arisen over whether syllabi or online course materials should be treated as a form of intellectual property and are, therefore, controlled under work for hire. If so, can the employer use them in any way they want to? In scientific journals, the various ways in which different researchers may contribute to a project has sometimes resulted in confusion regarding the levels of responsibility each author has (LaFollette, 1992), which led some journals to create guidelines for determining who is an author ('Uniform Requirements', 2010). In one case, a university was accused of plagiarizing its honor code from the Center for Academic Integrity, the director of the center defended the action, responding:

> Perhaps the key point is that originality is not a desideratum of an honor code. That honor codes on various campuses are the same – even word for word–is a good thing. (Wueste, 2008: para 6)

Inherent in all these cases is the question of who is the author and what rights does the author have. However, as the response from Rene Clair illustrates, much of the complexity in all these cases results from the inherent intertextuality of the writing process, that is, how the texts are weaved together with new ideas. In his essay, 'The Ecstasy of Influence', Jonathan Lethem (2007), echoing the words of Rene Clair, celebrates this complexity:

> Any text that has infiltrated the common mind to the extent of *Gone with the Wind* or *Lolita* or *Ulysses* inexorably joins the language of culture. A map-turned-to-landscape, it has moved to a place beyond enclosure or control. The authors and their heirs should consider the subsequent parodies, refractions, quotations, and revisions an honor, or at least the price of a rare success. (para 52)

Not everyone recognizes parody as an honor, as illustrated by the lawsuits by the heirs of Margaret Mitchell, the author of *Gone with the Wind*, against an African-American writer, Alice Randall, who parodied the novel by retelling it from the point of view of the slaves. As Mary Shelley's quote suggests, *chaos* is a useful word for describing the present state of the controversy over plagiarism.

All of these various forms of authorship problematize the question of what is the appropriate form of textual borrowing and, consequently, what should be considered plagiarism and what should be considered a creative act. On one side of this debate are those who see plagiarism as a threat to the moral structure of academic integrity. On the other side, there are those who see plagiarism as part of the learning process and even a new form of textuality (Howard, 1999; Pecorari, 2008). The controversy has been intensified by the growth of new forms of digital literacy on the world wide web, some of which have been developed through the integration or 'remixing' of existing internet materials and, in turn, greatly exacerbating the problem.

According to Lessing, one of the most often cited examples of the transformative power of remixing texts can be seen in 'The Grey Album', which was created by the rap artist Danger Mouse. In this remix, music from the Beatles 'White Album' is mixed with music from Jay-Z's 'Black Album'. Johnson-Eilola and Selber (2007) have argued that these remixes can be considered a new form of textuality, which requires new concepts of plagiarism that incorporates the unique characteristics of the genre. Patchwriting (e.g. Howard, 1999; Hull & Rose, 1989) itself can be seen as a form of remixing or as a form of what has been called 'mosiac plagiarism'. The migration of terms like 'patchwriting', which originated in the field of college writing, to discussions in scientific journals describing the problem with the replication of articles (e.g. Couzin-Frankel & Grom, 2009) also illustrates how far this debate has spread.

Despite the concern for these various forms of textual borrowing, the concept of plagiarism has not been well understood either by students or even experienced faculty (Roig, 2001; Roy, 1999). Pecorari (2001) found in a study of the official policies toward plagiarism in the United States, the United Kingdom and Australia that even when there was a universal agreement that plagiarism was wrong, there were many variations and omissions in views about exactly what constitutes plagiarism. Sunderland-Smith (2008) similarly found wide disagreements within her department in Australia.

At the institutional level, it is often difficult to implement a consistent definition. In an interview, which will be discussed in more detail later, the head of the Committee on Academic Misconduct at our university expressed dismay over the variety of definitions professors had used in their accusations of plagiarism since this inconsistency had made it difficult to find appropriate and consistent penalties. Understanding the boundaries between the appropriate and inappropriate use of texts may not be clear even to experienced writers. As the American author Kevin Kopelson (2008) wrote:

> Is there–for me–a difference between... [the] 'creative process' and 'simple larceny'? Or rather, between creative process and not so simple larceny. Between process and, oh–just *write* it!' (to quote Elizabeth Bishop)–plagiarism. (para 5)

The task of translating this dilemma into a clear policy that students understand can be daunting.

Price (2002) found that even when there was a consistent policy, it was often vaguely defined and, despite various attempts, difficult to operationalize in the classroom. For example, she argued that the meanings of statements such as 'write in your own words' can be problematic even for native English speakers. It can be difficult to define what 'in your own words' mean? Trying to decide how many words constitute an act of plagiarism has likewise been frustrating. Given the large number of 'chunks' or lexical bundles that exist in English (Hyland, 2008), which words should be counted in trying to determine plagiarism can add another level of complexity.

As will be discussed throughout this book, the growth of the internet has undoubtedly raised new questions about how traditional boundaries apply to new forms of digital literacy. Do rules for attribution to print-based texts hold true for blogs or multimedia forms of literacy? What about tweets and text messages? How do these new technologies challenge our definitions of plagiarism? Such inconsistencies can cause confusion and consternation, particularly among students who may feel that the system is unfair. Such complexity, along with the fears of the 'piracy epidemic' and the 'plagiarism epidemic', has sometimes constrained teachers from using intellectual property found on the internet. For example, many teachers restrict student use of the internet, both because of their own relative lack of experience with using it and a fear that student use may result in charges of plagiarism and violations of intellectual property law.

Instances of plagiarism can spark intense and highly emotional debates, particularly those surrounding highly controversial political issues. The firing of an instructor in Texas who publicly humiliated students whom he had accused of plagiarism by publishing their names set off an emotional debate both inside and outside the university over whether administrators were responding strongly enough to what they considered to be a plagiarism epidemic and, on the other hand, whether student rights had been violated (Jaschik, 2008).

The depth of the emotion can often be illustrated by the metaphors used to frame the discussion (Lakoff & Johnson, 1980). The frequent use of such terms as 'epidemic', 'piracy' and 'thievery' has often framed acts of copying as a moral action, regardless of the motivation for the action. The criminal narrative implied in this metaphor often appears in discussions of plagiarism. In this posting, in support of the faculty member who had published the name of students caught plagiaizing, this commenter wrote:

> I've always thought it strange that university administrations (a) say that students need to be severely punished for plagiarism as a deterrent

to others, and (b) keep the punishments secret when they are imposed. The identity of criminals is not kept secret in the outside world, so why in academia?

Many who participated in this discussion used terms like 'thievery', 'criminal activity' and 'fraud' to defend the actions of the professor. Given this moral framework, publicizing plagiarists in the same way one publicizes other criminal acts would seem logical, regardless of the issues related to the privacy of the students and, perhaps more important, the pedagogy of teaching writing.

All such instances of copying, ranging from handing in a paper downloaded from the internet to copying a few words or sentences or even taking someone else's ideas, have been uniformly seen as a 'crime', whether it be 'stealing' or 'fraud' (Posner, 2007). This passion reflects the widespread concern over plagiarism that it is a threat to both academic integrity and the learning process in general. As Couser (2009) writes in an 'open letter' to a student who had plagiarized in his class:

> The reason that plagiarism like yours makes professors so sad – and, yes, sometimes mad – is that it entirely defeats our attempts to educate you. We work hard to put you in a position to reach understandings that you would not otherwise be able to attain. (This is what makes a real course a *course*.) Cannibalizing a source like *SparkNotes* [a website that provides summaries of literary works] is not 'extra research' for which you should be lauded (as you claim); on the contrary, it's a *substitute* for (and the very antithesis of) the intellectual work that you were asked to do, and which your professors see as being at the heart of a liberal arts education. The opposite of academic honesty is not actually academic dishonesty; it's dishonesty that is decidedly unacademic. To commit it is to suggest that you don't understand, or don't value, the kind of education for which you (or your parents) are paying so much. The problem is not so much rule breaking as point missing. (para 11)

Many other teachers and researchers, however, feel this professor's indignation is misplaced and that plagiarism is not as clear-cut as he implies. Thus, teachers are often left with many questions, as well as emotions, regarding the instances of possible plagiarism they frequently see in their classrooms.

Why Do Students Cheat?

It is no wonder, therefore, that the question 'Why do students cheat?' has long been of great interest, both as a means for understanding the nature of plagiarism and as a basis for creating policies for dealing with such accusations. McCabe *et al.* (2001) identified a variety of moral factors (e.g. the presence of an honor code, pressure from peers, perceptions of the chances for being caught) that contribute to deciding whether a student cheated. McCabe, the founder of the Center for Academic Integrity (http://www.academicintegrity.org), argues that plagiarism arises from a 'cheating culture' that exists on many campuses. He states:

> I think for many students it is a question of fundamental fairness. They see other students cheat. They are convinced that the faculty member knows what is going on. They don't see the faculty member do anything about it, and they decide for themselves they don't want to just sit there and watch these students get better grades and better GPAs, get accepted into better colleges, and have their parents happier about their academic performance.... Almost, an indirect, subtle peer pressure. (cited in Levine, 2001: 12)

A variety of other factors have also been explored as possible causes for plagiarism. In Marsden *et al.*'s (2005) study of different types of 'cheating' among Australian students, they found that 81% plagiarized, which they attributed to a variety of factors (e.g. sex, age, year of study and self-efficacy).

Other approaches examine the culture of the university as a factor in influencing plagiarism. Blum's (2009) study of plagiarism in an American university examined many aspects of university life, ranging from attitudes toward copying and grades to personal concerns about time and finances, as potential contributing factors to their attitudes towards plagiarism. Some students copy simply to 'get by', by appropriating textual material to fulfill what they see as the requirements of their course assignments. Students may be encouraged to cheat if they feel they will not be caught. Szabo and Underwood (2004) found that a large number of students felt that their tutors could not detect their plagiarism. Such attitudes and perceptions could become part of the decision-making process regarding the use of intellectual property by disregarding the potential risk of committing plagiarism. In such situations, the cooperation that both faculty and their students want in their relationships breaks down.

Blum uses the term 'performance self' (61) to describe how students, who feel they are under tremendous pressure to do well on assignments they have no vested interest in, will plagiarize to complete the assignment in the most efficient and beneficial way. Ritter (2005) has argued that this detachment from the goals of the classroom as well as from the institutional norms of the university can cause students to use paper-mill sites like schoolsucks.com to download papers that they could later pretend they had written.

Often students do not share or understand the goals their teachers have for their writing assignments. Plagiarism may also result from developmental factors. Students may not have the level of reading or writing skills necessary for university-level work (e.g. Pecorari, 2008). In their study of native English speaking writers, Howard *et al.* (2010) present data from their 'Citation Project' (http://citationproject.net) that show that the problem can be found in the difficulties students have in understanding and summarizing the source texts they are using in their writing.

Students often seem confused about the standards expected of them. As one student wrote in our class blog about his experiences with plagiarism:

Yes, frankly I plagiarized so many time in my former school. ...
Sometimes, I plagiarized by cut and pasted the paper ... and sometimes
I listed the internet sources or magazines to my research paper. ...
Moreover, I just turned in somebody's paper to the professor by changing
original name to my name. ... I knew that was not good but I did not
realize that it was against academic rule and it was a plagiarism. ... I also
did not get an education about plagiarism. That is why I did it. And,
sometimes when I did not have any idea about the paper or assignment
and I did not have an enough time to finish of it, I plagiarized.[1]

This student expresses a variety of, and sometimes contradictory, reasons for an action that many consider to be a simple act of theft. The student's response also raises complex questions about student attitudes toward plagiarism. How should teachers judge the work of students who plagiarize but have seemingly little understanding of what they did? Is such plagiarism a moral problem, a pedagogical problem, or a combination of both? Should this student's plagiarism be seen as an act of laziness or unwillingness to do the assignment or an act of resistance to the frustrations students may feel about assignments they cannot understand? Did he understand how plagiarism was defined? Did he commit plagiarism with the intention to cheat or because he was frustrated by the assignment and did not know how to cope with that frustration? Should students be punished for such actions? If so, Should any of these concerns matter when determining a punishment?

Another student in their study felt that international students, such as herself, lacked experience in using source materials in a way that meets practices in UK universities, and, therefore, do not understand the nature of plagiarism. She relates, 'It never occurred to us that we needed to go out to look for materials and references to prepare for our writing, which was very important in writing essays here' (349). Sapp (2002) discusses how EFL teachers working in China may encounter not only many instances of what they consider plagiarism but also an attitude among students that there is nothing wrong with what they have done. Pecorari (2008) found many instances of students from different cultures who thought that such copying was an important part of the language-learning experience.

Teachers often feel frustrated by the seeming intractability of the problem. On a listserv for English as second language (ESL) teachers, one teacher posted a message about how the problem has persisted despite spending considerable class time discussing the topic:

> Many of us have had the experience of discussing plagiarism and its repercussions, then teaching paraphrasing, summarizing, using citations, etc.–only to find that students don't take this matter seriously. Last semester, I nailed a grad student for plagiarizing much of a section and if I had had the time, I probably could have found more instances in her paper. While her advisor was fairly appalled, he seemed to think that because she had cited her sources (even though she had failed to paraphrase) that her offense was of a lesser nature. Her defense was 'I didn't have enough time', which was probably true because I knew she was behind in her reading and her first draft was extremely weak. (Meltzer, cited in Stanley, 2002, para 15)

This teacher's narrative illustrates how such cases are conflated into one moral issue. Although there could be many possible explanations for the problem, this teacher feels that the students did not take the lessons about plagiarism 'seriously', as illustrated by their repeated offenses. This use of expressions such as 'nailed' reveal the moral nature that is pervasive in this discussion about plagiarism. The teacher seems to feel even more frustrated that the advisor, while being 'appalled' by the plagiarism, does not seem to feel that this particular act was serious since the sources were cited and, therefore, presumably, there was no intent to defraud, which can be a factor in determining plagiarism as well as the severity of the act (e.g. Posner, 2007). Of course, copying itself may sometimes be a creative act and not simply an act of deception (Boon, 2010). However, not everyone would agree as to what is the boundary between acceptable and unacceptable copying. Cultural differences in defining copying, as will be discussed next, may further complicate the distinction.

Cultural Perspectives on Plagiarism

In the 'stories' about plagiarism narrated previously, there is an interesting intermingling of developmental and cultural factors that are recognized by both teachers and students as possible causes of the problem. Culture has long been in the foreground of how we think about plagiarism. Lunsford and Ede (1994) discuss culture in their argument that the teaching of plagiarism has been often tied to the type of writing instruction that values solitary and individualistic authorship over collaborative authorship, issues that have been tied to cultural differences.

The studies by Hull and Rose (1989) and Blum (2009) have examined plagiarism as a cultural phenomenon that has arisen, at least in part, in the conflicts between the norms and values of the students and their teachers. Hull and Rose describe the case of an African-American nursing student who they felt plagiarized as a means of appropriating a new language to see how she would later sound as a member of her new social community.

Culture has been seen as an even greater factor when discussing students whose home cultures may differ from the dominant Western cultures that have largely shaped attitudes toward plagiarism and intellectual property. Of all the factors underlying the discussion of 'Why do L2 writers cheat?' culture has probably been the most prominently discussed. Often when L2 writers plagiarize, it is the cultural, not the developmental, factors that are primarily given as a possible cause of plagiarism by non-Western writers. The discussion of cultural factors in second-language writing has its origins in what Robert Kaplan (1966) first called contrastive rhetoric. Since then plagiarism has been one of the critical areas of controversy in the general study of what Connor (2004) defines today as intercultural rhetoric.

How one views the role of culture in the study of plagiarism will ultimately depend on how one views the plasticity of culture. Assumptions about culture have often depicted issues such as plagiarism as being deeply hardwired into our practices; that is, these practices are uniform and unchanging. However, alternative metaphors for the transmission of culture, such as the use of 'memes' (e.g. Dawkins, 1976) to conceptualize culture as packets of information like DNA are transmitted from one generation to the next. These packets can affect behavior but do not determine it. Therefore, culture can be viewed as being more plastic and changeable.

The historical study of intellectual property, as will be discussed later, can show how attitudes and practices toward the use of intellectual property have changed over the years and challenge the more deterministic connections between culture and attitudes toward intellectual property law and plagiarism. What then is it about the culture that affects how writers integrate source texts into their own writing? Culture can affect the rules for citation, how a student learns a language, or the nature of the educational system in which the writer has been taught. As a result, there can be variations in attitudes even among individuals who share the same cultural memes, which does not mean that there will be no cultural differences, since no two cultures will necessarily share the same history. However, the recognition of this historical factor, as will be argued in more detail later, remains important for our understanding of how plagiarism can be addressed in the classroom.

One of the first articles that identified culture as a factor in the discussion of plagiarism was written by Matalene (1985). She argued that among Chinese students, plagiarism could result from the traditional practice of copying and memorizing texts, a learning strategy dating back to the teachings of Confucius. Matalene linked these cultural practices to how the Chinese viewed intellectual property as collectivistic as opposed to the Western view of intellectual property as individualistic, a dichotomy that has since been sharply criticized as being overly simplified and essentialized in how it defines non-Western rhetorics (Bloch, 2008b).

Despite the criticism, the importance of these cultural factors has persisted. The growing economic competition between China and the West, for instance, has highlighted the importance of these cultural differences in both their educational approaches and their treatment of intellectual property. It is perhaps inevitable that developments in these areas have taken differing paths because of the different social, historical and economic events occurring in different cultures. In their study of traditional and contemporary Chinese rhetoric, Bloch and Chi (1995) discussed examples of classical Chinese disputation where writers would intertwine various texts from the canon of the sages with their own arguments, with no obvious forms of attribution, a process akin to patchwriting. Patchwriting has, of course, long been valued in cultures such as Chinese (Bloch, 2008). In this kind of rhetorical context, where there was a small, clearly defined audience, the authors may have felt that attribution was not necessary since there is assumed to be a high level of familiarity with the source texts, a strategy that can reflect an important cultural perception of the audience.

However, this approach can be problematic when transferred to Western academic practices because of the lack of a consistent view of attribution. In my study of plagiarism among Chinese students, one writer recalled how during the Cultural Revolution, a time when misquoting the correct political line could be extremely costly, he plagiarized the writings of the Communist Party (CCP) leaders to ensure he expressed the correct ideas. For this student, plagiarizing was a valuable means of survival as well as being consistent with traditional approaches to learning (Bloch, 2001).

For L2 writing teachers, questions regarding all the uses of intellectual property can be seen as an extension of larger issues regarding the role English plays in global contexts (see Brutt-Griffler, 2002; Phillipson, 1992). Speaking of EFL writers, Pennycook (1996) argues that how texts are borrowed covers a variety of social and cognitive aspects of second-language learning, including the development of an authorial voice, views of varieties of English across the world and differences in the historical development of intellectual property. He is particularly concerned with how Western perceptions of these issues are often forced upon students in non-Western cultures.

This 'otherness' of non-Western cultures often perpetuates certain stereotypes of international students. Our university handbook for international students seems to confirm this view that students from non-Western cultures are 'different':

In the United States, ideas are considered the property of their author. It is considered stealing to use the ideas of another in a paper or presentation without giving the credit to the originator of the idea. . . . Americans value originality and individual achievement. These values are reflected in the rules of academic honesty. (p. 14)

That this apparent dichotomy between Western and non-Western values requires such a precise definition can easily be interpreted by international students as meaning that other cultures, including theirs, do not value originality and, therefore, may be 'inferior', when, in fact, originality may be defined differently in the same way that different fields or genres may define originality in different ways (Bloch, 2008b).

Recent cases of plagiarism involving international students in the United States have highlighted the possible problems that such perceptions of culture may pose. For example, a large group of international students at Ohio University were accused of plagiarizing parts of their dissertation, and in turn, the degrees of some of them had been rescinded (Lederman, 2006). Often international students seem to be subjected to a double standard regarding plagiarism. At Duke University, although a large number of students were accused of plagiarism, only the international students among them were expelled (Redden, 2007).

The differences in the severity of the punishment raise both pedagogical and legal questions of whether it was fair that international students were penalized more than the students who are native English speakers. The lawyer for the international students argued that they may not only have misunderstood the definition of plagiarism but also may not have known the appropriate way to apologize, which may have been another cultural reason so many students were expelled. In the previous discussion of the instructor who posted the names of his students, it was noted that all of the students had Spanish surnames, although the implications of this incident could not be determined.

Even institutions that may be trying to demonstrate a certain amount of sensitivity to these 'differences' often become perpetrators of such cultural stereotyping as our university handbook illustrates. Not everyone, of course, believes that culture should even be considered a factor in judging cases of plagiarism, particularly when such differences may undermine traditional values. In response to the incidents at Duke, one anonymous commentator posted that culture was no excuse for plagiarism:

> American universities, especially the elite ones like Duke, are the most sought after in the world. Their graduates should exemplify high ethical standards and values. (Etter, cited in Redden, 2007)

The language of this posting illustrates the threat that some see plagiarism posing to the moral standards of the university as well as the concern for upholding traditional values against the 'threat' that comes from other cultures.

The value given to collaboration in writing is another factor frequently used to explain the cultural differences. For example, our university's handbook for international students implies that:

> [i]n many cultures, it is common for students to collaborate on papers and projects. In the United States, it is forbidden to do so unless the professor states that the paper or project is to be worked on in groups. ('International Students': 4)

This assumption itself is highly controversial, since there are clearly many areas of writing where collaboration is the norm (e.g. Howard, 1999). In business or technical writing, both of which are of particular importance in ESP (English for specific purposes) teaching, collaboration is the norm. In academic writing, the degree of collaboration can vary greatly across disciplines. Moreover, what is meant by collaboration can vary according to both genre and discipline. Collaboration in a blog often refers to a group of individual voices contributing to a single form, while collaboration according to a page in Wikipedia refers to a blending of voices. Writers working collaboratively in the social sciences may mean something different than working together in the natural sciences, where each individual may have a specific role. Therefore, there may be a false contradiction between individualism and collaboration that can place students in a cultural bind between their own cultural values and those being imposed by the institution, which is why some see plagiarism as a form of resistance to being forced into such a bind (e.g. Pennycook, 1996).

Traditional approaches to discussing cross-cultural differences in such varied and complex contexts have often been criticized for ignoring the more nuanced nature of intercultural comparisons (Connor, 2004). Contrary to the often stated attitudes that there is no concern with plagiarism in the Chinese educational system, it has been found that the issue predates the concern for plagiarism in the West by more than 1000 years. For example, the establishment of the examination system in China during the T'ang dynasty (618–907) for advancing in government positions led to numerous cases of plagiarism. Miyazaki (1976) writes that if there were so many identical answers that it appeared that each was copied from the same model, all candidates were failed for 'recopying' (*lui-t'ung*). There is an old Chinese poem about the creative act that perhaps sarcastically reflects this concern for copying:

Memorizing 300 poems from the Tang dynasty,
Even if you don't know how to write,
You can steal the pieces to write a poem. (cited in Bloch, 2008: 223)

Unlike what is commonly assumed in the West, such 'cutting and pasting', which may be considered in Chinese education a useful first step in the writing process, is not considered to be the highest level of creativity.

Today, the Chinese view of plagiarism is far from monolithic. As the often intense debate over recent cases of plagiarism has shown, there is clearly a concern for plagiarism even though plagiarism may not be defined in the same way it is defined in the West. The problems of plagiarism in China has even been a topic for the National Unified Entrance Examination (NUEE), which is a test (*gao kao*) given once a year to determine which students can enter college and which college the students can attend. In the

Chinese language section of the 1984 examination, the following prompt was given:

> Some students say, 'When we are to write a composition, we often feel that we have nothing to say and can only hash some empty talk or cook up some materials to make a cut-and-paste essay.' On the other hand, some of the teachers said, 'Every time the students write compositions, I take great pains to correct and comment on them. However, the students do nothing more than glance at the score, paying little attention to the problems in their compositions. Therefore, they make little progress in writing.' (23)

This kind of 'cut-and-paste' writing strategy seems also to be as great a concern to Chinese educators as it is to their Western counterparts.

My own interests in studying the subtle cultural relationships directly resulted from the article by Matalene (1985). When I was teaching in China, my aunt mailed me the copy of *College English*, the journal where the article was published, which I then, perhaps ironically, had copied and given to my students who were preparing to be English teachers. A few hours later, a group of them, who had been offended by what she had written, were banging on my door, demanding to know whether I agreed with Matalene (Bloch, 2008a). I was fascinated by their passion for the topic, although my cultural linguistics professor would later remind me that when you tell someone they are 'different', they often interpret such differences as meaning they are 'inferior'.

A second incident would then reinforce how emotional this relationship between culture and intellectual property was for me. At a dinner with my then new Chinese father-in-law, a professor of art history, I remarked how consistent Chinese painting had remained for more than 1000 years. He stingingly rebuked me, saying, 'There is nothing consistent about it.' From this rebuke, I painfully learnt that what one may see as imitation in one culture may be seen as something highly original in another culture. Similar to how cultural differences have traditionally been discussed in regard to plagiarism, I assumed that the Chinese perception of originality was considered the 'Other' of the Western concept. What I missed by focusing only on the differences was how much the artist went beyond copying. As Confucius put it thousands of years before, copying is easy, but reflection is much more difficult.

In this exchange, I was guilty of assuming a monolithic view of Chinese culture. Speaking of the view of Chinese language sometimes found in Western culture, Tong (2008) writes that '[t]he Western idea of the

Chinese language is a system of quotations; quotations are repetitions. It is a remarkably unitary discourse, at least because it is a system of quotations' (508). These quotations are at the center of the cultural controversy. Are they simply copying them or are they interweaving their own ideas, 'standing on the shoulders of giants' so to speak.

There are many contradictory arguments to the role culture plays in this discussion. Pecorari's (2003, 2008) studies of patchwriting seem similar to what Howard and her colleagues have found in their study of first-language writers in the Citation Project. Thus, patchwriting could be seen as primarily a developmental issue. However, Pecorari found that there were cultural reasons for patchwriting, such as a greater importance to copying as a language learning strategy, which may not be applicable to first-language writers. Shi similarly found variations in attitudes toward textual borrowing between native English speakers and Chinese speakers (2004) and among L2 writers with different cultural backgrounds (2006).

Since we are concerned here with the connection between plagiarism and intellectual property, it is useful to note that this interaction between history and culture can be also seen in the assumptions regarding cross-cultural attitudes toward intellectual property. It is often assumed, for example, that the widespread copying of information and instances of piracy have meant that the Chinese have no concept of intellectual property; however, a closer examination of the historical trends of intellectual property in China challenges that assumption. Alford (1995) argues that the Chinese have a long tradition of intellectual property but that these concepts were based upon a Confucian tradition that deemphasized authorship and a political tradition that emphasized the state control of the distribution of ideas, a situation unlike that found in the United States, where concepts of intellectual property developed from both an acknowledgment of the economic rights of ownership and the desire to spread information for the betterment of society.

The role of culture in regard to plagiarism and the nature of intellectual property, therefore, can be a complex issue that is difficult to pin down. However, there may be differences in the reasons for the strategies L2 students have for the use of intellectual property, a distinction that may have important pedagogical implications as will be discussed later. Taken in conjunction with the problems with paraphrasing that all developing writers have, avoiding plagiarism can be an especially daunting task for L2 writers. While this argument was intended to demonstrate the plasticity of these cultural issues.

Regardless of how one views culture in the study of plagiarism, the impact of culture can remain a serious pedagogical problem for teaching the use of textual sources. The role of culture in this discussion can be further complicated by its link to developmental issues in the students' writing ability, raising a complex series of questions related to their use of source texts. Do students have sufficient background to understand what is meant by plagiarism? Do they understand what the writing assignment expects of them, what are the linguistic and rhetorical requirements required to cope with the demands of textual borrowing and what are the possibilities for negotiating these demands?

In his autobiography about his experiences working with basic writers, Mike Rose (1989) narrated a number of stories of the difficulties they have in entering the academic community, with plagiarism being a common consequence. In one story about Marita, an inner-city student attending a major academic institution, Rose felt that she too was placed into a double bind by her writing instructor, in part resulting from a possible contradiction between the cultural norms that she had learned from her family regarding when it is appropriate to speak and the demands of an assignment that required the student to speak as an expert on subjects about which she knew little.

The resulting misunderstandings, which in some cases may simply result in a low grade, can also lead to 'criminal' charges, as it did in the case of Marita. Culture, however, cannot simply be viewed as a deficit in this discussion. Students often bring with them long traditions of textual borrowing that they can draw upon in their writing (Bloch & Chi, 1995). They may also bring a strong sense of voice that manifests itself differently in different contexts or technological environments. Nevertheless, the interweaving of these factors with developmental problems in using the language can still place L2 writers in a difficult position as they enter a L1 community of practice.

Plagiarism and Technology

The term 'disruption' has characterized many discussions of the effect of technologies such as the internet on our lives. Such disruptions have been noted since the time of Plato. Technology has long played such a role in how intellectual property is viewed, dating back to the invention of paper and, particularly, the printing press (Eisenstein, 1979). Today, technology can influence how we listen to music and watch movies, how we create and share information and, perhaps most importantly, how we teach. Today, as the YouTube films of the cultural anthropologist Michael Wesch have attempted to show (e.g. 'A Vision of Students Today', 2007; 'Web 2.0 ... The Machine is Us/ing Us', 2007), the nature of the students entering the university today is continually or (constantly) changing.

More and more discourse on the internet can be accessed by anyone with a connection to the world wide web. Our concepts of literacy have been extended by the growing use of email, listservs, Facebook and Twitter. Such new literacies have raised a host of new questions about the possibility for different definitions of plagiarism in different literacy contexts, a problem that will need to be incorporated into any pedagogy dealing with this issue. From its inception, the internet has provided a space to write, from email and online chat to new forms of literacies such as Facebook and Twitter. The world wide web was designed to encourage the publication of new types of texts by new types of authors (Berners-Lee, 1999). Berners-Lee, who was one of the principal designers of the web, has often argued that his goal was to allow the web to be a space for the production of texts.

The continual controversies around the distribution of intellectual property on file-sharing sites like Napster, Grokster (Devoss & Porter, 2006) and Pirate Bay have been cited as leading contributors to the culture of sharing that some feel has devalued the moral authority of private property. Turnitin.com, one of the leading plagiarism detection sites, lists a variety of popular sites that are used legitimately for searching for information (e.g. Wikipedia) or sharing information (http://www.slideshare.net) as the most popular sites for plagiarizing ('Plagiarism and the Web', 2011).

The growth of the internet has frequently been cited as another answer to the question of 'why students cheat.' Often the blame is placed on the ease of cutting and pasting or the attitudes students bring toward sharing music and movies. In a study of students at an American university, Schrimsher et al. (2009) argued that internet plagiarism resulted from a concept that material on the internet is 'free'. The ease by which information can be shared online has led to one of the most famous aphorisms about the internet – Richard Stallman's (Williams, 2002) oft-quoted saying that intellectual property on the internet should be 'free as in free speech, not as in free beer', which argues not that the use of intellectual property should be without charge but that its creators should make it readily accessible for everyone to build upon and transform.

However, in the writing classroom, perhaps the most important factors are the new types of literacy spaces that have challenged the traditional boundaries of genre (e.g. Prior, 2005) and traditional attitudes toward the use of intellectual property. These new forms of digital literacy are reflected in various forms of texts, which can mix visual, print, audio- and video-clips. These new forms have led to new perceptions of authorship, audience, voice and expression, all of which have disrupted traditional concepts of intellectual property law and plagiarism.

These forms of multimedia are not new, but technology has facilitated the ease with which these forms can be created. Now, free programs such as Audacity allow even the smallest pieces of music to be edited and mixed with segments from other artists. Programs like MovieMaker and IMovie allow audio texts to be mixed with images and video to create new forms of multimodal texts. The growth of 'remixed' texts, which permeate internet spaces like YouTube, have raised new questions about how such texts can be appropriated and or cited: should traditional views, standards and laws for traditional print texts be applied to digital texts? (Hyde, 2010; Lessing, 2008; Post, 2009). The ease with which texts can be created and widely distributed on sites like YouTube or Facebook has had dramatic effects on some people's lives while causing tragedy to others.

Remixing has had one of the most profound effects on how we view the appropriation of texts on the internet. As Reyman (2010) argues, the rhetorical narrative of the antipiracy movement attempted to reify the dichotomy between the creator and the consumer. The role of the consumer is completely passive, contributing nothing but money to the creative process. Remixing, on the other hand, shatters that dichotomy, transforming the consumer into a creator of new texts.

This disruption to these traditional dichotomies has raised a host of questions for teachers. What are the relative values of these forms of discourse? What norms, values and customs will be applied to these different kinds of discourse? What then does Fisher's concept of a 'just and attractive' society mean in any particular discourse community or language classroom? How well do the traditional attitudes toward the use of intellectual property apply to these new genres of digital texts? What are the ethical challenges raised by these new forms of texts? (Harrington, 2010).

Many of the controversies surrounding the use of intellectual property arise from the nature of the architecture of the internet (Lessing, 1999). As many have pointed out, the internet was designed for sharing information quickly in a decentralized manner that could not be controlled from a single space. With the internet, educators quickly recognized that the ease with which a user could cut and paste from the internet made plagiarizing both simpler to accomplish and more difficult to understand. Old-fashioned paper mills evolved into new high-tech websites (Ritter, 2005).

Although there is no strong central authority governing these appropriations of texts on the web, many countries have created intellectual property laws to constrain the publication and distribution of creative content in both their own countries and the developing countries many of our students come from. As Lessing (2004) has argued, such laws have extended the dominion of intellectual property to actions far beyond what has ever been conceived before. One of the many moral dilemmas is that these laws were often created by governments acting to safeguard their power or in the interest of a few large corporations who control the creation and distribution of intellectual property to constrain the economic development of these countries.

The internet has transformed every use of intellectual property into an act of copying since every time a webpage is opened a copy is made. The growing use of mobile technologies – cellphones, smartphones and tablets – may further challenge how intellectual property is viewed. Perhaps more important, the internet has globalized the production of information, so it cannot be readily subjected to the laws of a single country. The decentralized nature of the internet, where a centralized computer system was replaced by an interconnected series of computers located all over the world, has changed how networks are developed, how connectivity among people is valued, and how information is shared. No longer could the legal and ethical mores of one country govern how the same information would be treated in the rest of the world, which would have a profound effect on how intellectual property is viewed. Weinberger (2002) wrote that traditional views of behavior, authority and boundaries no longer held, which is a concept that can be applied to our attitudes of plagiarism as it has been to our attitudes toward intellectual property.

It is the goal of this book to help students and teachers better understand the complexity of these questions and why this term 'plagiarism' brings such fear and confusion to everybody involved and how to create classrooms where students can safely confront these issues. In the remainder of this book, I further examine how new ideas regarding plagiarism and intellectual property have led to alternative ways of discussing plagiarism and a teaching methodology that incorporates these new perspectives. Chapter 2 examines the connection between intellectual property and plagiarism. Chapter 3 discusses alternatives to what can be called the *stealing* metaphor that has for so long dominated the discourse about both plagiarism and intellectual property. Chapter 4 looks at pedagogical approaches to helping students better understand plagiarism. Chapter 5 focuses on the search for new metaphors to frame both teaching and researching plagiarism. Chapter 6 examines how new metaphors impact the design of an academic writing course for teaching about plagiarism. Chapter 7 concludes with a discussion of the implications of these new approaches.

Note

(1) All student writing is unedited.

2 Intellectual Property Issues and Plagiarism: What the Debate over Both Means for First- and Second-Language Writing Teachers

This book contends that understanding plagiarism begins with an understanding of its connection to intellectual property law. If intellectual property was considered to be the same as physical property, which many content creators proclaim, the controversies regarding the attribution of intellectual property might be reduced. While both concepts are often linked to the theft of physical property, it is the differences between intellectual and physical property that are at the root of the confusion over plagiarism.

One difference between a physical property and an intellectual property can be found in the concept of the relative differences in their respective 'scarcity'. While the amount of physical property is by nature limited and the loss of a piece of physical property can require its replacement or compensation, the availability of intellectual property is unlimited; that is, its loss may cause a loss of potential income or control, but the property itself remains with its 'owner', often with no indication that it had ever been borrowed or used without seeking permission.

Although plagiarism does not usually diminish the value of the original creation, such cases could result in the more abstract loss of the integrity of the academy and its role as a place for learning. As these issues show, both teachers and students must confront an increasingly complex series of ethical considerations in their use of intellectual property that cannot simply be adjudicated by existing laws.

The Historical Development of Intellectual Property

To better understand this complexity, it is important to examine the historical contexts in which these concepts have evolved. These contexts are important for helping to create a broader perspective for this discussion. As a counterbalance to the determinism often found in the discussion of cross-cultural attitudes toward plagiarism, for example, a historical perspective views both plagiarism and intellectual property in more fluid ways. As Barthes (1972) argued, historicizing an issue can be used to critique claims that, while thought to be 'natural', are in fact affected by historical change and continually evolving conditions.

Although the Bible might give some guidance for the use of intellectual property (Green, 2002) with the injunction 'thou shalt not steal', this connection between intellectual property and physical property is of a more recent origin. While terms like 'piracy' make that link with the biblical injunction appear seamless, Johns (2010) argues that the term 'piracy' became a dominant metaphor for the inappropriate use of intellectual property only during the late 16th and early 17th centuries. The current framework for the use of the 'stealing' metaphor for both intellectual property and plagiarism developed at the same time as did the laws that treated the theft of intellectual property (e.g. Boyle, 1996; Feather, 1994; Jaszi, 1994; Lunsford & Ede, 1994; Vaidhyanathan, 2001; Woodmansee, 1994).

During the same period that intellectual property laws were being passed, the word 'plagiarism', which is derived from the Latin word *plagium* meaning kidnapping or plundering, was introduced. Many of the views held today have been or are closely tied to the development of intellectual property laws in the 18th and 19th centuries with the expanding opportunities for profiting from the sale of books (Jaszi, 1994; Rose, 1994). Previously, the authorship of intellectual property was primarily used to identify, not reward, the author, and was often used to determine whether the author was a heretic, not a property owner (Boyle, 1996). The dominant view then was that since authorship was divinely inspired, there could be no claim by an individual for ownership of the creations of others (Woodmansee, 1994).

Vaidhyanathan (2001) argues that during the 18th century there were numerous court cases that attempted to resolve the tension between the rights of the publisher to profit and the rights of the author as creator. Jaszi points out that the publishers were the first to argue for the concept of 'author/genius' as the basis for granting them exclusive control of intellectual property, just as it has been the record and movie companies who today have led the fight against downloading intellectual property from the internet. The rights of the publisher were formally codified in the Statue of Anne in 1709. However, there was an important social provision that required the publisher to donate copies of each book to libraries across England, thus making the information available for the common good a prerequisite for being granted ownership.

Other countries, such as France, made the moral rights of the author the center of their intellectual property law, a concept having its roots in the medieval view of the author as a 'sower of seeds' (Rose, 2002). Still others, as exemplified in provisions for 'fair use' in the United States, have given more weight to the needs of the society. For writing teachers, authorship is often seen as the most important factor in making legal and ethical decisions regarding the use of intellectual property, although as will be argued later, the economic and social factors are equally important. The various motivations for these laws reflect the tension between the publisher, the author and the society that still governs our views of intellectual property and how it is used.

Underlying this focus on authorship was the romantic concept of the author as an isolated individual, as exemplified by romantic poets such as Wordsworth, who were considered creative geniuses 'rising above the masses' and therefore deserving of the ownership of their property (Jaszi & Woodmansee, 1994). This new view of authorship emphasized the amount of labor expended in the creative process. John Locke's treatise on the value of labor as a natural right has sometimes been cited as a basis for awarding ownership to the author of this intellectual property. For example, in his *Two Treatises on Government*, Locke argued that by mixing one's labor with the resources held in common one has the right to claim a property right and then pass this right on to others. While the applicability of Locke to copyright law is controversial, his writings were frequently cited both in Britain and in the United States in their early discussions of authorship and intellectual property.

The growing importance of the connection between economic and moral rights can be metaphorically seen in the use of the word 'piracy', whose usage increased with the growth of the commercial potential of books and the expectations of their readership for access to the latest and most popular ones (Johns, 2010). As Johns points out, these expectations grew with the invention of the printing press. He argues that the use of the 'piracy' metaphor emerged from the resulting economic tension between the commercial centers of publishing and the outlying agents, whom he metaphorically refers to as the 'barbarians at the gates' (14), who wanted a share of the publishing profits.

Changes in how the economic system rewarded authors further affected the status of intellectual property. The breakdown of the patronage system and the growing importance of publishers placed a greater monetary value on such property. The growing power of the stationers and publishers in Britain during the 17th century provided the impetus for the debate over who controlled the publication of what would later be called intellectual property. Artists could no longer rely on the wealthy patrons for support and had to turn to publishers to distribute their work, which created a marketplace for new ideas. It was a period, as Georg Lukács (1983) pointed out in his study of Balzac, when art became a commodity that was bought and sold in the marketplace like any other commodity. In response to this commoditization, the artist was often viewed more as a transcendent figure above the crass commercialism of the times. Nevertheless, ownership was given primarily to the publisher, not the author, which placed a greater emphasis on the economic value of the property instead of the author's moral rights to its ownership (Rose, 1993).

This concept of intellectual property, according to Hardy (1996), was further developed in the utilitarian views of Jeremy Bentham. For Bentham the idea of private property encourages individuals to create more property or improve the existing property. This argument supported the proposition that intellectual property law was intended to help develop new goods that are available for appropriation in the 'public commons' (Boyle, 2010: 8). This utilitarian principle can be understood in two ways, both of which have great importance for understanding plagiarism. One is that creators and owners of intellectual property retain certain rights that constrain its use. The second is that intellectual property laws should help increase socially valuable goods and that these goods should be distributed to increase the 'net pleasures that people reap from them' (Fisher, 1998: para 29).

These utilitarian principles, in fact, would become the basis in the United States to use intellectual property law in order to encourage the development and spread of ideas. Fisher points out that following the utilitarian views of Bentham, copyright law in the United States was designed to protect the free flow of information in order to contribute to the development of democratic institutions. Netanel argues that copyright laws provide incentive for any creative expression that supports a democratic culture and does so by freeing this expression from a reliance on the state or the elite (cited in Fisher, 2001).

This view of intellectual property was also incorporated into British law, with the passage of the Copyright Act of 1814 (Feather, 1994). It has been argued that this law was needed to stabilize prices in the book industry (Vaidhyanathan, 2001). Ownership, however, was not the sole motivation. Intellectual property rights could provide incentives to the creation of more intellectual property, thus providing a societal benefit, an argument that is prevalent among media companies today.

Beyond its use in the discussion of the utilitarian value of intellectual property, the 'commons' metaphor was applied to the question of governance, particularly in regard to whether the intellectual property should be governed by users or by the state (Hyde, 2010). As Hyde points out, this question was debated in Great Britain for hundreds of years as the control of the common property shifted from the individuals who used it to the state and private interests. Hyde (2010) extends this argument to the situation today where governance has become the center of the controversy, both between different cultures and between the consumer and the producer.

The Evolution of Authorship and Intellectual Property

There has been a long, though uneven, evolution in the relationship between the text and its author, often related to the development of new technologies. Walter Benjamin's (1968) view that the easy reproduction of texts, whether they are written texts or artistic images, changes their intrinsic nature can be extended to the even greater ease of reproduction the internet affords. Today, we often discuss the 'death' of the romantic concept of authorship (e.g. Lunsford & Ede, 1994; Sunderland-Smith, 2008); however, in reality, it is difficult to discuss authorship as a single, monolithic concept. These differences can often be seen in contexts where authors work together and have to share credit. In Hollywood, for example, it is impossible to tell how screenwriters may have collaborated since credit is given depending on the percentage of words each writer contributed. Perhaps nowhere is this variation in definitions of authorship greater than in scientific writing. Biagioli (2003) argues that even with scientific disciplines there can be different concepts of authorship, often depending on the various ways scientists are rewarded for their work.

Gross (2006) discusses how such rewards have evolved as the ownership of scientific intellectual property developed during the 17th century, in part due to general economic developments, that created increased value given for the priority of publication in the establishment of a claim. He argues that in the early part of the 17th century greater emphasis was placed on the cooperative nature of scientific endeavors, as exemplified in the writings of Francis Bacon in his utopian novels such as *The New Atlantis*, which was considered a model for the cooperative nature of scientific culture.

In such a cooperative context, who first claimed a discovery was of little importance. What was more important is achieving not only the goals of cooperation but also related political concepts such as transnationalism; however, these ideals proved to be utopian as conflicts over the priority of a claim would influence attitudes toward plagiarism and intellectual property. Gross describes the often vicious fights between Isaac Newton and Gottfried Leibniz over claims to the discovery of calculus as signaling the end of this spirit of cooperation. Soon, greater importance was given to establishing ownership and protecting that ownership from inappropriate use by others.

Interestingly, according to Gross, this debate evoked some of the earliest claims of plagiarism, although the term was not used in this context.

However, the growing influence of written discourse in scientific culture gave even greater importance to concerns over the priority of a claim. Although initially the establishment of the priority of a claim could be made equally by oral or written presentations, its publication eventually became the primary means for establishing priority (Gross, 2006), which opened the way for greater profits for the publishers. The role of intertextuality in scientific publications was evolving as well. Early publications, such as Newton's *Optiks*, did not have any citations, and while some early scientists, such as Joseph Priestley (1733–1804), championed the use of citations, the practice did not become widespread until the 19th century (Bazerman, 2009b).

As Gross argues, the growing importance of publication can be seen within the wider context of the rise of industrialization and commercialization, and perhaps more important for this discussion, the rise of Great Britain as a military and economic superpower as well as a publishing one, which established the British view of intellectual property law as dominant. At that time, much of the American publishing industry was built upon reprinting 'pirated' editions (Johns, 2010), a practice about which Charles Dickens vociferously complained (Vaidhyanathan, 2001).

The evolving nature of authorship continued throughout the 19th century, further expanding the definition of plagiarism. However, then as today, changes occurred in different countries at different times. Until 1891, it was legal in the United States to copy materials imported from other countries (Post, 2009). Johns (2010) argues that from the American perspective, the British copyright laws were seen as an 'imperialistic' attempt to control the distribution of information, thus putting the Americans at a distinct economic disadvantage. Johns cites an American economist of that period, Henry Carey, as arguing that the 'centralization' of intellectual property, as codified in intellectual property law in Britain, constrained the production of new intellectual property, an argument that Lessing (2004, 2009a) and others have also made today.

Such constraints not only make the property scarcer and, therefore, more valuable to the publisher but also inhibit the social and economic growth of the culture. These British laws were also seen as contradicting the American ideal that every citizen should be able to afford to purchase reading materials cheaply. From this perspective, the use of the 'piracy' metaphor by British publishers and authors could be seen as their response to such resistance.

These attitudes changed as the United States became a more important producer of intellectual property, a process accelerated by the introduction of new technologies and industries such as those associated with the development of motion pictures which, in the early part of the 20th century had a profound effect on how such issues as 'corporate ownership', 'derivative rights' and 'work for hire' were viewed (Vaidhyanathan, 2001). It is not surprising that one of the strongest advocates of strengthening the intellectual property laws was Mark Twain, who William Faulkner called the father of American literature (Jellife, 1956), and therefore, was perhaps the first truly American creator of intellectual property.

Vaidhyanathan (2001) argues that Twain felt that the lack of a copyright law allowed for the cheap reproduction of novels that crowded out the development of American authors, an argument that was the opposite of the position Carey had earlier taken. In 1886 Twain wrote that:

> [t]he statistics of any public library will show that of every hundred books read by our people, about seventy are novels – and nine-tenths of them foreign ones ... this fascination [with these novels] breeds a more or less pronounced dissatisfaction with our country and forms of government, and contempt for our republican commonplaces and simplicities. (cited in Vaidhyanathan, 2001: 61)

Twain's argument for laws giving authors perpetual copyright to protect 'American culture' by protecting its authors still resonates among many in the artistic community today (e.g. Helprin, 2009).

As the United States became a net producer of intellectual property, Twain's goals have become more the norm although perpetual copyright has never become law. During the early part of the 20th century, a combination of laws and court rulings continually extended the rights of copyright holders. Throughout the century, the duration of the copyright increased, sometimes dramatically. What initially began as a 14-year period of protection became a 70-year period. The Copyright Extension Act of 1998, which extended copyright protection for an additional 20 years, was motivated, at least in part, by the pending loss of the copyright of Mickey Mouse by the Disney Corporation (Lessing, 2004).

Jack Valenti, who, as the spokesperson for the Motion Picture Association of America, argued for stronger and longer-lasting laws to protect intellectual property beyond what had originally been proposed in the Constitution, argued to the US Congress that there were few, if any, valid reasons for removing the strongest protection from a piece of intellectual property:

[a] public domain work is an orphan. No one is responsible for its life. But everyone exploits its use, until that time when it becomes soiled and haggard, barren of its previous virtues. Who, then, will invest the funds to renovate and nourish its future life when no one owns it? How does the consumer benefit from that scenario? The answer is, there is no benefit. (cited in Litman, 2001: 77)

Valenti's use of metaphors such as 'soiled' and 'haggard' to denigrate the value of the public domain may seem somewhat disingenuous, given that the Disney company, who was one of the strongest backers of copyright extension, has also been one of the greatest legal exploiters of the public domain, whether it be fairy tales, legends or novels (Lessing, 2004). His argument exemplifies how a dichotomy has been created between the producers of intellectual property and its consumers. In this win–lose situation, benefit to one side means a loss to the other. The resistance to this dichotomy, on the other hand, has become a strong motivation to change attitudes toward intellectual property and plagiarism so that both sides can benefit, as will be discussed later.

What becomes copyrightable and what does not can also help illustrate this interaction between culture and history. Fisher (1998) illustrates how translations, which are now fully protected under copyright law, were not considered to be violations through much of the 19th century. In a federal Circuit Court decision concerning a translation of *Uncle Tom's Cabin*, a book about slavery by Harriet Beecher Stowe, the court argued against copyright protection for such derivative works:

A translation may, in loose phraseology, be called a transcript or copy of her thoughts or conceptions, but in no correct sense can it be called a copy of her book. (Woodmansee & Jaszi, 1995: 772)

It was not until the late 19th century that copyright protection was extended to translations and then to sequels and other derivative works. In other cultures, however, such translations were not viewed as original, not as derivative. For example, Chinese translators developed an approach referred to as 'butterfly literature' (Link, 1981) where the author could embellish the translation of the work to such a degree that it was considered a separate work of art.

Today, nothing better illustrates the relationship of historical and cultural factors than the issue of governance both of physical and intellectual property. From the American perspective, governance is deeply rooted in its history. Post (2009) compares the current controversy over the global governance of intellectual property law to the situation faced over 200 years ago when President Jefferson purchased Louisiana and much of the territory west of the Mississippi River, what is called the Louisiana Purchase. Post argues that Jefferson believed in localized governance and, therefore, was not concerned so much with the question of how such a vast, unchartered territory could be governed. His opponents, who believed in a strong centralized government, argued that such a large and chaotic territory could not be governed and, therefore, opposed the purchase.

The historical and cultural factors that shaped this controversy are still in play today. Post sees the battle over the internet governance as between the traditional content providers, such as the record and movie companies, who want a strong centralized authority to protect their products, and those who like the Jeffersonians before them, prefer local control. Joseph Ellis, a biographer of Jefferson, called cyberspace 'a perfect Jeffersonian environment', which is 'all decentralization and disorder, growth and expansion, a frontier that is constantly expanding and seemingly illimitable' (cited in Post, 2009: 117). The Jeffersonian viewpoint attempted to balance maximizing the wealth derived from intellectual property with the social benefit that could be derived from the distribution of that property.

Even advocates of reform often situate their rhetoric in this economic framework. As Lessing (2009a) has argued, openness in the spread of intellectual property does not necessarily mean there is no profit. Some content creators have, in fact, embraced changes in distribution and have encouraged the sharing of their music, which they may feel will increase its value in the long run. Alternative models of distribution, such as open-access models, have sometimes brought greater exposure and even large profits to new ideas and artists.

Such open-access materials, on the other hand, are important in the globalization of language teaching where many teachers and researchers do not always have access to online materials locked in what are called 'gated communities'. Such restrictions can result from political and cultural concerns as well as economic ones. The ongoing blocking and filtering of sites such as YouTube, often under the guise of a crackdown on 'pornography', can reflect such concerns for cultural differences in how intellectual property is viewed (Helft, 2009).

Changes in how information is gathered and how research is funded have also changed how intellectual property has been distributed. A few authors, particularly those advocating changes in intellectual property law, such as Lessing (2002, 2004, 2009a) and Jonathan Zittrain (2008), have also placed their books online to download freely. Sometimes, opposing sides using similar tactics for different purposes. The open textbook movement has attempted to place a variety of types of textbooks online for little or no cost while traditional publishers must reduce cost or inconvenience in order to maintain market share. Open materials have challenged how scholarly journals control the distribution of papers. The citation of information considered open for the public use, such as that produced by the Human Genome Project or the Hubble telescope, has become problematic for scientific journals. Such frameworks need to be explored to discover their relevance for discussing plagiarism. In the Open Source perspective, for example, traditional views of authorship are even more strongly challenged since each new contribution is valued on its own merit without regard to whether it is properly 'cited'. Jaszi (1994) argues that the traditional view of copyright loses sight of the importance of these 'serial collaborations', works resulting from the successive elaboration of an idea.

These alternative approaches to governance illustrate how views of culture need not be as monolithic as is often described. On a global level, the same kinds of cultural differences have been seen in conflicts over governance. The importance given to local control has often been overridden by a growing harmonization that has been imposed from the top down in both laws and international economic treaties as well as changes in perceptions of self-interest. This harmonization has tended to be unidirectional, from those countries lying at the center of the economic hierarchy to those on the periphery, which has been dominated by the laws and ethics of the United States. Sometimes this harmonization has been forced upon the countries on the periphery, such as the pressure placed on China to crack down on the reproduction of intellectual property as a prerequisite for joining the WTO. In other cases, governments have attempted to import ideas but modify them to reflect their own local conditions.

The Canadian government, for example, has proposed strict regulations regarding the circumvention of digital protection, such as passwords (Geist, 2008), which are similar to those found in the American Digital Millennium Copyright Act (DMCA), which is a highly controversial US law that attempted to respond to some of the effects of technological changes on the distribution of intellectual property. They also imported American concepts of fair use, which embodies the Jeffersonian ideal of a balance with social benefit and individual reward, but with a somewhat different approach that they would call 'fair dealing' (Geist, 2010). The New Zealand government passed a more restrictive law holding internet service providers responsible for identifying users who are downloading movies by denying them service, a tactic the American media companies have advocated but have not achieved (Anderson, 2009).

The international codification of intellectual property rights can be found in agreements such as the Berne Convention for the Protection of Literary and Artistic Works, which legally enshrined the moral rights of the author; these date back to the 19th century but were not ratified by the United States until 1988:

> Independently of the author's economic rights, and even after the transfer of the said rights, the author shall have the right to claim authorship of the work and to object to any distortion, mutilation or other modification of, or other derogatory action in relation to, the said work, which would be prejudicial to his honor or reputation.

The Berne Convention made everything in a fixed medium copyrightable, which served to reinforce the centrality over governance. Both print and digital texts have been given equal status because both kinds of property encompassed the principles of creativity (Johns, 2010). However, unlike inventions covered by patent law, copyrighted materials need not be completely unique but rather show only 'a modicum of creativity' ('Working Group', 25) to receive protection.

Since the acceptance of the Berne Convention, copyright in the United States has been granted automatically without any formal application to the government unless it has been anticipated that there may be future lawsuits in which case the copyright need be registered. Moreover, copyright protection is not discriminatory; that is, every work, whether it is an email message or a novel, has equal status, which means that every piece of intellectual property is copyrighted in the same way (Halpern, 2001).

The Berne Convention would later be applied to the governance of intellectual property on the internet. Although the internet was developed initially in the United States, its governance has moved to international organizations such as The World Intellectual Property Organization (WIPO) and The Internet Corporation for Assigned Names and Numbers (ICANN). The increased globalization of communication, often with English as a *lingua franca*, along with the ease with which digital copies of music and movies can be distributed, created inevitable conflicts in how intellectual property should be governed.

On the other hand, because of the changes in the variety of languages represented on the internet, these organizations have been the center of discussion on how the architecture of the internet can be changed to reflect the growing importance of these languages, which are often written in non-Roman scripts. International copyright laws can reflect other differences, although a country may not provide more protection to its own citizens than to foreign nationals. International law, however, does acknowledge that in different cultures, there may be different definitions of what can be copyrightable although the legal implications are not always clear (Merges *et al.*, 1997).

The conflation between the cultural and historical factors can be no better illustrated than how local cultural and economic differences are reflected in the different perspectives over the purpose of intellectual property law. Recent battles between the Chinese government and Google as well as controversies over censorship of the internet illustrate the greater importance the Chinese give to controlling the flow of ideas. Google's conflict with the Chinese government, which seems to be primarily concerned with the control of information, illustrates the conflict over the flow of intellectual property. Google itself was caught in this conflict between its corporate culture, as epitomized in its motto, 'do no evil,' and its economic goals for creating profits. However, it should be noted that the importance given to controlling the flow of intellectual property was not unknown in the West either where, as Johns (2010) points out, at the time the printing press was invented, both the church and the state felt the desire to control the flow of literature by licensing its publication.

These conflicts have been equally applied to plagiarism as well as intellectual property. Intellectual property rights have become as contentious in the US–China trade relationship as plagiarism has in the debate over the possible causes of plagiarism among Asian students studying in the West. Just as there has been a rash of 'crackdowns' involving plagiarism among Asian students, the United States has been pressuring China to crack down on reprinting or be denied membership in the World Trade Organization (WTO).

This conflict also illustrates how difficult enforcing these laws can be, an issue that has equally confounded teachers and intellectual property owners. Even if one country cracks down on the bootlegging of intellectual property, another country will take its place since there are many countries that have real economic reasons, as well as cultural ones, for resisting the imposition of a universal copyright law, just as the United States had resisted during the 19th century. A copy of Windows, which may cost a US professor a couple of hours of wages, can cost a professor in China a month's wages. Therefore, there can be strong economic incentives for copying intellectual property, which even the owners of the intellectual property have sometimes recognized. Michael Eisner, who was the head of the Disney Corporation, admitted that 'history has shown that one of the best deterrents to pirated property is providing legitimate product at appropriate prices' (cited, in '2600 News', para 18).

When I first worked in China in the early 1980s, one place I was forbidden to visit were the backrooms of Chinese bookstores where the cheap reprints were kept. It could be argued the economic, technological and intellectual development of China today had its roots in these backrooms, similar to what Carey argued occurred in the United States during the 19th century. Today, a similar but more high-tech process is occurring with the hacking of online databases to either 'steal' or 'liberate' depending on your perspective, valuable information necessary for future research (Young, 2011). Is such a violation a result of lazy approaches to research or creative and necessary approaches to progressing knowledge? This question is equally applicable to the discussion of plagiarism, as will be discussed later.

The Impact of the Internet

The importance given to the internet for 'the plagiarism epidemic' may have its roots in the differences between how digital and print texts are created, distributed and utilized. Such differences are directly related to how the internet was originally conceived. The internet was created by the US Defense Department as a decentralized network that could not be taken out by a missile. When Arpanet, the forerunner of the internet, was developed, there was little concern about the formal rules for determining the legal status of these digital texts or for the rules for their citation.

However, as large numbers of people have come to populate the internet and the use of texts rapidly grew, new concerns arose as to the use of intellectual property. Although this decentralization began in the United States, it has since spread throughout the world, further complicating the legal and cultural status of digital intellectual property. The problem has been further complicated by the fact that the architecture of the internet and the world wide web further has encouraged the copying and sharing of information.

The problem of 'the piracy epidemic' has, in turn, been complicated by how the architecture of the internet and the world wide web has further encouraged the copying and sharing of information. Advocates of radical changes to how intellectual property on the internet should be viewed have taken strong positions that these technological differences have led to new conceptualizations of text ownership and distribution.

John Perry Barlow (1994) has argued that digital texts can and should not be regulated by traditional intellectual property laws:

> The riddle is this: If our property can be infinitely reproduced and instantaneously distributed all over the planet without cost, without our knowledge, without its even leaving our possession, how can we protect it? How are we going to get paid for the work we do with our minds? And if we can't get paid, what will assure the continued creation and distribution of such work? (para 2)

Many of the recent laws passed to adapt intellectual property law to the digital age have likewise limited its usage. One of the most well known is The Digital Millennium Copyright Act (DMCA), which some have argued has created new restrictions on the use of digital material than there had been on print material (e.g. Samuelson, 1999). The DMCA, for example, has created laws preventing circumventing encryption that has increasingly restricted the flow of information (Samuelson, 1999). If, for instance, I had purchased a subscription to the print version of a magazine, I could distribute my copy to whomever I please without obtaining the permissions, based on what is referred to as the first sale doctrine, which allows owners to do what they wish with the property they purchased.

Under this new law, on the other hand, one could purchase an online subscription and instead of passing the paper around, the purchaser of the online version could give the password to as many people as she wanted. The publishers have argued that this wider distribution could be a greater economic threat and should be curbed. These approaches to intellectual property law could have detrimental results for its use in education.

These issues regarding the further restrictions on intellectual property have so permeated our global society that, as Boyle (1966) has argued, everyone must become involved in the discussion about intellectual property law in the same way they are involved with other critical issues that can greatly impact their lives. Despite the confusion, the access and use of intellectual property on the internet has become a central question both inside and outside the classroom. Global access to the internet no longer simply means the ability to log on. As information becomes more crucial, access today also includes the ability to receive uncensored and unfiltered information, which means that governments allow the free flow of intellectual property to and from their countries without restriction. The new technologies that have been developed for the world wide web provide teachers both with new tools for teaching writing and new forms of rhetorical contexts that students may need to master to become literate. The development of newer ways of connecting people and the various artifacts that populate the web may further complicate the pedagogical problems that new forms of intellectual property have caused.

The Legal Cases Shaping the Metaphors of Intellectual Property in Cyberspace

Cyberspace has become an important factor in the discussion of plagiarism not simply because students use it to search for information that can easily be cut and pasted but also because it has evolved as a physical space for writing. One approach for understanding how the use of intellectual property, whether it is from ethical or legal perspectives, can be found in the study of the various court cases that have contested the control of intellectual property on the internet. These cases are important for writing teachers both because they have provided the constraints for using and distributing teaching materials in the classroom and because they helped create some of the metaphors that frame how we think about plagiarism and intellectual property.

The concept of 'copying' has been at the heart of the discussion of metaphor. Digital texts, for example, are copied and distributed in different ways than are print texts. Elkin-Koren (1998) points out that in cyberspace, texts are not physically distributed; rather users are granted the right to access the intellectual property. While the author of a printed text essentially loses control of the property once it is copied, the author of a digital text can use a variety of technological means to retain control and deny further access. However, as the problems over the removal of unwanted materials from the internet have shown, the ability to control such reproduction is limited (Zittrain, 2008).

In some of the first cases on copying, the court decided (e.g. *MAI Systems Corp. vs. Peak Computer*) that the transmission of intellectual property over the internet involves making copies at every stage of the transmission and, therefore, falls under the influence of intellectual property law (Hayes, 2000). Since copying was considered an integral part of the nature of the internet, it was considered legal. The question was then raised as to whether the copies created during transmission over the internet should be considered fixed. Fixation is part of the definition of what is considered copyrightable, so this question considered whether online intellectual property would be considered in the same way as other forms of intellectual property. The White Paper on Intellectual Property Rights published by the US government in 1995 argued that 'a transmission, in and of, itself is not a fixation. While a transmission may result in a fixation, a work is not fixed by virtue of the transmission itself' (cited in Hayes, 2000: 364). As Hayes points out, legal cases (e.g. *Lewis Galoob Toys Inc. vs. Nintendo of America, Inc.*) confirmed this point. These cases seemed to confirm that online intellectual property was, in fact, copyrightable.

The nature of copying has continued to be an important topic. For example, the caching of a web page, which occurs continually during internet browsing, constituted making a fixed copy that might not be legal with physical forms of intellectual property. The courts indicated that web browsing does, in fact, create fixed copies that could be subject to existing intellectual property laws. However, since such copying was found to be an integral part of the architecture of the internet, it was not considered an infringement of the copyright holder's rights. Such rulings raised a new question: if such copying is legal, then who controls the copies?

The control of 'copying' is, of course, at the heart of the concern over plagiarism. Although the implications may be different from that of copying intellectual property law, there is an equal concern for how it denigrates value, often of the educational process if not the original itself. In his letter to a student who had plagiarized in his course, Couser (2009) expresses concern that copying denigrates the value of the student's education. A similar concern for the 'denigration' of the value of intellectual property that raised alarms about distribution. Since caching was only temporarily and therefore did not affect the value of the property, it caused no loss to the owner. However, the owners of intellectual property feared that the ease of distribution, even though it may not result in the actual loss of property, would reduce its value by reducing its scarcity. Cohen (1998) believes that this argument assumes that the value of property is only the sum of wealth generated by its transactions, and consequently, intellectual property laws should maximize the amount of wealth that could be generated by the property. Cohen, for example, argues that these 'cybereconomists' have attempted to replace the social contract that allows for the fair use of intellectual property in exchange for copyright protection with a purely economic one where the sole criteria is the maximization of profit. Receiving such a copyright restricts (1) reproducing the work, (2) creating a derivative work, (3) selling the work for the first time and (4) performing the work in public (Legal Information Institute).

The debate over the economic value of intellectual property has greatly impacted how the relationship between creativity and commercialism in the technological world is viewed, a conflict that inevitably arises with the introduction of each new technology. It is not surprising that in the earliest days of the personal computer, a young Bill Gates attacked software sharing in a now famous letter to the Homebrew Computer Club, where many of the early developers of the personal computer gathered, arguing that such views of openness would retard the development of new software (Freiberger & Swaine, 2000). However, the most well-known example of this drive to limit sharing has come from a company, the Disney Corporation, whose creativity has always depended heavily on 'borrowing' many of its most famous cartoon and animation characters while simultaneously arguing against any application of fair use and for the expanded duration of copyright (Lessing, 2009a).

Another example of litigation that reflects this battle of metaphors was the question of linking. As with copying, linking can threaten the control over the intellectual process, similar to what Bolter (2001) found with the reading and writing process. Although linking, also like copying, is part of the intrinsic nature of the internet, it too can result in the lowering of a property's value if it is used to bypass advertisements, for example. A link within a website that bypasses the front page of the site can block the reader from seeing an advertisement placed on the front page, so there may not be any revenue generated from the ad.

Conflicts over the use of these links have provided important perspectives on how online intellectual property can be viewed. In *Intellectual Reserve v. Utah Lighthouse Ministry*, the courts ruled that distributing intellectual property by linking to it was considered a violation of copyright law. Such linking cases were also important for establishing the nature of online intellectual property. Some cases were concerned with whether it was legal for a website to link to any page on another website, thus perhaps bypassing that website's homepage and the advertising on it (*Shetland Times Ltd. vs. Dr. Jonathan Wills and Zetnews Ltd*). In such cases, the question was whether a website could be considered the same as a physical property whose entrance could be controlled by the owner, other cases have involved the right to link to a second website within a frame of the first website (*Washington Post vs. Total News, Ticketmaster vs. Microsoft*). Framing was the practice by which one site could place another site inside a frame, thus substituting its advertisements for those of the linked website. This practice was referred to as deep linking. It was argued that this ability to link texts is a fundamental principle of the organization of the internet. Oppenheim (1996) writes:

The copyright owner made a deliberate choice to place his web site online, with full knowledge (presumably) of how the system operates. Linking of web sites to one another is extremely common and is, arguably, both the *raison d'etre* of the WWW and the reason for its success. It is custom and practice, and so if a copyright owner puts up a web site, he must expect others to link into his site. Services such as web search rights could not operate without this ability. (para 26)

This argument raised an important principal that appeared in a number of related issues: whether such actions are considered an inherent part of the architecture of internet and, therefore, could not be restricted even though these actions might be considered an infringement in the print world. In discussing intellectual property in Cyberspace, Okediji argues that it is necessary to consider 'how the technology determines modes of communication' (164). As Okediji goes on to argue, downloading webpages, forwarding email and creating hypertext links can all be considered a normal internet activities and, therefore, cannot be judging to be offending usages.

Even when revenue is not involved, the issue of control remains. This issue arose in the field of teaching writing when the On-line Writing Lab (OWL) at Purdue University sought a cease and desist order to stop a for-profit tutoring company from deep linking to its website (Kolowich, 2010). The university became concerned when the tutoring company framed the OWL as part of its resources page, so it may appear that the university was connected to this company.

The metaphorical importance of these arguments over controlling copying and linking is crucial to determining whether websites should be considered the same as private property where the owner can control the use of the intellectual property. If a website is conceived metaphorically as private property, for example, the website owner has the same right as a owner of a department store to determine where a user can enter into store premises (Hardy, 1996). The counterargument, as discussed below, is that the internet should be considered as a 'commons' and could be accessed anywhere the user wanted to. As will be discussed later, this argument over how intellectual property should be metaphorically viewed has shaped many of our discussions about plagiarism.

Metaphors for the Governance of Intellectual Property

This battle over control is central to understanding the controversy over metaphor, as it applies to both intellectual property and plagiarism. Control has long been an issue in the teaching of writing. One of the central tenets in what are called academic literacies (Street, 1995) is the question of who controls what is brought into the classroom – the student, the teacher and/ or the institution. From this perspective on academic literacies, the attempt to value what the student brings to the classroom may conflict with the institutional goals of the classroom, an issue that is important in defining acceptable and unacceptable uses of intellectual property.

The responsibility for the creation and dissemination of intellectual property has also been at the center of controversy. The prominence today of the music and the movie companies in prosecuting the 'pirating' of intellectual property might indicate that the publisher is most prominent, an issue dating back to the Statue of Anne. During the 19th century, it was clear to the British publishers that the American publishers were the 'pirates'. Who were their equivalents today? Litigation has focused on the users; the websites used for distribution, such as Napster, Grokster and Pirate Bay; and the Internet Service Providers (ISP), who were responsible for transporting the content.

Initially, the publishers focused on threatening and suing the ISPs. Even the threat of a lawsuit, which was expensive to litigate, could force the ISP to restrict the distribution even before the legality could be established in court. A series of rulings, however, held that the ISPs were not liable since they had no ability to monitor every piece of information published on their servers (*Cubby vs. CompuServe*) although in other cases (e.g. *Stratton Oakmont vs. Prodigy Servs. Co.*), the courts ruled against the ISPs if they were found to monitor or screen information (Caden & Lucas, 1996). Overall, however, they were not considered to be actively participating in any illegal activity, much like the phone companies, who are not liable for what is spoken over their lines.

More central to the problem of plagiarism is the decentralization of possible offending publishers or distributors. Is there actually a publisher at a specific location or is anyone posting on the internet a publisher? Unlike the traditional publishers, who are located in a physical space, these publishers, like our students, are located all over the world. Texts can be published anywhere in the world, making it difficult to enforce local intellectual property laws, particularly if each locality's laws are grounded in a unique set of historical, economic and philosophical issues (Post, 2009). Can publishing and distribution ever be controlled and even if it is possible to do so, could the laws or rules be harmonized to respond to the economic and cultural differences of so many users? Writing teachers have asked the same question about the attitudes and rules regarding plagiarism.

Alternative Forms of Metaphor

The attempt to answer such questions has spurred a variety of alternative metaphors to better capture the complexity of these issues. The legal battles over copying and linking have corresponded to the metaphorical battles over the shape and form of the internet. For instance, we often speak of the web as a place we 'visit' or 'enter', making the web analogous to a physical property where the owner of the website can exert property rights just as the owner of a house or building can (Hardy, 1996).

Today, with the development of new technologies such as cellphone cameras and social networking websites, it has become easier to post and distribute intellectual property, and, consequently, the public-private division has become subject to a different set of constraints. This development has made it more difficult to control what is publicly distributed. In some cases, the choice of terms can confuse the situation when two different forms of communication are linked metaphorically, such as the relationship between 'mail' and 'email'. Many people, for example, regard their email as private, similar to a letter sent through the mail, even when the email has been posted to a listserv or newsgroup and has been read by hundreds or thousands of people. However, email is often considered to be public messages placed in a fixed medium and, therefore, can be used under the same conditions as any other copyrighted message. Okediji (2001) has pointed out, in practice, the courts have considered reposting email, like caching websites, to be an intrinsic part of internet usage and, therefore, may not be in violation of copyright law. This perspective has also meant that in a business setting, the employer has the right to read their employees' email, thus making the status of email as intellectual property much different than traditional forms of mail.

One of the central works in this debate over metaphor has been Eric Raymond's 'The Cathedral and the Bazaar'. Raymond (1998) proposed two competing metaphors to frame this discussion of intellectual property. The 'cathedral' metaphor refers to a massive structure to which the public may be invited to enter but who can only use one designated entrance. This metaphor frames the flow of information as being strictly controlled. The 'bazaar' metaphor, on the other hand, reflects an open space where people can enter and exit wherever they please. This 'bazaar' metaphor highlights new ways of sharing the flow of information, which would later be called 'open access', and of gaining incentives and rewards for its production (Boyle, 2010; Lessing, 2009a; Zittrain, 2008); the open-access movement calls for the 'free' access to the development and sometimes the use of the software, not the absence of assigning a monetary value, the same distinction as found in Stallman's 'free as in free speech' metaphor.

With the 'cathedral' metaphor, the creator works in isolation; however, in the bazaar view, they collaborate so that each problem can be more easily solved. Here, authorship is distributed throughout a network. While Raymond's use of the 'bazaar' metaphor mainly concerned open source software projects like Linux or Mozilla, it can also be applied to any variety of collaborative projects, where many authors with different agendas and approaches can work on the same project without a clear delineation of what belongs to whom.

However, Raymond argues that this alternative view of authorship does not reduce creativity to being the product of a committee-like collective:

> This is not to say that individual vision and brilliance will no longer matter; rather, I think that the cutting edge of open-source software will belong to people who start from individual vision and brilliance, then amplify it through the effective construction of voluntary communities of interest.

Nor does this concept of authorship eliminate the rewards for the creation of intellectual property; rather it assumes that collaboration can improve the product, which could bestow greater rewards in the community as a whole.

A variation of the 'bazaar' metaphor can be seen in the use of the 'commons' metaphor, which, as mentioned earlier, has been used in the debate over governance of both intellectual and physical property (Boyle, 2010; Hyde, 2010). Its use as a metaphor for framing discussions of social activity was popularized in the work of Garrett Hardin (1968), who discussed the possible destructive nature of the commons as individuals would overuse its resources without concern for its future or the rights of other users, such as what happens when overfishing by a few degrades the ability of the ocean to provide food for everyone. Hardin wrote, 'Ruin is the destruction toward which all men rush, each pursuing his own best interest in a society that believes in the freedom of the commons' (1244), which may warrant stronger intervention and regulation. Because of the dire nature of his vision of the destruction of fishing areas, Hardin argued for stricter laws to control access, much like the view today of those who see a relationship between 'the piracy epidemic' and 'the plagiarism epidemic' and call for stricter rules and better tools for enforcement. Intellectual property law, for example, can therefore serve to 'enclose' this commons by restricting who can utilize it and how it can be used (Boyle, 2010; Hyde, 2010). Institutional rules and, in particular the implementation of plagiarism detection software, can play a similar role in the attempt to clearly delineate acceptable and unacceptable usage.

As the internet has grown in importance and popularity, the 'commons' metaphor has been increasingly applied to the use of intellectual property on the internet since its negative factors, such as the increased piracy of intellectual property and the growing ease of plagiarism, were causing a similar degradation of the academic community and the society as a whole (cf. Benkler, 2006). However, Hess and Ostrum (2006) found that the 'commons' metaphor has been used in more complex ways for describing the variety of more positive social interactions that were taking place on the internet, most relevantly for the creation of knowledge. They focused more on the creative potential of an open commons for meeting the varied needs of internet users.

They argued that unlike other forms of the commons, this type of knowledge commons that was growing on the internet can be additive and 'creative' so that the more people use it, the greater the amount of good that is created. Unlike the example of overfishing used by Hardin, in the knowledge commons, the more people contributing information, the more vital a source of information the commons will become (Shirley, 2008). Wikipedia is often cited as the best-known example of this phenomenon as its relevance has grown with the addition of new contributors across a variety of languages. The fact that the commons is open, however, may not mean there is no governance (Hyde, 2010). In response to incidents of deliberate falsification and a number of other issues on Wikipedia, new regulations were implemented governing who could edit Wikipedia and the type of information that could be added, thereby modifying the architecture of the site to protect the integrity of the commons.

Moreover, Hess and Ostrum (2006) argued that even without institutionalized laws, the new knowledge commons is still being regulated and communally developed, so it can be in the best interests of everybody to maintain its integrity, an issue that can be applied to the writing classroom as well, particularly to the issue of localized control of issues regarding plagiarism. Differences in perspective on the value of the commons can, at least in part, result from changes in what has been called architecture or the code of whatever technology is being discussed (Lessing, 1999). This architecture can always be modified to accommodate changes in the goals. Changes in concerns for how the commons is being used, such as the regard for privacy in social networking sites or the ability to share information online, can be strengthened or weakened by modifying the code of the sites.

Rebalancing the Equilibrium

The great importance of the commons for our discussion on plagiarism is not the degree of responsibility these different metaphors place on the individual for the maintenance of the space. Under the 'commons' metaphor, there may be a greater need for each individual to understand and participate in how the commons is managed. The pedagogical implications of such a shift can be framed in what the 'gaming' metaphor refers to as the equilibrium among all the participants. According to the mathematician John Nash, an equilibrium is reached when the players in a game can make the best possible decisions, given that each player understands the strategies of the other players ('Nash Equilibrium,' Wikipedia).

There have been various attempts in intellectual property law to rebalance the equilibrium between the two distinct goals: rewarding the author and benefitting the society. These positions exist on a continuum between those who believe that the rules should be harmonized for all forms of texts (the 'Unexceptionalists') and those who feel they should reflect local conditions (the 'Exceptionalists'; Post, 2009). The unexceptionalists, whose ideas are sometimes referred to as copyleft, do not believe that intellectual property should be gated but that the holder of the copyright should allow anyone to use his or her intellectual property or modify it. As far as software is concerned, 'Copyleft says that anyone who redistributes the software, with or without changes, must pass along the freedom to further copy and change it. Copyleft guarantees that every user has freedom' ('What Is Copyleft,' 1999).

As Johns (2010) argues, this 'free' metaphor was not new but could be traced back to earlier arguments by Michael Polyani and Norbert Weiner over whether scientific advances should be patented. What this 'free' metaphor means has sometimes been ambiguous. Citing the famous quote from Steward Brand, 'information wants to be free,' and that of Richard Stallman, reformers of intellectual property law have questioned the ability of this process to govern existing practices on the internet. Negroponte argues, 'There is simply no way to limit the freedom of bit radiation, any more than the Romans could stop Christianity' (55–56).

Advocates for changes in intellectual property law and advocates for changes in how plagiarism is viewed share a desire for such new metaphors that contain more flexibility in how these concepts are viewed, often involving greater input from the users of the intellectual property. Speaking of traditional metaphors for intellectual property, Mark Rose (2002: 15) argues for such changes in how these metaphors are used:

[t]he issue of how we think about copyright is as much a matter of rhetoric as it is of logic. Paternity and property are very old metaphors, and they are deeply embedded in the way we think about ourselves as well as the way we think about copyright. We cannot simply escape from these metaphors because we cannot escape from history and from ourselves. A persuasive solution to the problems our metaphors pose will be one that does not simply reject the old tropes but finds new ways to understand them.

Deconstructing existing metaphors has also focused on the limiting effects of current frameworks for thinking about intellectual property. Patry points out that criticisms of the 'pirate' metaphor can be found in early 20th-century copyright debates in the British House of Commons:

> The Amendment to leave out the word 'pirated' and to insert the word 'unauthorized' is an amendment to which I attach the greatest importance. The use of th[e] word ['pirate'] is calculated to create a large amount of prejudice. (cited in Patry, 2009: 88)

Boyle (2010: 162) draws upon Greek mythology for a metaphor to ridicule the one-size-fits-all approach to intellectual property that the 'piracy' metaphor seems to assume:

> Procrustes had a bed to which he fitted its perspective occupants, whether they liked it or not. The tall were trimmed down. The short stretched on the rack. Intellectual property lawyers have many similarities to Procrustes. The technologies that are brought before them are made to fit the conceptual boxes the law provides, boxes with such names as 'copyright' and 'patent'. Occasionally, new conceptual boxes are made, but – for very good reasons – most of the time we stick with the boxes we have. As with Procrustes, things do not always fit and the process can be distressing for its subjects.

Boyle argues that the Procrustean metaphor from a view of intellectual property where the governance has been taken away from the creator and standardized to make its application simpler.

Boyle's Procrustean metaphor of being 'shortened' or 'stretched' fits well with how plagiarism has been traditionally viewed. The idea that all copying, from a few words of text to an entire paper, can be treated in the same way can confuse and frighten students who do not know when they can borrow intellectual property and how much property they can use. It is no wonder that Abasi and Graves (2008: 228) use the term 'anxiety' to describe such student fears.

To allay such anxieties, writing teachers need to create a new equilibrium that can acknowledge the differences in the views of copying that students bring to the classroom as well as providing a better understanding of the rules related to the particular genres being studied. Therefore, for both explanatory and argumentative purposes, it has become necessary to find better metaphors to frame these new pedagogical practices.

Formulating New Metaphors

As Lakoff (2004) argues, it is not enough to only deconstruct an existing metaphor to change attitudes but it is also necessary to propose alternative metaphors. The battle over the control of intellectual property has provided a plethora of alternative metaphors to counter the 'stealing' or 'piracy' metaphors. Therefore, the challenge is to incorporate all these new contexts for authorship and textuality. Litman (2008), for example, has proposed that intellectual property law should be seen as a 'fence', which is not a static structure but a flexible boundary that can adapt to the contour of the space. Individuals can bump against the fence, climb on top of it and sometimes even jump over it. This metaphor looks at intellectual property law from a more fluid perspective, allowing for local variation to match the conditions of the land, a possibly useful way for also looking at plagiarism.

These new metaphors do not present a monolithic view of these issues but often reflect the interaction between the new and the traditional norms and values that have evolved, and continue to evolve, in the culture of the community. The term 'open access', for example, addresses both the traditional views regarding the benefit of intellectual property for society and the collaborative nature of research. Unlike the traditional economic reasons for incentivizing the creation of new intellectual property, open access assumes that the rewards result from the ability to collaborate on problems that no one individual can solve alone, that there is increased security since the ideas will be under close scrutiny and that there will be increased reliability of these ideas because of the large number of individuals working on the same problem.

Moreover, traditional monetary results are not ignored (Lessing, 2005). For example, despite the fact that open source projects such as Linux are free, numerous for-profit corporations have sprung up adding new features and services. For many creators across a variety of fields, the ability to publish freely has given them the exposure that they could later benefit from. Social benefit is, therefore, not necessarily derived from the accumulation of wealth but from the access to a wide variety of ideas, which in turn allows the development of new ideas from which society can benefit (Cohen, 1998).

Robert Merton (1973) also argued that the overprotection of scientific knowledge was antithetical to the communal process by which it was produced. However, it should be noted that Merton endorsed a strict definition of plagiarism because he felt that plagiarism contradicted the importance of reputational capital upon which scientific progress was based. Open source and *Creative Commons*, for example, both of which were created outside the traditional systems of software development and copyright law, provide alternative ways for students and teachers to use intellectual property regardless of their location and alternative metaphors to think of textual borrowing. Similar to how different cultures may make different determinations as to what belongs to the individual and what belongs to the culture, these metaphors, in much different ways, attempt to rebalance the rights of the society ownership with those of the creators of intellectual property.

Creative Commons has attempted to achieve this balance in a more moderate way by shifting the governance of intellectual property to the creator, who can choose the type of copyright that may be more suitable to the creator's goals and values than the one-size-fits-all model. For example, they can designate that their materials can be freely used but that they must be attributed and cannot be resold or altered. For example, an author can choose a Creative Common license ('Attribution-Share Alike Unported 3.0') that allows a user to copy, remix and/or distribute the work while requiring attribution according to the guidelines of the author.

Lessing (1999) argues against the more radical viewpoints, saying the internet is not a place of infinite freedom but one that can be regulated far more than traditional media. Some regulation was seen as necessary so that further regulations, as exemplified by the DMCA, could be mitigated. Creative Commons allows the creators to make their own distinctions as to future copying or distribution. These types of licenses apply a new set of rules to the governance of the commons that reflect a different set of norms and values than do traditional copyright laws. These norms value the sharing of property among the users while the creators can exercise some degree of control over how the property will be used. As discussed earlier, these licenses can be adopted to create rules for specific contexts, reflecting cultural differences in defining the appropriate use of intellectual property. As Lessing (2004, 2009a), one of the founders of Creative Commons, has put it, new forms of intellectual property and new ways by which intellectual property is distributed require new approaches to protecting this property.

The term 'Creative Commons' also provides a useful metaphor by combining two fundamental principles, both applicable to the discussion of plagiarism, which are antithetical to traditional views of intellectual property. First is the argument that 'creativity', and not simply 'ownership', should be the basis for governing the use of intellectual property. Second, as does Raymond's (1996) use of the 'commons' metaphor, 'creative commons' implies that there should be decentralized controls over how intellectual property is used rather than a centralized form of governance. It should be noted that these new approaches have been strongly opposed by many of the media corporations and some artists who believe that perpetual ownership is still the right of the creator (e.g. Helprin, 2009) and that these new approaches cannot provide for a steady income for creators.

Writing teachers have often faced a similar dilemma of how to maintain their standards and educational goals while responding to the particular needs of their communities. We can evaluate metaphors based on their sensitivity to these needs. The use of new metaphors, such as 'creative commons', 'open access' and 'open source', speaks directly to the changes in the creation and distribution of intellectual property, which are particularly important in the globalization of language teaching where many teachers and researchers do not always have access to online materials locked in the 'gated communities'.

Most important is how well the metaphor addresses the kinds of pedagogical problems teachers face. How then can a consistent standard for responding to plagiarism be maintained when some students clearly have a greater difficulty in understanding plagiarism. A student who repeatedly copies even after multiple warnings may not understand or have the ability to paraphrase well. Is that an ethical issue that needs to be decided by an academic misconduct committee or is that a pedagogical problem that should be dealt with in the classroom? How does a teacher distinguish a student with this kind of problem from one who cuts and pastes to avoid doing the assignment? For some teachers, these questions may pose a dilemma between choosing a centralized 'cathedral' approach or a decentralized 'commons' approach.

Fair Use, Intellectual Property Law and Plagiarism

One of the most powerful alternative metaphors regarding the use of intellectual property for students and teachers to consider is what in the US parlance is called 'fair use' ('Fair Use', 2009). Under the US law, all creators have some rights to use the intellectual property of others; however, for many commercial and artistic purposes, the use of this intellectual property has been constrained by various laws and court decisions, leading to what has been called 'the permissions culture' (Boyle, 2010).

There are four principles in section 107 of the US Copyright Code that are used to judge whether a particular usage is covered by fair use:

(1) the purpose and character of the use, including whether such use is of commercial nature or is for nonprofit educational purposes,
(2) the nature of the copyrighted work,

(3)   the amount and substantiality of the portion used in relation to the copyrighted work as a whole, and

(4)   the effect of the use upon the potential market for, or value of, the copyrighted work. (http://www.copyright.gov/fls/fl102.html)

Variations in fair use have been adopted throughout the world. Canada, for example, adopted a less broad approach to fair use, which they call 'fair dealing' (Geist, 2010). Even in countries without specific fair use laws, educators have had special, though usually unspecified, rights to use intellectual property without permission. Our ability to borrow texts without permission illustrates one way how intellectual property differs from physical property. The goal of fair use is to protect the balance between the creator's rights and the users' rights. While the roots of copyright law may have been impacted by the romantic view that the authors deserved to be rewarded for their creations (Lunsford & Ede, 1994), its development in the United States was equally based on, as Litman (2001) put it, *a quid pro quid* whereby the author is granted certain rights to control his or her creative work for a limited period in exchange for giving the public various rights to use the work with certain restrictions.

The Working Group on Intellectual Property Rights has defined fair use in this way:

Fair use is an affirmative defense to any action for copyright infringement. It is potentially available with respect to all unauthorized uses of works in all media. If it is proven, then the use may continue without any obligation on the user's part to seek the permission of the copyright owner, pay royalties, or the like. The doctrine of fair use is rooted in some 200 years of judicial decisions and is, in general, most likely to be found when a user incorporates some of a pre-existing work into a new work of authorship.

The concept of fair use seems to undermine the argument that intellectual property can be viewed as being the same as physical property, which in turn undermines the blanket use of terms like 'piracy' or 'stealing' for every act of borrowing intellectual property.

Legal scholars have argued that this distinction is derived from US Constitutional demands for a 'public benefit' for intellectual property in exchange for copyright protection (Bell, 1998). Fair use in the United States was first explained in article 1, section 8 of the US Constitution, 'To promote the Progress of Science and useful Arts, by securing for limited Times to Authors and Inventors the exclusive Right to their respective

Writings and Discoveries'. The concept of fair use has been best expressed in a letter Thomas Jefferson wrote to an inventor named Isaac MacPherson in 1813. In this letter, he expresses the essence of the difference between intellectual property and real property:

> He who receives an idea from me, receives instruction himself without lessening mine; as he who lights his taper at mine, receives light without darkening me. That an idea should freely spread from one to another over the globe, for the moral and mutual instruction of man, and the improvement of his condition, seems to have been peculiarly and benevolently designed by nature, when she made them, like fire, expansible all over space, without lessening their density. (Koch & Peden, 1944: 577)

The same issue arose in Britain a few years later, although fair use would never have the same impact as it did in the United States. In a debate over copyright in the British Parliament in 1841, Thomas McCauley, like Jefferson, questioned the natural right of ownership of intellectual property, arguing instead for any rights being based on their usefulness to society:

> I own ... that property is the creature of law, and that law that creates property can be defended only on this ground, that it is a law] beneficial to mankind. (cited in Patry, 2009: xvi)

Such contradictions between the rights of the author and the rights of the public have contributed to the overall confusion of how intellectual property can be legally or ethically used. What rights, therefore, do authors have to control their property and what rights do the public have to use this intellectual property has never been clear, or as recent court cases have shown, stable.

Fair use, as Post (2009) argues, can be viewed as an implementation of the Jeffersonian ideal of balancing the protection of the rights of content creators as an incentive to create new intellectual property with the need for the widespread access of the public to that same intellectual property. In one of the first important cases in US intellectual property law, *Sheldon vs. Metro-Goldwyn-Mayer,* Learned Hand, a Supreme Court justice in the early part of the 20th century, argued that when analyzing whether intellectual property law has been violated, a judge must take into account 'the very web of the author's dramatic expression' (Vaidhyanathan, 2001: 109). While trying to understand exactly what is meant here can be difficult, Hand's choice of words illustrates how transformative principle is an important guide to deciding when the use of intellectual property is justified.

The first factor depends on whether there has been a transformative use of the work. The legal appropriation of intellectual property can be determined by the extent the original piece is 'transformed' in the new piece. The degree of transformation required for a work to be considered 'original' is often ambiguous, leading to a great number of court cases. What constitutes transformation, however, is often extremely subjective. In one case (*Gaylord vs. The United States*), an artist sued the US Post office because his statue was included in an image used on a postage stamp. The Court ruled that even though the photo altered his likeness, the alterations were not considered enough to invoke the fair use provision (Artflaw, 2010).

The growing importance of technologically enhanced forms of expression has further challenged this relationship between transformation and originality. A case involving the artist Shepard Fairey's use of a photograph of then presidential candidate Obama to create a new image that was used extensively in his campaign raised a number of issues about the degree to which his transformation of the image is his own and not the property of the photographer (Lessing, 2009b). Such uses are complicated by the fact that though his initial intent may have been artistic, the popularity of the new image generated a fair amount of revenue, an issue that would seldom be the case with the work of our students.

Today, this debate often has centered on 'sampling', a form of music that is stitched together with short pieces of music (e.g. Girl Talk at http://www.youtube.com/watch?v=Dzu ILGFDtm&feature=fvsr). Sampling allows pieces of audio or video to be reedited to create a new form. For some, this kind of creativity reflects the power of the internet, as well as the sharing of intellectual property, to create these new forms of expression (Lessing, 2005, 2009). For others, sampling epitomizes the denigration of traditional forms of art and the artists who created them by allowing anyone to rip their work apart without permission (Rosenthal, 2011).

In education, fair use has become one of the principal methods for both protecting and constraining these kinds of uses of intellectual property in the classroom (Aufderheide, 2011). While traditional forms of textual borrowing, such as citing authors in a research paper, does not need to meet these standards of transformation, new approaches to literacies that incorporate images and video may be affected. Principle 2 is concerned with the benefit of the work to the public. For example, work that can be used to illustrate or comment on a claim may have a different status than work used for decoration (e.g. Herrington, 2010). Principle 3 focuses on the amount of differentiating required between copying a few pages, a couple of chapters and the entire book, which a teacher may make when handing out materials to students in a class.

Here, again the context of the delivery of the material can be important; for example, handing a copy out in class may differ from posting it online, depending upon who can access it. While there are guidelines for how much text can be used without permission when publishing a book or an article, the relevance of amount to the teaching of writing is less clear. The issues are more complicated when using these new forms of digital literacy since, for example, it is more likely that a student would use an entire image than use an entire portion of text. However, the focus on the amount used could be mitigated by the degree to which its usage transforms its nature. Thus, it is important that all the principles be taken together in deciding whether fair use applies (Nimmer, 2003).

Principle 4, which many feel is the most important in determining whether a usage is covered by fair use, is concerned with whether the creator is losing money, which may not apply if only a limited amount is used, and whether the user receives money, which is rarely the case for teachers or students unless they themselves try to publish these materials to make a profit.

While fair use is often the reason we can use the materials in ways that may be considered plagiarism, the principles underlying them can differ greatly. Clearly, the metaphor of 'purpose and character', is not relevant to the use of physical property, but as Okediji (2001: 270) argues, 'if communication is the goal, then fair use will help distinguish between communication that is the *sine non qua* of the internet and mere exploitation of another's property,' regardless of whether the property is in print or on the internet. While these cases are not directly concerned with plagiarism, they illustrate how the debate in intellectual property law can be applied to the writing classroom as well.

It is often difficult to determine whether fair use applies unless there is a specific legal precedence directly applicable to the existing situation. Both teachers and students, therefore, are often placed in situations where they must make legal and ethical decisions without an appropriate level of understanding. Terms commonly used in fair use discussions, such as 'appropriation', 'transformation' and 'harm', are not always clearly defined and have been subject to a great amount of litigation over the years.

In making judgments about whether copyrighted materials can be used without permission or payment in either the physical or virtual classroom, it must be determined whether their usage conforms to or is consistent with at least some of the fair use provisions. In theory, fair use can be viewed as a set of arguments for justifying the appropriation of copyrighted material. In practice, Nimmer (2003) found that even judges often apply these factors in an ambiguous and contradictory ways. He argued that judges, in order to decide the case, sometimes use these provisions rhetorically to support their arguments.

One area where intellectual property can be used without permission is in parody, as illustrated in one of the most frequently cited court cases on fair use, *Campbell vs. Acuff-Rose Music, Inc.* The publisher of the popular rock and roll song, 'Oh Pretty Woman,' sued the creator of a parody of the song, a group called 2 Live Crew, for copyright infringement. It was decided that the intent was to parody the song, thus satisfying Principle 2. Okediji (2001) argues that this decision illustrates the importance of the purpose and character of the use of intellectual property in determining whether fair use is applicable.

Another area where fair use has been shown not to apply is in the use of copied materials sold to students. One highly influential decision that has affected classroom teaching in the United States was the case of Kinkos (now called FedEx Office), which is a popular place for making copies. The court ruled in *Basic Books vs. Kinko's Graphics* that Kinko's had violated copyright laws by making copies of articles with 'no literary effort. ... to expand upon or contextualize the materials copied' (cited in Jaszi, 1994: 49). This decision is important since Kinkos was a for-profit operation; therefore, the decision illustrates the importance of financial exchanges as mitigating claims of fair use, a decision that would later be applied to court decisions regarding file-sharing sites such as Napster. As long as teachers are not charging students for copies, however, this decision may not apply. A more controversial application of fair use can be seen in how it was used to defend the right of the copy detection program Turnitin.com (*A.V., et. al. vs. iParadigms*) to store the essays that were submitted by teachers and students to check for plagiarism. The controversy over what constitutes transformation can be seen in the decision over the legality to store the texts submitted for plagiarism checking because the judge ruled that storing the texts in order to use them to judge plagiarism was considered transformative and, therefore, covered by fair use.

Beyond its obvious connections to textual borrowing, fair use has come to reflect the rights of individual governments to create laws that reflect local concerns. Unlike the spread of intellectual property law, which has often been imposed through treaties, the development of the concept of fair use, or whatever term is used, often reflects unique historical conditions, such as the Jeffersonian ideals. The overall concern that fair use embodies for balancing different values and goals can be highly applicable to questions on plagiarism.

In all these ways, fair use has come to reflect how, even within a specific culture, the idea of copying can vary a great deal. Coupled with the cultural and economic differences, we can see how its role in writing has become so complicated. That is why so much is at stake in the debate over fair use and why it provides an interesting metaphor for thinking about plagiarism. Much like the rules regarding plagiarism, fair use places constraints on textual borrowing that can greatly shape the use of these texts. Both require users to continually think about how to transform the materials they have borrowed to satisfy their communities' guidelines for using them. How can we balance the need for norms governing the citation of intellectual property with the need to encourage learning and experimentation without the fear of harsh sanctions that may constrain the writing process?

Differences between Intellectual Property Law and Plagiarism

Despite their common origins and their epistemological importance in constraining the use of intellectual property, there are also divergences in how they have been viewed and implemented. Violations of intellectual property laws, as witnessed by the ongoing litigation by the RIAA against those it feels are illegally downloading music, are dealt with through court cases while plagiarism is generally not (Green, 2002). Court cases involving plagiarism often involve a demand for redress from those who feel they have wrongly been accused. In one case, a student sued a classmate, who he claimed had plagiarized his work without his knowledge, causing him to be accused of plagiarism and suspended from university. The court awarded him $100 in damages, as well as $25,000 in legal fees, which provides an interesting perspective on what a plagiarized paper is worth. In a recent case at The Ohio State University, a recent graduate student was sued for plagiarizing a dissertation, which perhaps has more economic value than does a class paper. The student not only had her degree rescinded but also had to pay in $15,000 restitution (*Montana C. Miller, PhD vs. Elisabeth Nixon, PhD*).

Although there is a tremendous imbalance in the number of court cases regarding intellectual property and plagiarism, the former are important for understanding where the concepts are interconnected and where they are not. The court has made a clear distinction, for example, between what kind of information can be copied and what cannot be copied. As former Supreme Court Justice O'Connor put it in *Feist Publications vs. Rural Telephone Service*, a decision that put the names in a phonebook in the public domain, '[t]he distinction is one between creation and discovery: the first person to find and report a particular fact has not created the fact; he or she has merely discovered its existence' (cited in Merges *et al.*, 1997: 336). Thus, granting authorship to an idea involves more than simply the investment of time or effort but rather something more creative and transformative (Price & Pollack, 1994).

In an often cited intellectual property case, The Harper Row Company sued *The Nation* magazine for printing in a book review of the autobiography of President Gerald Ford 300 words that were deemed to be in violation of their intellectual property rights. Of particular concern was one sentence dealing with his pardon of former president Nixon. They successfully argued that the publication of a specific piece of information undermined the economic value of their publication, thus overturning a lower court's ruling that fair use principles allowed the publication.

Determining the amount of copied text that would trigger charges of plagiarism is equally confusing. Merges *et al.* (1997) cite former Supreme Court Justice Learned Hand writing in the early part of the 20th century that 'no plagiarist can excuse the wrong by showing how much of his work he did not pirate' (*Sheldon vs. Metro-Goldwyn-Mayer*). Despite Justice Hand's admonishment, the amount of textual appropriation constituting plagiarism is often as ambiguous as the amount needed to be taken to violate intellectual property law. Charges of plagiarism could be levied even if only one sentence was not attributed (Lumley, 1995). Copying a sentence can be viewed the same as copying an entire paper and turning it in as one's own. Writing about his own struggle with how much copying is acceptable, the Canadian novelist David Carpenter (n.d.) asks:

> How much is too much? To make judgments on this question the literary sleuth looks for an entire pattern of stolen words and ideas done with unmistakable cunning. But hovering up a plot (or an idea, a maxim, a character, a technique, a moral dilemma, a phrase) for one's own use is as common as breathing for the writer. Tracing the process of lifting or any other legitimate kind of influence leads us into labyrinths as byzantine as the human mind. At best this is a fascinating exercise in the impossible.

Carpenter discusses how he realized the extent to which he had borrowed material for his novel from another Canadian writer, Robertson Davies. The irony of this accusation for Carpenter was that he had previously accused Davies of 'borrowing' material from the British novelist, Iris Murdoch, who, he points out, had borrowed material from classic Greek literature. As Carpenter points out, there is not only a fuzzy area of demarcation between what is plagiarism and what is not but also between what is a good and creative use of intertextuality and what is not, the latter often referred to as being 'derivative'. In this case, the problem of plagiarism is not so much a moral issue but a creative one; that is, how well can a writer transform existing texts into new ones.

Carpenter here confronts, as have many writing theorists, the impact of intertextuality on the concept of authorship and its relationship to plagiarism. On the other hand, unlike many contemporary writing theorists, such as Howard (1999), Carpenter views writing as essentially a lonely and isolated process; however, he does seem to agree that this isolation is mitigated by the collaboration between the writer and all the texts the writer is familiar with.

From both a creative and legal perspective, judging the value of a text is influenced by how much transformation the author or authors add to the original texts. What constitutes acceptable transformation or patchwriting is often unclear. The extent of such collaboration makes defining plagiarism, such as by using an artificial definition of copying more than three words per sentence, a less-than-satisfying approach. As discussions of patchwriting (e.g. Howard, 1999; Pecorari, 2008) indicate, there may be gaps in how students and teachers are judging the 'originality' of a piece of text. It is difficult to isolate ideas as belonging to a particular source as one might establish his or her ownership of a piece of physical property by using a receipt or bill of sale. Gladwell (2004: 48) denounces those 'who encourage use to pretend that . . . chains of influence and evolution do not exist and that a writer's words have a virgin birth and should have an eternal life'. Even the most sophisticated copy detection programs, even if they may be useful for tracking simple copying, would not be able to find the source of an idea, which can further complicate the issue if the source is falsely identified.

An often highly contested difference between intellectual property law and plagiarism is the question of intent. What does it mean when a student copies a piece of text but changes only a few words? Does the student feel that this is an acceptable paraphrase or is this an attempt to mask the intent to plagiarize? For many teachers, plagiarism is not concerned with the intent of the writer (cf. Percorari, 2008). The individual who deliberately takes the words of another writer and the individual who claims that an alleged instance of plagiarism was an accident could be considered equally culpable (cf. Pecorari, 2008). If plagiarism is considered 'stealing' or 'kidnapping', then such 'crimes' can never be 'accidental'. On the other hand, in cases such as parody, intentional copying is protected by law. Traditional views of plagiarism, on the other hand, admit no such distinctions although some have used the cultural or developmental background of the student for having a different view of plagiarism.

Plagiarism is different than violations of intellectual property in another important way. Intellectual property protection has a specific, though often controversial, duration after which this property enters the public domain and then can be reproduced and distributed freely. Walt Disney could exploit the public domain by taking 19th-century fairy tales and novels and transforming them into animations without having to ask permission or pay royalties. Lessing (2004) argues that a law further extending the duration of a copyright law was specifically passed to protect Mickey Mouse, a character Lessing feels may have itself been taken from a popular silent film star of that time, Buster Keaton. Supreme Court cases, such as *Eldred vs. Reno*, however, have confirmed the rights of the government to extend the duration of copyright.

Definitions of plagiarism can also be extended beyond what is covered by intellectual property law, such as seen in the use of the term 'self-plagiarism', where someone is accused of intentionally repurposing their own intellectual property without substantial transformation. Under intellectual property law, however, the owner of the property can do whatever he or she wishes with it. Terms such as 'self-plagiarism' (Scanlon, 2007) contradict this concept. A student can be accused of self-plagiarism for handing in his or her own paper to different classes. Faculty can be accused of self-plagiarism for submitting the same paper to different journals in order to 'pad' their resumes.

Perhaps, one of the most controversial differences can be found in acts of 'ghostwriting'. Ghostwriting usually refers to a person hiring a writer to produce a text that is subsequently claimed by that person, an arrangement considered acceptable in contexts such as in speeches written for politicians or businessmen but not in contexts where the originality is being judged. Ghostwriting can be considered plagiarism if the audience believes itself to be defrauded (Brandt, 2007; Posner, 2007). A major controversy arose among the readers of the educational journal *The Chronicle of Higher Education* when a 'ghostwriter' published an article under a pseudonym describing how he helps students with custom-made papers that cannot be checked for plagiarism in traditional ways:

> You've never heard of me, but there's a good chance that you've read some of my work. I'm a hired gun, a doctor of everything, an academic mercenary. My customers are your students. I promise you that. Somebody in your classroom uses a service that you can't detect, that you can't defend against, that you may not even know exists. (Dante, 2010)

For some students, there is no difference between what this person does and what a speechwriter does for a president or prime minister. For many in the university, however, such a distinction is of the greatest moral significance.

3 Connecting Intellectual Property Law and Plagiarism in the Writing Classroom: The Impact of Intellectual Property Law on Teaching Writing

Teachers are no longer sheltered from these issues regarding the use of intellectual property but must continually confront them in their classrooms. Much of what teachers do in the writing classroom is affected and, to some extent governed, by intellectual property law. In the past, the discussion of intellectual property by writing teachers was limited to needing to judge a relatively small number of situations, such as whether they could make copies to hand out to the students in class. Teachers, however, now have a variety of ways of distributing these copies, including posting them online, giving out URLs to their online locations, burning copies to CDs or posting the materials on an online reserve. With these changes have come more complexities in judging the rights and regulations affecting these actions. As Litman (2008) has pointed out, it has only been in recent times that the reach of the law has expanded to cover almost every use of intellectual property. As a result, teachers and students must be aware of not only what regulations may be imposed on them but also what rights they have.

One cause of the confusion is that the goals for providing protection to intellectual property can be contradictory. One goal was to protect the economic development of the country. Another goal was to give creators an 'incentive', but not necessarily a moral right, to create. A third, sometimes contradictory, goal, as the discussion of fair use illustrates, is to support learning and the flow of ideas. What can further confuse the situation is that there have been few specific court rulings that cover all the uses teachers have for intellectual property. For example, are you allowed to rent a DVD and show it to your class? Many of the answers to these questions are 'maybe' or 'perhaps, depending of the circumstances'.

Concepts such as fair use can, therefore, have great pedagogical impact on how writing, as well as how many other subjects, are taught. Therefore, as Rife (2008) has argued, fair use, as well as the multitude of other laws and provisions that sanction the use of intellectual property, is of great importance in the teaching of writing. Even in countries where there is not a formal tradition of fair use, these concepts can help teachers focus on the rights, and not just on the restrictions, for using intellectual property.

Much of the controversy has resulted because of the growth of new forms of texts on the internet. The written nature of many digital texts has meant that certain forms of communications, which may once have been oral, have now become written and, therefore, have become forms of intellectual property subjected to the same rules as do print texts. The proliferation of email, chats and blogs, and now Twitter and Facebook, have demonstrated tremendous pedagogical potential, both as a tool for helping with conventional forms of writing and as new forms of digital literacies (Bloch, 2007) and multimodal texts (e.g. Kress, 2003). Many new genres of digital literacy rely on accessing materials from the internet. New approaches to teaching grammar rely on greater degrees of specificity in the types of examples given (e.g. Hyland, 2000b). Teachers can distribute authentic materials drawn from a variety of different genres and disciplines, ranging from samples of grammar to published academic articles, movies and podcasts.

The growing availability of these materials and the ease with which they can be copied have made cutting and pasting and freely distributing intellectual property much easier. Some types of such copying may be legal and ethical, and some may be considered illegal and unethical. The latter types have been the center of the 'plagiarism epidemic'. As Szabo and Underwood (2004: 196) argued, a majority of the students in their research at a British University would 'give in to Internet plagiarism' in the right situation. But are all such acts of 'giving into' illegal and unethical? Or are some acts both legal and ethical?

At the same time, the growing importance of these texts have raised new ethical concerns regarding plagiarism because of the ease with which information can be cut and pasted and new rhetorical concerns because of the different contexts in which these texts are found and possible differences in how such texts should be cited. Writers need to consider new kinds of questions. Do internet texts, such as blogs, carry the same degree of credibility as do print texts and how may any differences affect the credibility of the writer? Should these texts be then cited as an authored text or personal communication or are they like private conversations that may not need attribution (Kolko, 1998)? Should email postings, for example, to a listserv be considered as common knowledge or cited in the same way as are other forms of print texts? Should a cite like Wikipedia be considered as trustworthy as traditional print-based encyclopedias?

Intellectual Property Law in an Educational Context

In the United States, education has had a privileged space in intellectual property law. Fair use has had perhaps its greatest impact in the educational use of intellectual property, reflecting what Jefferson said more than 200 years ago that 'the nations which refuse monopolies of invention, are as fruitful as England in new and useful devices.' The Jeffersonian ideal that the primary purpose of these laws should be to promote the spread of ideas balances the Lockean argument that authors had natural rights as creators, which would become the basis for granting strong rights to authors and their publishers (Post, 2009).

On the other side of the issue is what Reyman (2010) calls the 'rhetorical narrative' that links intellectual property with physical property has further served to confuse both students and teachers by denying that there are rights to use intellectual property. As a result of these conflicting narratives, teachers and students are often confused about their rights. The ratification of the 1976 copyright act not only had a profound effect on the use of intellectual property in the United States schools and universities but also created much confusion about how intellectual property laws could be applied in the classroom.

One attempt to resolve some of this confusion can be seen in the guidelines created after the 1976 Copyright Act by a group of interested parties to ensure that teachers have some limited rights without the threat of being sued, although it has never been clear how limited these rights are. For example, the distribution of copies was 'subject to the rigorous limits of "brevity," "spontaneity," and "cumulative effect" ' (Crews, 2001: 617). However, as is often the case, these terms have never been clearly defined. Teachers have often been told that although they could make a copy of a piece of intellectual property, they could distribute it only once. As Crews points out, the purpose of such guidelines was limited to providing a 'safe harbor' for universities and its employees to use intellectual property for nonprofit and educational purposes without the fear of endless lawsuits that these institutions did not have the resources to fight.

Unfortunately, these guidelines have often confused teachers as much as they have provided a safe harbor. Crews points out that while the courts have sometimes used these guidelines rhetorically as a legal argument for limiting usage (e.g. *Basic Books vs. Kinko's Graphics*), their implementation remain ambiguous and was not universally accepted within the academic community. While some universities accepted these guidelines, other groups, such as the American Association of University Professors, did not (Grayson, 2001). The difficulty of subsequent attempts during the 1990s to reconcile these differences showed that deep divisions still existed (Crews, 2001).

Teachers are still often placed in the position of needing to be intellectual property lawyers in order to decide whether they are abiding by the law. As Crews (2001) puts it, teachers count the number of words in an article before they distribute it to their class. Writing teachers, like judges, are faced with laws that are becoming more difficult to enforce or to understand. There have been some court decisions that provide clear guidelines, such as the *Kinko* case. Although many of the cases decided in for-profit contexts provide interesting frameworks for discussing the nature of intellectual property, these decisions may not apply to the classroom.

The Impact of Technology on the Pedagogical Use of Intellectual Property

The legal questions regarding the distribution of copyrighted materials to students, for example, were first related to technology advances, such as mimeographs and later copy machines, which made the distribution of large amounts of materials easier and more available whenever the teachers needed them. A long list of new technologies, from the internet to the use of email, digital stories and concordancing programs, have been introduced into the writing classroom, each raising new issues regarding the use of intellectual property.

Not everyone has found these developments to have a positive impact on creativity or education. Lessing (2005) tells the story of how John Phillips Sousa, the American composer of marches, complained to Congress at the turn of the 20th century that the invention of the phonograph would change the nature of music in such a way as to discourage people from singing. Much like Plato's lament that the introduction of writing would negatively affect memory, Sousa seemed to partially understand how technology could change the use of intellectual property but could not anticipate how new technologies could change our creative processes, including how we sing.

The introduction of newer technologies for the distribution of intellectual property has again further complicated the issue. Often the boundaries for fair use can depend on how well the materials are protected. For example, a recent case where a group of publishers sued Georgia State University over posting materials on online reserves was argued on the basis that not only could the students who registered for the course access the materials but that they were available for others as well (http://www.nacua.org/documents/ CambridgeUPress_v_Patton.pdf). Although the site was password protected, there were gaps that allowed non-registered users to access the materials. Had the materials been protected so only registered students could receive them or had copies been handed out in the old-fashioned way, then there may not have been a case. There are a number of ways to accomplish this level of protection, including the use of gated learning management systems. However, such an approach can make it difficult to extend the course beyond the walls of the classroom, as can be found in some new approaches to online education.

This case illustrates how teachers can find themselves in a legal quandary about which they may have little understanding. In this case, for example, the teachers were deposed by the plaintiffs' lawyers in often grueling depositions over whether each of their uses of intellectual property was covered by fair use.

Such cases illustrate the importance for teachers to understand both their rights and the limitations for intellectual property usage. On the other hand, despite what seems to be a growing number of restrictions, sometimes the law changes to better accommodate these new pedagogies. Driven by the economic potential of online teaching, new laws, known as the TEACH ACT, in the United States were passed to clarify the use of intellectual property in online courses. Despite its intentions, it has been felt that these laws have further complicated and restricted fair use.

The growth of the world wide web has intensified concerns over the relationship between technology and academic misconduct. Besides making plagiarizing easier, the internet has made the 'ghostwriting' of student papers easier than ever. Students have long been able to buy texts they could submit as their own (Berlin, 1984; Bledstein, 1978; Russell, 1991), but they were always limited by time and place. On the other hand, the internet has given students more options for purchasing papers and has made the transactions both easier and less traceable. Newer social networking sites, such as the Mechanical Turk (https://www.mturk.com/mturk/welcome), which legitimately allow hiring for all kinds of work, can also provide a different, and again highly controversial, means of bypassing traditional middlemen to find ghostwriters.

As the amount of pedagogical materials has increased on the internet, there have been more and more calls by content creators for greater restrictions. As

Boyle (2010: 60) argues, the 'Internet Threat' has caused content creators to demand that protection increase as the costs of copying decreases, which resulted in such legislation in the United States as the DMCA and the Sonny Bono Copyright Term Extension Act, both of which have been seen as limiting the traditional rights engrained in the US Constitution for the use of intellectual property (Lessing, 2005). The late Jack Valenti once commented that copyright should last 'forever less a day'. New technological developments have raised calls that even these new laws are not strict enough in protecting the moral rights of the author (Rosenthal, 2011).

It has been argued that such limitations contradict the reasons intellectual property was given legal protection in the first place. As Boyle (2010: 8) argues, '[c]opyright, intended to be a servant of creativity, a means of promoting access to information, is becoming an obstacle to both.' He goes on to argue that if copyright restricts creativity, then it is no longer serving its utilitarian function. A similar argument can be applied to the classroom: If copyright law constrains teaching, then does the law contradict its original purpose for supporting the spread of ideas.

As the Georgia State case illustrates, teachers are often caught within this debate. The list of questions teachers must face about the use of intellectual property is endless. In a letter to the TESL-l newsgroup, a writer forwarded a question from a student about whether titles of books are copyrighted. Another letter writer asked whether it was okay to copy messages from the TESL-l listserv and use them as classroom materials. One asked whether movies could be shown in class. A new controversy has emerged over whether students can post their class notes on sites like Course Hero (http://www.coursehero.com; Kolowich, 2009) or their teachers' lectures, which can easily be recorded on cellphones and published on YouTube. The legality of these new forms of distribution rested on a sometimes subtle distinction between oral texts, which may not be considered intellectual property, and written materials such as PowerPoint presentations that are in a fixed medium.

Teachers, therefore, want to know whether they can copyright their lecture notes or whether they or their students can sell them online. Teachers can also find websites where faculty can post their syllabi. Even such simple acts raise new questions. Can faculty borrow each other's syllabi without their permission (Sinor, 2008)? This controversy will not go away as students become more reliant on the internet for their writing. The growing numbers of the so-called digital natives (Palfrey & Gasser, 2008; Prensky, 2001), those who have grown up with internet, has meant that students may have experiences with an ever-growing myriad of technologies that are used outside the classroom and may also be used for educational purposes. On the other hand, the older so-called digital immigrants may not understand these technologies as well, which sets the stage for inevitable conflicts.

The ability to easily publish online, which can have a profound effect on the writer's concept of audience, has brought with it a new set of legal and ethical concerns. The growth of the read/write web (Berners-Lee, 1999) has made it easier for digital natives as well as digital immigrants to publish, whether it is on YouTube or in an online journal. Teachers and students who wish to publish often face a complex and changing set of intellectual property issues regarding who owns the work both before and after it has been published. Journals and publishers vary greatly in how they treat copyrighted material. Some journals allow the author to retain copyright. Others require authors to relinquish their ownership of copyright. Still others reserve certain rights for the author. These requirements have raised additional concerns over whether the author can republish his or her work or even send a copy to a friend.

These developments in digital media raise questions about posting and sharing texts rival the changes that the printing press brought to the nature of literacy (cf. Eisenstein, 1979; Johns, 2010). New approaches to teaching with digital media similarly can also affect attitudes toward using and sharing intellectual property. How music, images and video are used in online texts has forced teachers to become experts in intellectual property law.

We have attempted to integrate digital stories (Lambert, 2010) into our writing classroom. With digital stories, writers can choose images, videos and music to develop their written texts. The use of each of these forms of intellectual property has raised new questions about the use of digital media, both in terms of how students can remix materials found on the internet with their own materials and how these materials can subsequently be distributed as both students and teachers find new audiences for their work. While these new approaches can make the question of intellectual property in the classroom more complex, they can also provide new opportunities for teachers and students to explore both the new issues resulting from these technologies as well as the older issues but from new perspectives.

The Use of Intellectual Property Outside the Classroom

The expansion of the uses of intellectual property has been extended far beyond the classroom. Open-access materials, such as books or journals, have become more prevalent as some content creators have either eschewed financial rewards or have sought to be rewarded in other ways. New open-access journals such as *Language, Learning, and Technology* (llt.msu.edu) and *The Journal of Writing Research* (http://www.jowr.org) have allowed new research to be easily shared at little or no cost by teachers and researchers all over the world.

The growing amount of open-access materials is both a product of the discussion of the differences in online intellectual property and the consequences of the expanded ability to disseminate this material on the web. It is, therefore, not a coincidence that universities such as MIT (http://ocw.mit.edu/courses/electrical-engineering-and-computer-science) and Carnegie Mellon (http://oli.web.cmu.edu/openlearning/index.php), which have long been in the forefront of research in science and technology, were among the first to make teaching materials freely available online. Some of these providers hope, as do many online companies who put part of their product online and charge for upgrading, that students will be encouraged to come to their universities to study in the old-fashioned way with the professors whose materials they have already been exposed to online. On the other hand, there have already been charges that a university in China plagiarized online courses posted by Yale University (http://oyc.yale.edu/) raising questions similar to those I had encountered years earlier with print texts. Regardless of their intent, the availability of such materials has already had a global impact on both education and research.

At the same time, much of the fear many educators have of the 'epidemics' from the concern about how often people like our student have used the intellectual property they have access to. As a result, the use of plagiarism detection programs has proliferated as a technological response to plagiarism. More restrictive laws for distributing online materials have served to limit the sharing of information even more than traditional print copies could. These could be global restrictions such as the controversial proposal by Google to digitize books online. They could also be local issues as well, such as a teacher who might want to share the pdf file but may be as guilty of violating intellectual property law as the person who shares the mp3 file of a song. Such restrictions have raised new questions regarding the use of intellectual property. Does it matter, for example, whether these materials are posted in a password protected context or are open? Teachers are often afraid of distributing materials, perhaps because of the ethical concern that their use may be illegal in the same way students may fear charges of plagiarism for using online materials.

While some technologies have increased accessibility, others have restricted it. Some of these restrictions have already resulted with the introduction of electronic book readers, such as Amazon's Kindle, which are growing in use both inside and outside of the classroom. The ability of Amazon to delete two of George Orwell's books from its Kindle book reader shocked readers who were unaware of this 'tethering' (Zittrain, 2008). Electronic books, in fact, come with a number of new restrictions. Whereas with a print book the reader can access it as many times as desired, sell it, lend it or give it away, and perhaps even make a copy, with the Kindle, all of those uses can be restricted. Strict limitations on the distribution of intellectual property could further extend the gap between the haves and have-nots in their ability to conduct research. As Lillis and Curry (2010) argue, such global access gives researchers a tremendous advantage in conducting publishable research. Open-access materials, on the other hand, have been important for reducing that advantage.

Another issue related to accessibility occurred when publishers restricted the ability of Kindle to use its text to voice features. This restriction limited its usefulness for readers with sight problems and has hampered its adaption in the university because of concerns over how these restrictions can violate the rights of disabled students. While there are certain work-arounds that have been agreed upon with publishers for use with disabled students, other cases can make compliance difficult. Moreover, even the work-arounds may not be considered legal by all the content publishers.

The Role of Writing Teachers in the Debate

Teachers and intellectual property lawyers are often involved in the same conflict between maintaining the integrity of the institution and fostering learning and creativity, whether this integrity refers to a student in a writing class or a musician or software programmer. One of the more exciting results of these discussions has been that writing teachers have begun to take a central role in these controversies. The Committee on Intellectual Property (http://www.ncte.org/cccc/committees/ip), which is sponsored by the National Council of Teachers of English (NCTE), provides writing teachers a forum for discussing issues on the use of intellectual property. Teachers wanting to incorporate any new form of media face these issues, whether it is digital stories or sampling hip-hop music or integrating both (Nelson & Hull, 2005). In response, The Center for Social Media has produced a number of free online pamphlets outlining the fair use rights (http://www.centerforsocialmedia.org/fair-use/best-practices). Even for teachers working in countries without fair use laws, these pamphlets provide a valuable insight into the relationship between creativity and intellectual property law.

Calls for reform of the attitudes and policies toward plagiarism are often met with strong opposition. An article by Rebecca Howard (2001), for example, entitled 'Forget about Policing Plagiarism, Just Teach' was attacked by some who felt that such a position undermines academic integrity. One university administrator responded:

> Don't believe it, and don't accept it. Plagiarism remains an individual decision and an act of fundamental dishonesty. Apologies and recommendations like Howard's will do nothing to decrease plagiarism.

How does a teacher or an institution differentiate his or her or its approach toward plagiarism where there are such concerns, particularly when they come from administrators, for academic integrity, regardless of the constraints that such concerns may place on learning?

An interesting way for thinking about these issues can be found in what Boyle (2010) calls the 'Jefferson warning' – that in the United States the rules regarding copyright were established as a means of promoting creativity as well as providing an incentive to create – a concept that can be applied to plagiarism as well. Teachers, particularly those working with creating new forms of media and multimodal forms of literacy, have turned toward these new approaches as a means of protecting their students from violating intellectual property law and charges of plagiarism, by focusing on the transformative nature of the creative process. A connection can be found between having students transform intellectual property and having students cite texts for rhetorical purposes and not simply to acknowledge ownership. In such approaches, both intellectual property law and the rules regarding the attribution of texts can be regarded as an integral part of the writing process.

Rethinking the Relationship between Intellectual Property and Plagiarism

One dilemma that has arisen in this debate over intellectual property is the relationship between the creator and the user. Today record executives and teachers can find themselves struggling with how to deal with those people who are central to their work or who are their best customers but are seen to be violating their rules. Individuals sharing music are often the biggest purchasers of CDs and concert tickets (cf. Rosenthal, 2011) just as those responsible for plagiarizing are often those who most need help in developing their writing. The punitive nature of plagiarism has created the same type of contradiction between punishing and teaching that has been seen in how the courts punish those who most love the music but have been caught sharing it. Despite the legal victories of the entertainment industry in shutting down peer-to-peer websites and suing those who share intellectual property, there are still millions of people willing to 'steal' or 'pirate' it. In the same way, plagiarism has continued despite threats and the development of new technologies designed to stop it.

However, as Patry (2009: 24) argues, such criminalization will doom the content creators to a stagnation from which history has shown it is difficult to recover. He argues:

> Litigation has become a tool by which copyright industries deceive themselves into thinking they can avoid the inevitable stagnation that occurs when they fail to focus on the essential purpose of their business as a customer-creating and customer-satisfying organism.

Much in the same way that intellectual property law has been used to instill fear of litigation in children and their parents (Patry, 2009), as well as writing teachers, the threat of failure and punishment has been used to instill a fear of misusing texts, what has been referred to as the 'shock and awe' approach to teaching about plagiarism (Jascik, 2009), a metaphor taken from the US military's attack on Iraq. Even if the amount of plagiarism could be substantially reduced, using such approaches as copy detection programs, such a reduction tells us little about the students' writing processes.

The intent to instill fear can lead to unintended consequences, which may negatively impact the student's writing development. Our university used a variation of the shock and awe approach when it created a short play to be shown during the orientation program for international students depicting the process they may encounter if accused of plagiarism. In the play, an international student was berated by the committee on academic misconduct for failing to correctly use quotation marks even though the passage had been cited.

After seeing the play, some of our students admitted that they would never want to go through that experience, even though it was never clearly explained why the student needed to use quotation marks or why the penalty for such an infraction was so great. One student who admitted that he was scared by the play turned in a paper using quotation marks with every paraphrased passage even though such usage was unnecessary. Advocates for reforming plagiarism, as are those favoring reform of intellectual property law, are looking for a more restrictive definition of plagiarism as well as a reduction in penalties to make the laws and guidelines conform more to the actual behavior of the students and the pedagogical goals of the classroom.

Conclusion

In sum, the analysis presented here has led to a variety of questions and debates connecting intellectual property and plagiarism to which writing teachers can make a valuable contribution. Such connections include:

- Both have been used extensively to explain why international students 'inappropriately' use intellectual property and plagiarize.
- They have developed in response to historical changes in how authorship developed.
- They have evolved over the past 300 years in response to social, economic and historical forces, a process that has led to inevitable cultural differences as well as similarities.
- Their evolution reflects local unique cultures that have developed from different historical experiences as well as trends toward globalization that may harmonize these differences.
- They have been institutionalized in both legal and pedagogical contexts and then 'pushed' down on users, without necessarily considering local needs or customs.
- They have long been involved in struggles over governance.
- They share metaphors that deal with often horrific criminal or socially unacceptable activities.
- They have practices that have been criticized for stifling creative and pedagogical innovation.
- Their definitions have been extended over time to include more and more uses of intellectual property.
- Teachers may be confused because of the complexity of both issues.
- The shift from print to digital texts has raised questions about whether traditional approaches for governance are still applicable.
- They share the controversy over a top-down, centralized form of governance versus a bottom-up, localized form of governance.
- Reformers in both areas have sought new practices and metaphors for framing institutional change in an international context.
- The so-called digital natives and nonnative English speakers have been singled out for special attention. As Lessing (2009) argues, such attempts at eradication have only succeeded in criminalizing certain uses of intellectual property, often turning young people into 'thieves'

and 'pirates'. Similarly, plagiarism among our students has not been stopped, but they too have been similarly criminalized.

- Violations of intellectual property law and plagiarism have been difficult to stop.

Not everyone agrees that copyright reform and plagiarism reform involve the same principles. Lawrence Lessing (2009a), one of the foremost advocates for copyright reform, somewhat facetiously stated that '[p]lagiarism is... the only offense deserving the death penalty.' It seems difficult to escape relying on these metaphors to express one's opinions regarding plagiarism regardless of one's position. As I will argue, however, finding alternative approaches will inevitably require rethinking the nature of the metaphors we use.

4 A Pedagogical Approach toward Plagiarism

The search for the relationship between new pedagogical approaches and new metaphors raises the 'chicken and egg' question of which comes first. Given the linear nature of the printed book, one has to choose one, so we begin with the question of formulating new approaches.

The Development of Attitudes toward Plagiarism in the Academy

As with the questions surrounding the use of intellectual property, our search for answers can begin with a historical overview of plagiarism. The concerns with plagiarism in the United States seems to have its origins during the late 19th and early 20th century as attitudes toward intellectual property were expanding (Marsh, 2007). As Hyde (2010) points out, this was a period when American romanticism, as epitomized by the writings of Ralph Waldo Emerson, replaced the more socially orientated thinking that dominated American intellectual life in the 18th century. During this period, numerous incidents of plagiarism and the growth of paper mills were reported (Russell, 1991), including one incident that led to a shooting at Antioch College in Ohio when a professor confronted a student selling papers (Bledstein, 1978).

The question of why students cheat raised issues then similar to those discussed today. One such issue was that students did not necessarily see themselves as authors or even as part of a learning culture (cf. Blum, 2009). For the first part of the 19th century, attending university was often, though not always (Gold, 2008), seen as a social sinecure for future businessmen or clergy whose careers were guaranteed by their fathers' position and who, therefore, did not require a degree. The lack of seriousness given to obtaining an education, as illustrated by the social importance given to 'averageness' or what is sometimes referred to as the 'Gentleman's C' (Veysey, 1965: 299), was seen as a possible cause of academic misconduct. Veysey writes that 'the widespread persistence of cheating on examinations, with little sense of personal responsibility, bespoke the reality of continued alienation' (1965: 299). Academic writing during this period often had little importance for the student, beyond demonstrating having obtained a proper degree of literacy or a basic level of knowledge (Berlin, 1984; Russell, 1991).

This situation began to change with the development of new types of universities enrolling new types of students in the United States. Land-grant universities were developed during the latter half of the 19th century to educate students in the new technological developments in agriculture and industry (Gold, 2008). Many of these students returned to their family farms and, in general, did have the guaranteed social status that some of their counterparts had. As the university began to take on more responsibility for training students for jobs in industry, more emphasis was placed on teaching the written artifacts required for these jobs, such as articles and reports (Russell, 1991). Therefore, the teaching of writing began to increase in importance in the university curriculum as it began to compete with speaking as the dominant form of rhetorical instruction.

One historical aspect that affected how writing was taught was the influence of German universities on American higher education (e.g. Berlin, 1984). Connors and Lunsford (1994: 370) note that when American academics returned from studying in Germany, they brought with them the 'scholarly precision' of the German system to replace the 'gentleman-amateurism' of the British system, although there was no specific pedagogy for teaching writing (Brereton, 1995).

These various influences would greatly affect the relationship between research and the teaching of writing (Berlin, 1984). The growing professionalism brought an increase in graduate studies. Researchers at the graduate level may feel less alienation and, therefore, a stronger sense of authorship than their undergraduate counterparts, which would add a further emphasis to the need to create standards for plagiarism. As Johns (2010) argues, this push toward professionalization elevated the status of intellectual property and how it was treated. He finds that this connection was especially true in the sciences, where 'discovery' was a defining aspect the process and, therefore, should be rewarded by acknowledgment.

As Adam Sherman Hill, one of the principal designers of these new writing courses, wrote in 1879, the purpose of these courses was 'to teach boys and girls to use their native tongue correctly and intelligently' (cited in Elliot, 2005: 11). By the beginning of the 20th century, universities began to codify its rules in these courses regarding the attribution of both texts and ideas and to establish punishments for their violation (Brereton, 1995; Marsh, 2007). Brereton argues that such rules made it seem that these new writing courses were designed to put students 'on trial' (1995: 19). As Marsh points out, these new rules coincided with the passage of new copyright laws that granted greater protection to the author.

There were also changes in the role of intertextuality in academic writing, which enhanced the concern about plagiarism, as it has today. In his study of the research article in physics, Bazerman (1988) reports that in the 19th century, references were used only generally without necessarily referring to a specific claim; however, by the turn of 20th century more attention was paid to coordinating current research with previous research, resulting in both an increase in the number of citations and the length of the articles. Bazerman (1988) shows how these practices spread over the years, particularly to the social sciences as demonstrated by the codification of the APA style manual. This new attitude toward the importance of citations, as well as to what Bazerman refers to as its 'standardization', can be seen as another factor influencing the growing importance of plagiarism as a concern in American universities.

The more dynamic role of intertextuality can also be found in various genres of writing. Bazerman (1988) gives the example of how writing in the social sciences began to resemble scientific literature, particularly in their use of textual borrowing. The growth of scientific research, for example, placed a greater importance on the use of references as a rhetorical means of establishing the 'truth' of a claim (Bazerman, 1988), which in turn can increase the importance of the rules regarding the attribution of these references. Citation practices in science have similarly evolved along with changes in scientific practice and funding (Biagioli, 2003).

This historical relationship between the development of genre and the role of textual borrowing can highlight an important pedagogical consideration: the importance of teaching about plagiarism within the context of genre studies. At its essence, plagiarism is about the rules for textual borrowing and, therefore, plays an intermediary role in what Bazerman (2009a) calls the epistemological nature of genre. According to Bazerman, learning a genre is not just learning a form of organization but also engaging in the epistemological practice of the field. Attributing sources, as Latour (1988) points out from a much more social perspective, is part of that process.

Such historical changes can also be seen in the development of alternative attitudes toward plagiarism in other countries, which, at least in part, resulted from the shift in these nonnative English-speaking countries from publishing in journals in their native language to journals in English (Lillis & Curry, 2010). One of the earliest reports in China of the problems associated with this shift concerns two researchers accused of plagiarizing their literature review in a paper published in an English-language journal (Li & Xiong, 1996). According to the report, the writers seemed surprised at the accusations. Unlike Western academics who normally plead that they made an innocent mistake when caught copying, these researchers readily admitted plagiarizing but did not understand the concern since they felt that the literature review was highly formulaic and, therefore, did not need to reflect any original or critical thinking.

This example illustrates a number of important issues regarding the continually changing intersection of traditional cultural values attached to intellectual property and plagiarism with new attitudes toward the scientific process. For whatever reason they chose to publish in an English-language journal, they may not have been prepared for the implications of this historic shift, in particular the different rules regarding attribution or the demands of writing in a second language. Despite the apparent differences with Western standards, the criticism and their resulting punishment also refutes the argument that Chinese academic culture had no such standards for appropriate attribution, as is often claimed, although their standards, as well as the rhetorical importance of these citations, may not have been applied in the same way as is found in other academic cultures (Bloch & Chi, 1995).

As with the study of intellectual property, this historical perspective suggests that the principles shaping attitudes toward plagiarism are not necessarily 'hard-wired' cultural distinctions but more malleable ones that also reflect evolving social and cultural developments. This perspective, however, may not mitigate the problem for the L2 writer, who still may need to understand possible intercultural differences regarding textual borrowing. However, the historical nature of the relationship between plagiarism and intellectual property can demonstrate how such difficulties can be viewed in ways that allow for more flexible, and less moralistic, pedagogical approaches.

Both those supporting traditional approaches to plagiarism and those advocating the reform of plagiarism can learn a great deal from the battles over the governance of intellectual property. No aspect of this battle over the equilibrium of governance has generated more publicity or controversy than the control of online music. These new approaches will be important for our discussion of reforming plagiarism since they frame a shift from a general institutional control over those rules regarding textual appropriation that apply to every student in every context to more locally controlled approaches that can reflect the specific classroom goals of the teacher.

Nevertheless, there are still some aspects of authorship that seem to be affected by the differences in the program's code or architecture. The authorship of a web page may differ from the authorship of a blog, which in turn may differ from the authorship of a tweet or an email. The decentralized authorship of the webpage made it easy for the reader to control how the webpage is read (Bolter, 2001). Although a blog is architecturally similar to a web page in how it is coded, it has provided greater emphasis on authorship since blogs seem to allow the writer to focus primarily on developing his or her own thoughts.

On the other hand, micro blogs, such as Twitter, which limit the number of characters for each posting, may provide a different form of authorship since they limit the depth of the development of ideas. As Post (2009) argues, there is no better example of how the architecture of a website can affect authorship than Wikipedia, where without strong governance, an unpaid and largely anonymous group of authors has created a body of work that rivals traditional encyclopedias.

Even without considering the impact of technology, the nature of authorship can vary greatly across different genres. The debate over the nature of authorship has been seen as central to any discussion of plagiarism. As Sunderland-Smith (2008) argues, postmodern views of authorship and the relationship between the author and the reader/viewer, such as found in the work of Barthes (1967) and Foucault (1969/1980), has challenged traditional views of what is considered plagiarism. Despite these arguments, the nature of authorship, as has the nature of plagiarism, remains highly contested, particularly when new technologies are introduced, as has been the case since the time of Plato (e.g. Johns, 1998; Ong, 1982).

The introduction of new technologies, whether the internet, the motion picture camera or the record player, have all had a profound effect on how intellectual property is viewed (Lessing, 2003) and, consequently, how plagiarism is viewed. These new ways of thinking about intellectual property engendered by new technological developments show that now, as was found in the 18th century, we are in a new era where the previous laws may no longer be applicable. While the development of the internet and the world wide web has been a powerful force, this impact is not new. Ong (1982) has pointed out that literacy is a technology that affects the thinking process, as Plato has pointed out when he warned about how literacy affected memory adversely.

The introduction of a new technology into the discussion has often affected attitudes and concerns regarding plagiarism. By placing concepts such as 'author' and 'text' in their historical context, these constructs are less 'natural' but more 'social' in nature and, therefore, more easily subject to change. The basis of Howard's attack on conventional views of plagiarism is that changes in the view of individual authorship necessitate corresponding changes in the view of plagiarism. The same argument can be found in new forms of textuality. As the Critical Arts Ensemble (n.d.) put it:

> Readymades, collage, found art or found text, intertexts, combines, detournment, and appropriation – all these terms represent explorations in plagiarism. Indeed, these terms are not perfectly synonymous, but they all intersect a set of meanings primary to the philosophy and activity of plagiarism. Philosophically, they all stand in opposition to essentialist doctrines of the text: They all assume that no structure within a given text provides a universal and necessary meaning. No work of art or philosophy exhausts itself in itself alone, in its being-in-itself. (para 3)

As Howard and Pecorari have argued about patchwriting, this manifesto argues that plagiarism can be a positive force in the production of texts, although this view does not necessarily account for the rhetorical nature of authorship found in writing classes. Moreover, there is the question of the production of the text itself. Does how these texts are produced change how they are to be appropriated into new texts?

Variations in how texts are produced have had a profound effect on authorship across a variety of genres and disciplines. Technical writings, business communications and journalistic pieces all incorporate different concepts of collaborative authorship. The complexity about the collaborative nature of authorship can be seen in the debate over who is the 'auteur' (Bazin, 1967) of a movie. Many of us go to movies because we like the director. However, no art form is more collaborative than a movie, as witnessed by the long list of final credits. Bazin proposed a theory of authorship that held that certain great directors, such as Charlie Chaplin, were the real auteur regardless of how many other contributors were there. On the other hand, postmodernists, such as Barthes (1972) or Metz (1974), held that the interpretation of a text belonged to the reader/viewer and was not constrained by the intent of the author.

In other areas, we can see the same type of collaboration underlying traditional forms of authorship. The use of the term 'invisible college' (Crane, 1972) illustrates how academic knowledge is created in large networks that ranges from conversations in hallways to discussions at conferences and later publications. In some disciplines, how these different kinds of interactions are acknowledged as authors can be complicated. With the evolution of the internet, the ability to create even larger numbers of connections with large number of individuals and artifacts all over the world has further complicated the problem of defining authorship, even further complicating the rules for attribution.

The Pedagogical Problem Today

Traditional approaches for teaching about plagiarism, particularly when separated from the teaching of writing, seem to assume that students can understand the complexity of the rhetorical demands involved in textual borrowing simply by reading a passage from a handbook or watching a short film clip, an approach that can be referred to as the 'just don't do it' approach. This reliance on handbooks or simple lectures does not necessarily account for the complexities of plagiarism. As Angélil-Carter (2000: 2) argues, plagiarism is 'a complex problem about student learning, compounded by a lack of clarity about the concept of plagiarism, and a lack of clear policy and pedagogy surrounding the issue'.

Unfortunately, the confusion and sometimes resistance students express can greatly affect their lives, particularly if they come from educational environments where plagiarism was not a major pedagogical focus. As one of our students wrote on an exam question discussing appropriate punishments for plagiarizing:

> After arriving in America, the word 'plagiarism' often appears in my life. Teachers likewise can have anxiety over plagiarism. As one teacher bitterly put it:

> I am still very, very angry at the complete lack of back-up I experienced when I did my job as I was instructed by my supervisors. In what Bizarro world do we live where a known cheater can get a degree while an ethical educator gets the axe? No Ph.D. for me, but somewhere out there is an education major who thinks ctrl-c [cut] is an effective way you write a research paper.

For many teachers, instances of plagiarism can cause these types of emotional reactions, ranging from anger to xenophobia. For other teachers, making accusations of plagiarism can be a wrenching experience. Debora Weber-Wulff (2008), who regularly blogs about plagiarism and academic misconduct, recalls an angry response from a student she had accused of plagiarism.

> He threw back an email... saying that if I look hard enough I will find plagiarism everywhere I want to. He said it rather nastily, but he does have a point: If you find a lot of plagiarism, do you start (wrongly)

thinking that most students are plagiarists and seeing plagiarism everywhere? Or is plagiarism just so rampant that we absolutely must suspect it everywhere? (para. 4)

Beyond the institutional approaches, teachers often hope that there can be an explicit understanding or a 'social contract' between them and the students that could lessen the problem. In an article in a high school newspaper, one teacher told her students that she would make a honest effort to comment on their papers regardless of how she felt about them, but they had to stop plagiarizing regardless of how they felt about the assignment (Allen, 2008).

Both teachers and administrators can find themselves in this double bind between their goals for teaching and their perceived need to police their students. Panagiotis Ipeirotis, a professor at New York University, posted a blog entitled 'Why I will never pursue cheating again' about how his class became 'poisoned' when he accused a number of students of plagiarism, which he felt caused his evaluations to drop (Price, 2011). Hyland and Hyland (2006) found that teachers often do not confront suspected plagiarists out of the fear that a mistaken accusation of plagiarism may affect their relationship with the student. Abasi and Graves (2008: 229) found that professors, even if they feel they understand the rules regarding the use of source texts, may still feel conflicted about their role in enforcing them. They cite one professor as saying:

I felt like a security guard. . . . My aesthetic or affective response for not wanting to include it [a discussion of plagiarism] was because that's just not the way that I want to enter into a relationship with my students when I'm teaching in a class and am learning with them.

The problem this professor is describing has been greatly complicated in an intercultural context in which the writing is taking place, particularly when teachers from one culture attempt to impose their values on students from another culture. The importance of these values means that teachers are not simply gatekeepers and students are not just passive players waiting to be initiated into their communities of practice.

The connection between developmental and cultural factors can affect even the most advanced writers. In a study of plagiarism in the sciences (Long et al., 2009), questionnaires were sent to scientists accused of plagiarism. One nonnative speaker responded:

I am not a native English speaker so I do have many problems in expressing my ideas. . . . You and other English language speakers are lucky at least from this point of view that your language is the principle scientific language, therefore I and other persons like me expect you and your colleagues to help us overcome this obstacle.

Lillis and Curry (2010) have found a growing pressure for academics such as this scientist to publish in English for a global audience, which potentially places such academics at a disadvantage compared to their English-speaking colleagues.

This scientist's call for 'help' asks us to create new pedagogical approaches for understanding textual borrowing. One of the more interesting pedagogical problems is seen in the use of common knowledge in academic writing, which refers to information considered 'authorless' and, therefore, available for use without attribution although citation may be preferable in certain rhetorical contexts. It is not always clear what is considered common knowledge since its definition can be highly contextualized across different genres (Lunsford & Ede, 1994) and across various forms of discourse (Chandrasoma et al., 2004). A claim cited in one field may not need to be cited in another, or it may be acceptable to cite different individuals regardless of the origin of the claim.

Different scientific cultures may, in fact, have their own value systems for creating and citing claims. While new ideas in some areas may be rewarded financially, new ideas in scientific cultures may be rewarded through publication and then by attribution. The connection between cultural and developmental factors can also be seen as reasons for misunderstandings of what is common knowledge. Students may make judgments about the appropriateness of their own writing on the basis of a combination of such factors. Flowerdew and Li (2008), for example, found that Chinese writers would often copy words directly from their source texts if they felt these words were common knowledge, a process that Flowerdew and Li felt could help students learn about the conventions of academic genres through what they call 're-using' words to exploit the 'formulaicity of language' (460) in a genre-based pedagogy.

Pecorari (2008) saw some forms of what is called patchwriting as an honest attempt to learn the language by memorizing well-written passages. In this way, students are incorporating their own concepts of what is appropriate forms of imitation and orality, which can have roots in the cultural memes that are incorporated in the 'DNA' of their writing. Others, such as Howard (1999) and Pecorari (2008), have also seen more positive learning experiences in 'plagiarizing'. In Gu and Brooks' (2008: 347) study of international students in a UK university, a Chinese literature student discusses the pedagogical value of plagiarism: 'Sometimes I just want to improve my writing. I read some

articles and felt "wow, that was a wonderful sentence. I want to learn it."...
so I write it down.'

The value of such different learning strategies can be further complicated by different rhetorical assumptions concerning the nature of
audience. In her study of French rhetoric, Donahue (2008) found that a
more equal relationship between the author and the reader than what is
often found in other Western rhetorical traditions. Differences in this
relationship can cause confusion about what information can be considered
common knowledge and what should be cited. Drawing upon the work of
Bhaktin, Donahue (2008: 98) uses the term 'reprise-modification' to give
greater latitude to the idea that the creation of common knowledge is
an ever-changing process that creates different relationships between the
concepts of originality and copying that underlie traditional views of
plagiarism. This bind between their own learning goals and the rules
for appropriate attribution, therefore, is not simply a consequence of
cultural differences but one that can result from contradictory purposes for
common knowledge.

The term *common knowledge* can, therefore, be considered a cultural
construct with no strict definition; therefore, what types of information
can be considered common knowledge and what types are proprietary can
be unclear and, more important, can vary across disciplinary and rhetorical
contexts. Common knowledge in one field may need citation of its source in
another. Such confusion about the citation of common knowledge can be
seen in the frequent questions students raise about its attribution (Price,
2002). Angélil-Carter (2000: 74) reported on one student who responded to
a question of what he did with common knowledge by saying, 'I present it
as mine.'

At our university, a newly arrived international student was suspended
for plagiarism for copying what he considered common knowledge from a
textbook even though he argued that the textbook had already copied the
information from another source. Such students seem to understand that
information goes into the public domain at some point, but it may not
be clear where that point is or what are the appropriate rules for borrowing
it. Even information considered common knowledge may have to be
cited, not out of a concern for plagiarism, but to give credibility to a claim
or to demonstrate the author's familiarity with important texts (e.g.
Latour, 1988).

Latour describes this process in terms of the actor/network theory.
Writers situate their claims within the network in order to show support for
their work and establish what classical rhetoricians call *ethos* by demonstrating familiarity with key texts in the conversation about their topic. By

demonstrating such familiarity, the writer is considered a 'good' person whose arguments and claims can be trusted. Since the 'ownership' of an idea can be difficult to pin down, a writer may have to cite a certain text in order to demonstrate such familiarity. It may not be enough to cite 'somebody' as a means of demonstrating the ownership of an idea, as is often taught, but that a particular text needs be cited instead.

The definition of common knowledge can also vary as a result of cultural differences, with the term *culture* used in the broadest way to include 'big cultures' (e.g. being Chinese) or 'small' cultures (e.g. being a scientist). While here we are referring to 'small' cultures, the same problem regarding common knowledge can be found in 'big' cultures. Distinguishing these two forms of cultures is important because it can help us understand the different rewards a writer may receive for appropriate citation. While the general culture may value individualism and personal expression, a scientific culture may value communalism instead. Biagioli (2003) argues that scientific knowledge is created to be shared and built upon, comparing it to 'free software', thus evoking Stallman's 'free speech, not free beer' metaphor. Thus, common knowledge and proprietary knowledge both function in the knowledge creation process, although they may be valued differently and perhaps attributed differently as well. A critical difference, according to Bigioli, is that scientific reward is more often based on how frequently a paper is cited than on its publication.

This distinction between types of ownership may at times be blurred in different academic communities. Hyde (2010) argues that such communalism in American scientific culture began in the 18th century, as exemplified by how the work of Benjamin Franklin on electricity was shared throughout the scientific community, a process that greatly influenced how intellectual property was discussed in the US Constitution that was written during that period. The blurring of such distinctions can also be found in how different forms of intellectual property are defined. Some forms of intellectual property, often produced outside of the dominant economic cultures, are considered to be common knowledge, such as traditional folk materials and even recipes (http://www.copyright.gov/fls/fl122.html), and therefore, are not protected by laws.

Even within communities, the rules regarding citation practice are also defined by social relationships; thus, the application of these rules need not be universal, and, instead, such rules can be affected by the values that have been standardized in the genre (e.g. Bazerman, 1988). For example, readers of scientific writing may place greater importance on explicit citation than do readers of essays, popular writing or creative writing. The appropriate attribution of common knowledge has become a more complex issue with growth of such online sources as Wikipedia. How and when information from Wikipedia must be cited can be problematic because of the lack of a common understanding of the nature of this information. As will be discussed later, the introduction of all of these new forms of digital literacy has accelerated changes in this relationship between writer and reader both within and across cultures.

The Impact on Classroom Teaching

The controversies for the writing classroom have, in part, arisen from how these changes were manifested across different forms of literacy. Every form of literacy requires the creators to transform existing sources for new and, sometimes radically different, purposes. The New London's (1996) group use of the 'designing' metaphor for the creation of texts illustrates how texts are constantly transformed and repurposed to create new texts. While all forms of expression can be affected by fair use, each new technology has raised new and more complex ideas for classroom use.

The issues discussed here are not simply legal concerns but often go directly to deeply held personal concerns regarding how intellectual property should be used. One principle upon which these distinctions may result from differences in fundamental human needs and interests, which include 'autonomy, self-realization as an individual, self-realization as a social being, security and leisure, control over the presentation of one's self to the world, identity, and privacy' (Fisher, 1998). Thus, how teachers and students make judgments both about the rhetorical and the ethical use of intellectual property can vary greatly.

However, this principle can return us to old questions about culture, which seem to recur over and over again. Are these personal traits universal or are they particular to a culture? If the latter is true, should they or the laws and policies based on them be enforced on those living in other cultures that may have different personal values (Pennycook, 1996)? This question over the struggle between local and universal governance regarding the rules of plagiarism has been central to understanding the question of plagiarism among international students, particularly those learning English in their home countries, since the issue first arose.

Controversies over the governance of intellectual property connect the debate over intellectual property law with that of plagiarism. On one end is the institutional debate over the governance of the use of intellectual property law as illustrated by Post's (2009) metaphorical connection between the problems of governance faced by Jefferson over the Louisiana Purchase and the problems lawmakers have today with the vast and often uncharted world wide web. The same question can be asked about the governance of plagiarism. Can the same rules that have long been imposed by institutions on students still apply in the digital age or are new rules needed?

In February 2010, two events occurred in the same week that well illustrates the challenges that these new concern over intellectual property, plagiarism and cyberspace that teachers today must negotiate. In one incident, a well-known blogger was found to have plagiarized and immediately resigned his post. The blogger, Gerald Posner, responded by blaming the pressure that digital writing had put on him to produce articles:

> I realize how it is that I have inadvertently, but repeatedly, violated my own high standards. The core of my problem was in shifting from that of a book writer – with two years or more on a project – to what I describe as the 'warp speed of the net'. For the Beast [name of blog] articles, I created master electronic files, which contained all the information I developed about a topic – that included interviews, scanned documents, published articles, and public information. I often had master files that were 15,000 words, that needed to be cut into a story of 1,000 to 1500 words. (Posner, cited in Shea, 2010, para 5)

Writers often must sort through far more information in cyberspace than could ever be found in the print world, a condition that has been referred to as the 'long tail' of information (Anderson, 2006). The breakdown of gatekeeping, allowing for this almost unlimited supply of information has created new challenges for managing large amounts of data and tracking down individual ownership.

In the second incident a 17-year-old German writer was likewise accused of plagiarism. A few years earlier, there had been a similar case of an equally young American writer accused of plagiarism. She later apologized, and her publisher pulled her book off the shelves. However, in the case of the German writer, which raised an equal uproar, the writer did not even feel her work was plagiarism:

> I myself don't feel it is stealing, because I put all the material into a completely different and unique context and from the outset consistently promoted the fact that none of that is actually by me. (cited in Keen, 2010)

In essence, her argument was that she had transformed the older materials into a new form. The publisher apparently agreed since the book was kept in the competition for a prestigious award from the Leipzig Book Fair.

These different responses to copying illustrate how new concepts of 'originality' and 'authenticity' have emerged because of the ease with which digital materials can now be 'mashed up' or 'remixed' (Lessing, 2009a). These kinds of remixed texts embody alternative forms of authorship, some of them more explicitly relying on creative forms of synthesis and collaboration. New forms of authorship can involve different social relationships and different types of rewards.

Central to this debate is how these new forms of 'patchwritten' or 'remixed' texts should be viewed. As with the argument surrounding the value of 'patchwriting', Lessing (2009a) argues that taking pieces of texts to create a new text should not be considered the same as downloading and sharing music and films and, therefore, should not be treated the same in law. He claims that remixing is not only a new form of literacy but also a new form of democracy, one that is not defined by the institutional constraints imposed from above, an argument that can be applied to plagiarism as well. The implications of such views on the teaching of writing will be discussed further in the next chapter.

5 Searching for a Metaphor for Thinking about Plagiarism

The Battle of Metaphors for Framing the Discussion of Plagiarism

We have seen instances throughout this discussion of how different views about intellectual property can be expressed through the choice of different metaphors. As was the case with intellectual property law, new approaches to the pedagogical problem require new metaphors for framing how we think about plagiarism. Lakoff and Johnson (1980) argue that these types of what they call structural metaphors can affect how we perceive the world in which we live. Their often cited example about the difference between 'argument as war' and 'argument as dance' illustrates how the choice of metaphor can frame argumentation as either antagonistic or cooperative.

Lakoff and Johnson (1980) have argued that these kinds of metaphors are never neutral but provide frameworks for how concepts are perceived. They point out that while some 'conceptual' metaphors can be relatively straightforward, such as whether one gets 'in a car' or 'on a bus', others can be highly political and emotionally charged, such as indicating whether an act of copying is called patchwriting, textual borrowing or plagiarism. Both plagiarism and copyright law have shared the same metaphors regarding intellectual property that similarly frame an intimate link between the author and her 'creation', what Patry calls 'the creation-as-birth metaphor' (70). These metaphors, for example, directly connect creativity to individual ownership; however, one might imagine other metaphors as connecting creativity to the good of the community. An appropriate choice of metaphor can have a powerful rhetorical impact. Howard (1999) uses the 'standing on the shoulder of giants' metaphor in the title of her book as a way of reminding her readers, most of whom are academics, that all writing borrows from other texts.

As Lakoff (2004) has argued, the use of such metaphors frame the cultural narratives through which individuals can discuss and argue, as Howard's choice of metaphor frames her narrative about copying as an integral part of the academic writing process. On the other hand, terms such as 'thievery' or 'kidnapping' tell a much different narrative about the inappropriate use of intellectual property, connecting copying to the inappropriate use of real property, such as money or automobiles. Thus, choosing an appropriate metaphor is an important first step in framing an approach or pedagogy to respond to issues related to plagiarism.

Traditional Metaphors and Traditional Approaches

The frequency with which such metaphors are used indicate how deeply engrained they are in how we think. Expressions such as 'piracy', 'theft' and 'moral panic' seem to have 'naturally' emerged from this framework on intellectual property and have spread throughout discussions on these issues, particularly in the area of pedagogy. The 'stealing' metaphor is often explicitly found in advice given to students about plagiarism. As one handbook puts it, 'Plagiarism is literally a crime, a form of theft in which one steals the words of another' (Berke, cited in Leight, 1999: 222).

The connection between real property and intellectual property can also be seen in how the monetary metaphor has been applied to plagiarism, as it has to the sharing of intellectual property, although in the case of plagiarism, financial loss or gain is rarely a factor. In another handbook on writing research papers, the authors warn that 'since the currency of scholarship is ideas, it is not farfetched to say stealing a scholar's ideas is the moral equivalent of stealing from a bank' (McCuen & Winkler, cited in Leight, 1999: 226). Sometimes, the monetary connection is directly made as in this piece of advice: A person who plagiarizes as little as $2.39 is the same as 'someone who robs a bank' (Crews, cited in Leight: 225).

Such metaphors have so permeated academic discourse that even online paper mills, from which a student can purchase ghostwritten papers for classroom use, have used the stealing metaphor to promote their more expensive custom made papers. As one website puts it:

> Our custom essays and research papers are written in strict accordance with academic standards and your instructions. We've developed multi-level, plagiarism detection software, so all papers we produce are 100% authentic. (http://www.professays.com)

Another website in Great Britain (http://dissertation-service.co.uk) promises a 'free anti-plagiarism' report as a warranty on their services. The metaphorical nature of the term 'plagiarism' frames every act of copying, regardless of amount or intent, as a moral violation akin to stealing. Thus, no distinction can be made between buying a paper online, knowingly cutting and pasting text, or patchwriting.

The use of the 'stealing' metaphor reflects a deeply held belief that plagiarism is an example of moral decay rather than simply another pedagogical problem. While most of the research on plagiarism in both L1 and L2 journals have criticized this viewpoint, discussions among teachers on plagiarism inevitably bring out deeply emotional responses. In this comment on an article about a professor fired for publically humiliating students he had accused of plagiarism, one reader responded in his defense:

> I've always thought it strange that university administrations (a) say that students need to be severely punished for plagiarism as a deterrent to others, and (b) keep the punishments secret when they are imposed. The identity of criminals is not kept secret in the outside world, so why in academia?

Although there are also legal issues that involve student privacy that would apply in this case, it is the 'stealing' metaphor that frames much of these arguments: that students who plagiarize have given up their place in society as does a criminal. As another reader put it:

> I am horrified to see an administrator say that it 'is up to interpretation' as to whether a student who is found copying should receive a F. Sorry, that is no longer the student's 'work', none or limited learning has occurred, and it is cheating. That is a F for failing to complete the work as assigned.

The widespread use of these metaphors reflects how many of our daily activities are affected by intellectual property law. Litman (2001) points out that criminal metaphors such as 'piracy' have been greatly extended to more and more usages of intellectual property. She argues that while the term was once applied primarily to the mass copying and distribution of intellectual property such as movies and cassettes, it has now been applied to virtually every use of intellectual property.

In these ways, the 'stealing' metaphor has greatly impacted all the various ways teachers use and discuss intellectual property. As Crews (2001) points out, intellectual property laws can impose an authoritative standard on behavior (positivist), affect how individuals behave in specific contexts (normative) or can combine both concepts into a framework for using intellectual property. The 'stealing' metaphor frames all such acts as being the same. The imposition of such metaphors has meant that arguments regarding appropriate and inappropriate usage may seem to result from clear-cut legal or ethical standards even though these standards may actually be more nuanced or not generalizable beyond a particular context. The apparent clear-cut distinctions between appropriate and inappropriate usage of intellectual property has impacted traditional pedagogical approaches to discussing plagiarism. If plagiarism can be assumed to be an act of theft, the ethical concerns could be easily impressed upon students by comparing the improper citation of a text with stealing someone's wallet. As Litman (2008) points out, however, the uncontroversial application of these metaphors masks the fact the erasure of such distinctions may not accurately reflect either legal or ethical concerns. As a result, both teachers and students have become involved in these discussions often unaware that the ethical claims are often highly contested, and answers to questions about such appropriateness should often begin with 'It depends.'

Copy Detection Programs and the 'Stealing' Metaphor

One area of the plagiarism debate where these issues are most apparent is the use of plagiarism detection sites, such as Turnitin.com, MyDropBox (http://mydropbox.com), Glatt Plagiarism (http://www.plagiarism.com), PlagAware http://www.plagaware.com) and Ephorus (https://www.ephorus.com/en/home). These sites have variously been referred to as 'plagiarism detection', or 'copy detection programs', depending on whether one thinks their reports can define plagiarism. Many sites have also been developed for those in the arts and in business to search out what may be considered infringement of their intellectual property. Such sites make their ideological positions obvious. As Copybyte.com puts it on their website, 'Copyright Infringement is Stealing,' a metaphorical connection some, particularly advocates of fair use, might dispute. While some sites are free, the deployment of sites like Turnitin.com can be costly. Our university spent $70,000 a year for a license for Turnitin.com, in part from the fear among professors that plagiarism was spreading faster than they could respond to it.

These websites utilize algorithms that can match strings of text to determine whether they have been copied and are continually attempting to improve the old algorithms to improve the process. However, the usefulness of these programs has been highly controversial both in terms of effectiveness and whether what they are detecting is actually plagiarism (Weber-Wulff, 2011). The growing popularity of creating more effective and sometimes more lucrative programs has even spurred competitions that test their effectiveness (e.g. http://plagiat.htw-berlin.de/software).

Searching for instances of plagiarism has employed the 'stealing' metaphor to describe the process. John Barrie, the developer of Turnitin.com, uses the forensic term 'digital fingerprints' to describe the functions of these programs. 'We take digital fingerprints of individual documents and compare them to the digital fingerprints of existing documents' (cited in Ralli, 2005). The proliferation of these sites reflects a real concern about the difficulty of detecting plagiarism. In the incidents of plagiarism found in Great Britain (e.g. Pecorari, 2008) and in US universities such as Ohio University (Lederman, 2006) and Ohio State, one common factor was that the instances of plagiarism were initially unnoticed.

For overworked teachers, these programs have become a barrier to the breakdown of the moral fabric of the institution. Barrie compares the proliferation of plagiarism to the proliferation of corporate crime, giving the example of the downfall of the Enron Corporation, the once powerful energy company brought to bankruptcy because of corporate malfeasance. In response to Princeton University's refusal to adopt Turnitin.com, he stated, 'The disturbing thing is that Princeton is producing our society's future leaders, and the last thing anyone wants is a society full of Enron executives' (cited in Read, 2008: A1). Although there is clearly a great deal of hyperbole between the corporate malfeasance that bankrupted a company and leaving quotes off a citation, the 'slippery slope' metaphor from one 'immoral' action to another is made explicitly clear here.

Perhaps because of their controversial nature, some sites have been shifting their narrative away from one of purely moral concerns. Turnitin.com has claimed that its suite of programs also helps students become better writers and reduces the amount of time teachers spend searching for instances of plagiarism, both of which they argue improve student learning ('White Paper', 2010). Turnitin.com, for instance, also offers modules that help students collaborate. The website of the checker *Academic Plagiarism* (http://academicplagiarism.com) promises students that it will 'identify potential areas of plagiarism in your writing' and instructors that it will 'simplify your teaching', an issue that has been of concern to all teachers. However, despite this shift, it is questionable whether institutions would purchase the program solely for these reasons.

The popularity of these programs has spread throughout the world. The Chinese developed one copy detection program called the 'Plagiarism detection misconduct program' and another called the 'Academic Misconduct Literature Check'. The names of both programs give an interesting insight into the growing concern the Chinese university system has with plagiarism as well as the lack of concern for suppressing the true intent of the programs, as a name like 'Turnitin' does.

Opponents of the use of these copy detection programs have developed their own metaphors for highlighting problematic aspects of their usage.

The use of this 'forensic' metaphor has been at the heart of the criticism of such programs, which cannot distinguish between different forms or intents of copying. Marsh (2004: 434), for example, uses the term 'ethical drug test' to describe the process of submitting papers to the website. Others have compared the use of these programs in the classroom to an 'airport', where everyone is considered a potential terrorist until checked, and in the case of Turnitin.com, had their work appropriated and stored in the company's database. In Sunderland-Smith's (2008) study of attitudes of Australian teachers toward plagiarism, one teacher expressed concern that the use of Turnitin.com will lessen the importance of teaching by 'outsourcing' the detection of plagiarism. While these sites were already the center of an online metaphorical battlefield, they have also become the scene of a more literal online battleground between the program developers and those who want to hack it. The *Times Higher Education* website reports on how technologically savvy students can avoid detection, a problem that Turnitin.com felt was a minor concern that was being remedied (Fearn, 2011).

Multimedia Approaches to Teaching about Plagiarism

Technology has also been employed to educate students about plagiarism. The popularity of the web has motivated many universities to create websites, often using multimodal approaches, for providing information about plagiarism. Although their approaches using games, YouTube and other student-centered activities are new, they often incorporate the same metaphors to impress upon students the moral dimension of the problem. The San Jose State University plagiarism website (http://tutorials.sjlibrary. org/tutorial/plagiarism/tutorial/1origin.htm), for example, begins their tutorial with an animated burglar stealing words and being hunted down by the police while reminding students that the word 'plagiarism' is derived from the Latin word for 'kidnapper'. The School of Education at the University of Leicester site (http://www2.le.ac.uk/offices/ssds/sd/ld/ resources/study/plagiarism-tutorial) begins its animation with 'crime scene' tape familiar to anyone who watches police shows. The animation itself focuses on defining plagiarism and giving students strategies to avoid it.

Many of these websites incorporate this 'fear' approach, sometimes mixing in a bit of humor with moral reprobation, as a means of impressing upon students the moral dimension of copying. Many of the sites, at least metaphorically, present the most extreme of all possible punishments. The Acadia University website (http://library.acadiau.ca/tutorials/plagiarism) uses flash animation to depict a student caught plagiarizing being locked behind bars dressed in prison clothing, a situation that can only be seen metaphorically since plagiarism is usually not considered a violation of the law.

Other tutorials play on the fear that being caught plagiarizing can lead to problems in their future careers. The tutorial on plagiarism produced by the University of South Florida (http://www.cte.usf.edu/plagiarism/ plag.html) presents sometimes overly simple 'tips' for dealing with textual borrowing. Along with the tutorial, there is narrative description how plagiarizing in university can come back later to affect your future career (http://www.cte.usf.edu/plagiarism/scenario.html). As with the Acadia site, there are either real or cartoon characters with clearly Asian features, indicating that at least some of the potential audience may be international students.

Other universities feel that humor can help engage students with the problem of plagiarism. The University of Bergen in Norway created a somewhat risqué satire of 'A Christmas Carol' on YouTube called 'Et Plagieringseventyr' to warn students that, as Ebenezer Scrooge was warned, their futures are in grave danger unless they reform their ways (http:// www.youtube.com/watch?v = Mwbw9KF-ACY). In his fantasy, the plagiarist is arrested by a patrol of machine gun-carrying soldiers when he tries to hand in a plagiarized paper. Ryerson University (http://www.ryerson.ca/ academicintegrity/episodes) created a series of animations illustrating various aspects of academic integrity, including sharing and purchasing essays. Yavapai College (http://www.youtube.com/watch?v = n3 tin1ik6E) also uses a humorous You Tube video called 'Diagnosis Plagiarism', which uses comical doctors, reporters and secret service agents to explain what plagiarism is and how it can be avoided.

Many universities have used the internet to present information about plagiarism in the context of general writing instruction (e.g. Purdue University, http://owl.english.purdue.edu/owl/resource/589/01; Colorado State University, http://writing.colostate.edu/guides/teaching/plagiarism). Cornell University offers students a number of websites discussing plagiarism and other forms of academic misconduct (http://www-apps. umuc.edu/vailtutor).

Many of these websites attempt to teach students about specific, often complex citation practices. The 'Recognizing and Avoiding Plagiarism' website (http://plagiarism.arts.cornell.edu/tutorial/index.cfm) contains exercises that discuss, for example, differentiating between common knowledge and proprietary knowledge, using quotation marks and citing visual texts. The presentation is more prosaic than some of the others and, as is often the case, ignores the rhetorical dimension of these citation practices.

Some sites do make an attempt at educating students as to why they are borrowing texts in the first place. At another of Cornell's sites, there are a series of videos on plagiarism and intellectual property, including one with interviews and short trigger films discussing plagiarism (http://digital literacy.cornell.edu/integrity/dpl3320.html). The main argument that this website attempts to make is that the primary purpose of citations is for sharing resources and giving credit.

Other purposes of citation, however, such as its rhetorical dimension, are often ignored or presented in a more confusing manner. Often their explanations leave the topic murkier. At one point, the film attempts to explain what common knowledge is by comparing the fact that George Washington was the first president of the United States, which was common knowledge, and the fact that he lost his teeth at a young age, which was not. Such a distinction seems to assume that common knowledge is what everybody knows, but those facts that seem less well known need to be cited even though it is not clear whether the condition of Washington's teeth is proprietary knowledge and, therefore, needs citation. The film concludes with the aphorism 'when in doubt, cite,' a simple rhetorical strategy that may help students avoid plagiarizing but may not, for example, explain when common knowledge should be cited for rhetorical purposes or, more generally, why they are employing textual knowledge in the first place.

YouTube has also entered into the educational field with its YouTube Copyright School (http://www.youtube.com/copyright_school), which copyright infringers must view and then take a short quiz to have their violation expunged. The Media Education Project took a different direction in trying to explain the rights of fair use (http://www.youtube.com/watch?feature = player_embedded&v = CJn_jC4FNDo#at = 34).

There have been numerous other sites providing education as an alternative to punishment. The website of the Council of Writing Program Administrators (http://www.wpacouncil.org/node/9) lists a number of 'best practices' that can be used by writing teachers, including explanations of plagiarism, and the sequencing of assignments that could help student avoid the need to plagiarize and use sources in their writing.

Finding New Metaphors for Framing Plagiarism

In the age of student-centered learning, the 'criminal' metaphor reflects highly institutionalized norms that students are expected to obediently and, often blindly, follow without understanding why they exist. These norms are often created and enforced by the institutions for delineating the social roles that govern the relationships between the members of that institution. Some of the alternative metaphors have retained the moral dimension of plagiarism while recognizing that plagiarizing is not the same as 'stealing'. The alternative approaches depicted in these sites either contain or will require new metaphors. The Media Education Project's film ('A Fair(y) Tale Use') shows mashed-up images from the history of Disney animation into a new fairy tale depicting the rights of users (http://www.youtube.com/watch?v = CJn_jC4FNDo). The 'cartoon' metaphor was used to both show the creative power of remixing and to critique Disney's opposition to such an approach. Finding new metaphors is not a prerequisite for creating a new pedagogy, but such new metaphors can help to highlight changes in how such a pedagogy can effect classroom changes.

The challenge of formulating new metaphors is how to incorporate new contexts of authorship and textuality. In Lakoff and Johnson's (1980) terms, this framework needs to be accompanied by a change in the metaphors in order to conceptualize plagiarism in ways more consistent with the changes in pedagogy. In discussing the role of metaphor in political discourse, Lakoff (2004: 33) writes, 'If you keep their language and their framing and just argue against it, you lose because you are just reinforcing their frame.'

No term better illustrates the importance of alternative metaphors than 'patchwriting' to describe the use of often small pieces of texts within a sentence without attribution, a strategy more pejoratively referred to as 'mosaic plagiarism'. The use of the 'patchwriting' metaphor seems to view textual appropriation from a more creative perspective, making intertextuality sound more like a creative process for stitching together pieces of text into a collaboratively created quilt where no individual contribution needs to be attributed. Such a metaphor decriminalizes textual borrowing and can even legitimatize such borrowing as an appropriate writing strategy. Patchwriting can also be viewed as an important pedagogical tool for helping students acquire a new form of discourse (Pecorari, 2008) as well as a form of literacy (Howard, 1999). Howard writes:

[p]atchwriting is a form of imitation or mimesis in classical Greek rhetoric. It is a process of evaluating a source text, selecting passages pertinent to the patchwriter's purposes and transporting those passages to the writer's new context. Patchwriting accomplishes a (re)formation of a source text by providing a new locale and thus new meanings for the source material, as a form of verbal sculpture, molding new shapes from preexisting materials. It is a form of pentimento in which one writer reshapes the work of another while leaving traces of the earlier

writer's thought and intentions. It is something that all academic writers do. Patchwriting belongs not in a category with the cheating on exams and purchasing term papers, but in a category with the ancient tradition of learning through apprenticeship and mimicry. (xviii)

Drawing upon the role of intertextuality in writing, Howard argues that all writing is in fact 'collaborative' as writers are continually interacting with texts.

The introduction of the 'patchwriting' metaphor illustrates how the new metaphors can help frame new inquiries into the nature of plagiarism and new approaches for teaching about textual borrowing. Patchwriting has been viewed both as a developmental issue and a form of textuality. Initially, patchwriting was also seen as a developmental problem that existed in a social context or more specifically, a clash between different contexts. Hull and Rose (1989) used the concept as part of an educational process in their example of the nursing student accused of plagiarism. Similarly, the lack of the sophisticated language skills required in para-phrasing – the ability to find alternative vocabulary and to manipulate a variety of syntactic forms while maintaining the semantic and rhetorical intent of the sentence – cannot be viewed only in traditional moral terms but also as a pedagogical problem related to mastering the complex forms of language found in any writing genre (Pecorari, 2008).

The study by Hull and Rose (1989) laid the groundwork for helping teachers understand how the appropriation of texts can be an important step in the acquisition of identity that goes beyond the writing class. For many teachers, however, defining what is appropriate patchwriting may be as difficult as defining plagiarism, particularly in terms of what are the motivations of the students and how much of these texts were patch-written. Posner's (2007) 'fraud' metaphor eliminates the need for such judgements but retains the moral and criminal dimension of plagiarism. Such metaphors might be useful for specific acts where, as Posner has argued, the reader may feel a sense of fraud and violation. Posner (2007: 17) refers to plagiarism as an act of 'concealment', a metaphor that retains the moral dimension of plagiarism but allows for intent to be considered in deterring the severity of the action.

With this metaphor, Posner can distinguish between intentional and unintentional plagiarism, which has long been a point of contention in discussions on plagiarism. He argues that the 'fraud' metaphor can differentiate between the case when the 'copier is passing off the copied passage as his own' (6) and borrowing, which can lead to the creation of new work. He differentiates from the kind of appropriation found in

Shakespeare, which he feels is easily recognizable and, therefore, does not defraud the reader, and the type of plagiarism where the writer attempts to deceive the reader.

Posner's 'fraud' metaphor can be applied to different types of plagiarism, such as purchasing papers online, which cannot be tolerated just as how certain acts of misappropriating intellectual property that are not tolerated. This metaphor could be applied to patchwriting, particularly when the writer commits the same act over and over. Although Posner uses a wide brush for defining what is plagiarism, his 'fraud' metaphor can help incorporate the often deep, visceral emotions teachers may feel when they find that a student has plagiarized with at least some ability to differentiate among different forms of copying, which the 'stealing' metaphor cannot do.

However, the 'fraud' metaphor has its limitations as well. It does not capture the complexity of the issue for writing teachers or provides a framework for creating a pedagogical approach. This concept of 'fraud', moreover, can be highly subjective. As a Chinese teacher in Sunderland-Smith's (2008) study put it, what may seem to be fraud may in reality be a coping strategy for students learning English. There are other instances where new perspectives, and hence new metaphors, are needed to reflect a new pedagogy for dealing with plagiarism, one that relies less on punitive measures and more on teaching how each genre of writing contains a set of values that are integrated into the way that genre is socially constructed.

Angélil-Carter (2000) has more explicitly recognized the importance of changing these metaphors as a prelude to introducing new pedagogical approaches for teaching about plagiarism. Using the same distinction Lakoff and Johnson (1980) made between 'argument as war' and 'argument as dance', she chooses the 'dancing' metaphor to replace the 'stealing' metaphor. The 'dancing' metaphor eliminates the moral dimension to plagiarism and emphasizes the creative aspect of intertextuality, challenging the view that there are fixed, well-defined and unambiguous rules, regulations and policies regarding plagiarism. Much like Litman's (2008) 'fence' metaphor for intellectual property, the 'dance' metaphor presents a more fluid and changeable view of textual borrowing, which may help teachers explore new and creative directions for dealing with plagiarism.

As appealing as this metaphor is to reconceptualizing how plagiarism is discussed, other metaphors are needed to better frame pedagogical approach to the complexity of the issues related to plagiarism, particularly in some genres, such as some forms of academic writing, where the norms and values underlying the use of intertextuality are more formalized. All genres rely on textual borrowing but with different sets of constraints and practices for acknowledging the ownership of these texts. Such differences can also reflect different rhetorical purposes for the uses of the texts. Many artistic works do not directly acknowledge their sources, a practice that could be considered plagiarism in some genres of writing. Such differences in the rules for attribution in different rhetorical contexts should be an essential component of any attempt to reform the metaphors used in regard to plagiarism. Therefore, other metaphors are required for capturing these rhetorical differences while providing teachers with a framework for incorporating a pedagogy for teaching about plagiarism with the writing processes and genres taught in their classrooms.

The Use of the Game Metaphor

I would like to explore using another alternative metaphor, what can be called the 'game' metaphor, for incorporating a new perspective about plagiarism and, more important, for framing a pedagogical approach for teaching the purposes for textual borrowing and the constraints on its use. The 'game' metaphor used for framing discussions about plagiarism is not a new approach. Stanley Fish (2010) compares the rules regarding plagiarism to the rules of golf, which both have rather 'arcane' rules that are only important or often only understandable to those insiders who play or closely follow the sport. This comparison was strongly criticized for stripping the moral dimension from plagiarism. This argument may also upset some teachers for whom the term 'game' has a frivolous connotation that might reduce the seriousness of the issue. As Casanave found (2002), some teachers may feel offended at its use to describe the writing process. Angélil-Carter (2000) describes one teacher who felt the use of the 'game' metaphor particularly offensive.

> It is nothing short of outrageous to suggest that protocols against plagiarism are merely part of some academic game. The suggestion that a student becomes so immersed in the subject that he/she is unable to differentiate between his/her own ideas and those gained from research is worthy of nothing but derision. (cited in Angélil-Carter, 2000: 1)

This teacher seems to fault the use of the 'game' metaphor for seemingly stripping the moral dimension from the discussion of plagiarism. However, the underlying argument that something that is 'merely a game' should not be applied to the more 'lofty' goals of academic research seriously underestimates the complexity in which games are currently being discussed in fields such as mathematics, economics and the social sciences (e.g. Binmore, 1992a, 1992b).[1] Originating in the work of John von Neumann (1953), game theory has been defined as a process for understanding 'decisions that are made in an environment where various players interact strategically' (http://en.wikipedia.org/wiki/Game_theory), a definition that can also be applied to the decisions whether to attribute sources or a reader must make when determining whether a text is plagiarized.

If genre, for example, is seen not as a form that needs to be scrupulously followed, but as Miller (1984) puts it, as a series of socially mediated practices, so then its relationship with writing can be more clearly seen. Freadman (1994) used a 'tennis' metaphor to discuss genres. In this framework, the demarcation between where a ball can land and cannot land serves as a heuristic for deciding appropriate strategies. Atkinson (2003) explicitly uses the 'game' metaphor for L2 writing when he argues that teachers need to be aware of their participation in these 'language games' (57), which he defines as language environments where there is little 'innocent', decontextualized, skills-only teaching (60). Casanave (2002) argues that the 'game' metaphor is useful for framing how novices experience the unfamiliar practices that writing in an academic genre may entail, which is especially true for understanding the rules regarding plagiarism.

There are many aspects of game theory that could be discussed in relationship to plagiarism, but here I will only focus on a few issues that are important for framing the pedagogical questions regarding teaching about plagiarism and the rules and goals for attributing texts. Games have highly contextualized goals, such as winning a contest, receiving a high grade, writing a publishable paper or scoring the most points. Understanding the motivations for making those decisions that may be regarded as plagiarism can, therefore, help teachers as well as students create new perspectives on the nature of plagiarism and why students may engage in it. Blum's (2009) study on plagiarism illustrates a variety of motivations that students may have to plagiarize: the importance of the grade, their attitude toward their instructor and the course or their representation of the writing task.

Game theory as a metaphor is consistent with the process approaches to teaching writing. The connection between game theory and the writing process assumes that individuals are rational in deciding their goals and their strategies for achieving those goals. As Davis (1983) puts it, these decision-making strategies can be evaluated on the importance the players place on maximizing the value of the outcome (getting a high grade or the feeling of doing well on a paper) and minimizing the costs (the time spent writing or the frustration with the assignment). The assumption that actors/writers make rational decisions and gain expertise in making these decisions by learning more complex strategies had a great impact on early work in cognitive process theories of writing (e.g. Flower & Hayes, 1980).[2] Flower (1981) used the expression 'Problem-Solving Strategies' in the title of her writing textbook, with the term 'strategies' used to refer to a plan of action for achieving the goals for writing similarly to how the term has been used in game theory (e.g. Davis, 1983).

Game theory can provide a theoretical framework for understanding how these motivations can lead to specific outcomes: whether to purchase a paper from an online paper mill (e.g. Ritter, 2005) or to plagiarize from the internet. As Blum's work indicates, if a person chooses not to be a participant in the game or have goals that contradict the institutional goals, then there may be no motivation for following the rules. Detaching this relationship between the goals of learning and the rules can make such rules seem arbitrary and neutral, thus obscuring the specific purpose of each rule for furthering the goals of the game while simultaneously reflecting the norms for achieving these goals.

All of these actions encompass a sometimes highly structured set of rules that both constrain and support the achievement of these goals. Sporting events, for example, have rules that attempt to vary the degrees of balance between the offensive and defensive aspects of the game as well as to increase the interest of the fans. In writing an academic paper, the structure or 'rules' of a genre can play an epistemological role in motivating the writer to use these strategies to explore new areas in order to satisfy these rules (Bazerman, 1988).

The rules of a game can also have larger social implications for understanding the context in which they are implemented. The rules of the American courtroom – innocent until proven guilty – are often extrapolated into the society even though they might not always apply. From a different perspective, a rule can reflect a particularly interesting aspect of social organization. The rule from the television show 'Who Wants to be a Millionaire,' which allows the player to ask the audience for help, illustrates what is called the 'wisdom of crowds', a concept concerning the collective intelligence of a random group that has become increasingly studied with the growing importance of networked cultures (Surowiecki, 2005).

In applying the 'game' metaphor, it can be assumed that the nature of the rules reflects the social norms of the institution that has created the rules. As Fish's (2010) 'golf' metaphor implies, understanding the most 'arcane' rules makes you an insider even if you are not a championship-level golfer. Therefore, rules are neither arbitrary nor neutral: Each rule has a specific purpose for furthering the goals while reflecting the norms and values for achieving these goals. In American football, for example, the quarterback is considered the key player and, therefore, is allowed to do certain actions other players cannot do as well as being given additional protection to reduce the likelihood of injury that is not afforded to the other players.

Violations of the rules, on the other hand, must be punished so that the goals of the game can be better achieved. The rules are primarily designed to tell the participants 'who can do what and when they can do it' (Binmore, 1992b: 25). Once a punishment is assessed and an explanation is offered, the game can continue as before. Game theory can, therefore, provide a critical framework for thinking about punishment. Should a student, for example, be punished regardless of the degree of copying involved? The problem of creating appropriate punishments depending upon the severity of the violation was partially addressed by Boyle (2010) in his use of the story of 'Procrustes' as a metaphor for how intellectual property law treats all forms of copyright as the same and, therefore, may assess punishments accordingly. Game theory provides a rationale for creating varying degrees of penalties that suit the social context of the game, so the punishments can better reflect local contexts. For example, often, a penalty is given for a violation of a rule but with no moral stigma attached. Often play continues, and the players are allowed to return to the game. In the same way, a teacher can address certain acts of copying as pedagogical and not moral problems.

The nature of the penalty also addresses the decision-making process. Given the possibility of being penalized, how then does one decide whether to copy? Games involve different relationships among and between the participants and the institutional contexts where the games are being played out. Cost–benefit decisions may lead one to download a song or a movie or cut and paste a text for a writing assignment. However, deciding to break a rule could also result from not fully understanding the rules or not being able to fulfill the expectations of the rules. Thus, even in highly structured games like golf one may find different standards for professional and amateur players. How one judges whether an act of copying should be labeled as 'plagiarism' can be highly subjective, much like the judgment calls that often have to be made in a game.

Asking students to submit their papers to a copy detection program like Turnitin.com can change the social context in which decisions are made and alter the decision-making process by making students more aware of having their actions monitored. Changing the procedures of the game to make them more consistent with the abilities and backgrounds of the participants can also affect the decision-making process. Assignments that cannot easily be recycled can make it more difficult to find papers on the internet or force those students who can afford to purchase more expensive, custom-made papers from term-paper mills, thus increasing the 'costs' of committing plagiarism. Having students revise papers or allowing them to utilize the writing strategies they are most familiar with can also have an effect on reducing plagiarism without sacrificing the integrity of the course, the nature of the student–teacher relationship or the rights of the students, as is sometimes found with the use of programs like Turnitin.com (Marsh, 2004). As will be discussed in more detail, the most important step is to ensure that there is an 'equilibrium' among all the participants, teachers and students alike, in their knowledge of the strategies, rules and punishments for textual borrowing.

Students as Game Players

Inevitably, we must return to the fundamental question, 'Why do students cheat?' Much has been made recently of the relationship between the students' sense of themselves as authors and their decisions about whether to plagiarize. Blum (2009) studied the possible motivations for employing plagiarizing as a coping strategy for dealing with school work. These motivations may result from the student's perception of his or her social position within the university. The students Blum discussed studied at an 'elite' university and, therefore, could be assumed to have had good education before entering the university. However, other students, both native and nonnative speakers, may not have such backgrounds. They may not have enough knowledge to make a rational decision about whether to plagiarize or may view the institutional norms differently from how professors and administrators view them. Students from different cultures or from different economic or with different educational backgrounds may also lack the knowledge necessary to make these rational decisions.

As Rose's (1989) story about the first-year student accused of plagiarism illustrates, many assignments seem to assume that the students have an expertise in both the subject of the assignment and in the institutional norms for completing that assignment, just as an expert author would, when in fact they have knowledge of neither. As Rose sees it, this student may not have the appropriate knowledge to do anything but regurgitate what he or she read but without knowing the appropriate way of citing it. This double bind between students views of themselves as authors and the expectations their teachers place on them to act like authors can frustrate them, which in turn can lead to viewing themselves as 'outsiders' and make plagiarism appear to be a rational decision. If students see no value in writing a paper or are frustrated by the assignment, they may be more likely to only expend the minimum effort required to meet the goal as long as they feel there is no effective deterrent, which can be an argument in favor of plagiarism detection websites.

On the other hand, writers may be highly motivated to do well on an assignment but feel they lack the ability and so decide to plagiarize in order to attain what they see as a higher goal, as the example of the Chinese scientists discussed earlier illustrated (e.g. Li & Xiong, 1996). If students want to do well on an assignment, or if they find the assignment interesting enough to inspire them to feel like an author and not just consumers of information, they may be more willing to expend the time to achieve this goal but still not have the ability or, in some cases, the inclination to avoid breaking the rules. For example, the large number of mostly nonnative English speakers discussed previously who were found to have plagiarized their dissertations could have argued, as did the Chinese scientists, that their research was substantial, as their degrees would indicate, so why did their lack of writing ability hinder their careers.

Other students may make similar decisions but for different reasons. In one story our students read in their writing class (see Chapter 6), a high school student must decide whether to borrow texts despite being warned that her paper should contain only her own ideas or to plagiarize the paper so that it appears that all the ideas are hers (Heaton, 2003). Because the student could not use citations but still wanted to obtain a good grade, she decided to cut and paste her sources and not cite them. Unfortunately for her, the student did not know her teacher was using Turnitin.com and she was caught plagiarizing and eventually expelled.

In this case, the student argued that she cared about the paper but simply could not complete the assignment within the institutional norms and, without the knowledge there was a deterrent in form of a plagiarism detection program, chose to intentionally plagiarize. As will be discussed, many of our students were not sympathetic with her decision, but at least we can understand the possible motivations for her decision and how adjusting the assignments or the teaching methodology, in this case by allowing her to cite sources or write multiple drafts, could have prevented this problem. Simply judging this student to be immoral because of her plagiarism may not have led us to this understanding. Many teachers, on the other hand, see the value of copy detection software in that it frees them from making these kinds of judgments by, at least in their eyes, presenting their students with an 'objective' measure of the amount copied.

Even highly motivated students can fall into the trap of plagiarizing because of their desire to improve their writing. Unlike the students Blum interviewed, Pecorari (2008) found that highly motivated students who cared greatly about their work still made decisions that could lead to accusations of plagiarism. Pecorari argues that such students are often confused about the rules for textual borrowing and, therefore, can unintentionally violate them. These students could most benefit from having to write multiple drafts, so they can have more opportunity to work on their paraphrasing skills if their problems could be detected.

Not everyone, however, chooses to plagiarize even when knowing that the outcome may be negative. Goldstein (2006), for example, discusses a student who had been asked to revise a paper about which he knew little and seemed to care even less. Goldstein narrates how the instructor suggested that the student should do more research about the topic. However, because the student had such little interest and felt pressed for time, he resisted the suggestion and accepted the consequences for doing nothing. This student chose not to plagiarize, perhaps because of an ethical sense or the fear of being caught, but it seems that receiving a low grade was not a strong motivation either to revise the paper or to plagiarize. All these examples illustrate the complexity of both the decision-making process and the pedagogical modifications needed to address the resulting problems.

The 'Game Theory' Metaphor and Genre Variation

Game theory also directly addresses the problem of the contextualization of rules as they vary across different genres. Fish (2010) calls plagiarism an 'an insider's obsession' since the rules for what is considered plagiarism are of importance primarily to members of the community. As with his example of golf, such rules can vary across different contexts, which can make them even more problematic to understand. One example I like to give students is to compare American football and what Americans call soccer. One difference between American football and soccer is in whether players are allowed to use their hands to catch a ball. While in soccer, catching the ball is mostly forbidden, except by the goalie, and in American football catching the ball is encouraged for certain players since passing and catching the ball often provides the easiest method to achieve the goal of scoring points. As a result, in American football, there have been a wide variety of highly technical rules to protect players from being interfered with when trying to catch the ball. Despite the normative force of these rules, they can either be modified or changed.[3] This adaptability reflects an ongoing need to change the equilibrium between the different players in the game in order to better achieve a new equilibrium that better matches the current goals. Sports authorities, for example, are constantly tweaking the rules in order to, for example, change the balance between the offense and the defense in order to provide more scoring and, therefore, to become more appealing to the spectators.

These same factors can be found in the evolutionary nature of genre. The 'game' metaphor allows for such flexibility to be incorporated into the framework for teaching about textual appropriation. Research in genre theory has shown genres are both socially constructed around the norms and values of the academic specialty (Berkenkotter & Huckin, 1995) and are continually evolving to reflect changing values, such as how a greater emphasis on research in the field is manifested in changes in the forms of research papers and their use of citations (Bazerman, 1988). Therefore, a successful academic writer requires knowledge of how these variations are situated with the student's learning communities (Tardy, 2009).

Metaphors can help us focus on the different variations in nature of the rules across different contexts. Such variance of practices can be especially true for how textual borrowing is attributed. Much as how cross-cultural approaches to studying textual borrowing has shown that it can vary across cultures, attribution across different genres of writing can vary as well. In some forms of writing, such as in manuals and reports, there may be no attribution while in certain forms of academic writing, there may be large number of citations.

The result of this lack of focus has often been a disequilibrium, for example, between what the teacher and what the student knows about these rules. In order to be effective, either as a writer or a player in a game, one must not only know the rules but also be able to reflect on what he or she knows and on what they believe the other people in the game know and do not know (Geanakopolis, 1993). The game 'metaphor' can frame pedagogy for creating a better equilibrium in knowledge across these various socially constructed spaces where the rules and practices can be negotiated or resisted (e.g. Chandrasoma et al., 2004).

Game theory emphasizes the importance of what Geanakopolis (1993) calls the achievement of equilibrium in 'common knowledge'; that is, everyone, including teachers and students, know what everyone else knows about both these practices and these rules. Therefore, to avoid charges of plagiarism, or other forms of academic misconduct, students have to know a great deal about the context of the genre that is 'common knowledge' in their field: what is considered originality, what is the nature of authorship, how their work will be assessed and what the rules for attribution are.

In a perfectly symmetrical relationship, this information is equally known by everyone (Binmore, 1992a), but an asymmetrical relationship puts the player with less knowledge. Students are almost always at a disadvantage in relationship to their teachers, who usually better understand the rules regarding plagiarism. The limitations of many of the pedagogical approaches for teaching about textual appropriation can be seen in how they are often decontextualized from the type or genre of writing from which these norms emerge. Unfortunately, both theories and pedagogies developed for teaching genre seldom focus on the rules regarding plagiarism that are encapsulated in these genres. As a result, students often do not understand why they are using citations. Too often we see students who believe that if they pretend that an idea is their own, they will sound more authoritative. A student, on the other hand, may be more likely to cite a source if he or she understands the importance academic writing places on the relationship between his or her ideas and what has been published before, as the metaphor 'standing on the shoulders of giants' illustrates.

Often, even experienced writers feel that citing sources is only a proforma act and has little intrinsic value to the construction of their own claims. The two Chinese researchers mentioned earlier, wanting to publish in the English-language research community, were accused of plagiarizing the literature review of their papers. They responded to the accusations of plagiarism from their own department that they had difficulty writing in English, so they copied a literature review written in English. They went on to argue, 'what difference does it make, the data was original' (Li & Xiong, 1996). They felt that their failure in writing was not as important since their data was original and contributed something to their field, which reflects a very traditional value on the objectivity of science.

Although their paper had been, in fact, published, their response clearly indicates a lack of understanding of the rules regarding citation as well as their rhetorical importance. Similarly, in the case of the international students at Ohio University who were accused of plagiarizing their dissertations, most of the instances of copying were found in the literature reviews of their dissertations (Lederman, 2006). These students may have felt that the literature review was only a formulaic recitation of the important texts of the field rather than part of the rhetorical process of establishing the importance and necessity of their research, an assumption that was not contradicted by their professor, who either did not recognize the plagiarism or may not have closely read their papers.

Teachers, too, face a disequilibrium in their knowledge about the constraints and rights for using intellectual property. The importance of achieving these kinds of equilibriums has long been a consideration in intellectual property law. Teachers may tell a student they cannot make a copy, even though the copy may be covered by fair use or may not know whether a certain amount of copying should be considered plagiarism. Pecorari (2008) found that when advisors were confronted with their students' alleged instances of plagiarism, they were often ambivalent about this revelation, expressing neither shock nor anger. She found that even the readers of their texts, in this case the students' advisors, seemed puzzled about whether their students had, in fact, committed plagiarism. Pecorari (2008) attributed this ambivalence to the relationship the advisors had with the students as well as the fact that they could not recognize the extent of their students' copying. Teachers may also not wish to become involved in a time-consuming and emotional experience. Some may feel that reporting cases of plagiarism may involve too much trouble or may incur a career-damaging risk.

In the case mentioned above concerning a large number of plagiarized dissertations, the plagiarism was discovered accidently by another student who had gone to the library looking for a sample dissertation that had been accepted by his advisor (Lederman, 2008). Their advisor claimed that he did not notice the plagiarism and that he was not responsible for finding it, an arugument that won him a large settlement. Other faculty may feel that it is their duty to report every such case and make these cases a warning to others, regardless of the time or consequences. In the case of the adjunct faculty member who was fired for publicly humiliating students whom he had accused of plagiarizing, those who supported him felt the administration had abandoned its commitment to academic integrity, but those who supported the firing felt that the administration had acted based upon a more important set of legal and ethical concerns (Couser, 2009).

As Boyle (1996) argues, there is much in legal and social practice that is based on an assumption of the egalitarian distribution of knowledge. A contract can become void, for example, if it is shown that one party was at a disadvantage in his or her understanding of the details of the contract. The same problem of achieving equilibrium can be seen in a writing classroom. The most important pedagogical consequence of using the 'game' metaphor is the importance it places not just on learning the rules but learning them in the context of learning to write. While the rules of a game are important, the central focus of learning is on playing the game, whether it is learning to play football or to write an academic paper. To participate in the game, it is important for every player to understand the complexity of the rules. While in some cases it may be enough to just avoid violating a rule, it is also important to understand the norms and values underlying the rules if students are to become skilled and effective participants of their communities.

The same analysis can be applied to becoming a skilled and effective writer. What is acceptable in remixes or literary works may not be acceptable in academic writing. These differences may arise from differences in how various literacies are socially constructed within different communities (e.g. Lea & Street, 1998). The 'game' metaphor helps us see how the variations in the social contexts in which games are played affect their rules. Discussing plagiarism in this contextualized way instead of as an abstract universal value can help create a literacy pedagogy that connects the rules regarding attribution with the goals of academic literacy. Such a framework places a greater emphasis on teaching every participant what these rules are, how these rules reflect the norms of the community, how they reflect the social contexts in which the participants are learning and what strategies are necessary to achieve those norms. Thus, teaching about plagiarism embodies many of these aspects of the writing process, from macro-level concerns with voice and argumentation to micro-level concerns with lexical and syntactic choice. While the primary focus is on education, the 'game' metaphor does not obviate the need for penalties but contextualizes such penalties in the goals of learning. In the next chapter, I will discuss the pedagogical implications of employing this metaphor.

Notes

(1) The awareness of the general public about game theory dramatically increased with the release of the film *A Beautiful Mind* (2001), about John Nash, who had received a Nobel prize for his work on game theory to study decision-making strategies.
(2) Hayes's and Flowers' research into the cognitive processes of writing was greatly influenced by the work of Herb Simon, who had won a Noble Prize using games theory to study decision-making strategies.
(3) Sporting events can be used as examples of this interaction between rules and goals. These rules reflect a balance between the goal of promoting scoring, which is popular among fans, and the need not to make scoring too easy. If one wanted to change this relationship balance, one way to do so is to change the rules.

6 Rethinking Pedagogical Strategies for Teaching about Plagiarism

Developing a Pedagogical Framework Using the 'Game' Metaphor

This perspective on plagiarism as an evolving pedagogical problem and not just a moral one emphasizes the creation of 'an equilibrium' in understanding the rules among all the participants–teachers, students and administrators–in their understanding of plagiarism, the reasons the rules exist and the strategies for avoiding the often harsh consequences of being accused of plagiarism. If writing teachers want to consider their classrooms as 'safe havens' where students can try out different types of writing without having to worry about being labeled a 'thief', new metaphors are needed for discussing how intellectual property should be used. From this perspective, all pedagogies require an integration of the rules regarding textual borrowing. However, changes in writing pedagogy–for example, a greater emphasis on collaboration or introducing new forms of multi-media–will mean that there must be changes in how we teach about plagiarism (Howard, 1999; Lunsford & Ede, 1994). Lunsford and Ede argued that as collaborative models of writing have developed, there have been changes in conceptions of authorship and, consequently, in definitions of plagiarism.

Much of the research into teaching about plagiarism has concluded that a pedagogy dealing with plagiarism does not simply involve learning abstract set of rules for citation, as important as they are, but also learning every aspect of the writing 'game'. One such aspect considered central for dealing with plagiarism is the question of the writer's voice. Writers, for example, may lack a concept of identity in their writing, which can lead students to represent the writing assignment as simply regurgitating back information with little sense of being an author (e.g. Blum, 2009). Drawing upon the work of Julia Kristeva, Ivanic (1998) found that the failure to establish an identity within the constellation of texts a writer must draw upon when writing can lead to plagiarism. Ivanic has argued that plagiarism can be connected to the problem of acquiring a new voice as a means of identifying with an academic community. Ivanic describes plagiarism as 'a very emotionally charged manifestation of a more pervasive mechanism for becoming party to new discourses' (196). The extreme case occurs when students buy their texts from paper mills, but the problem can also be found in cases where students repeatedly plagiarize even after instruction.

This problem regarding authorship can be especially acute for L2 writers. Abasi *et al.* (2006) found that L2 students do not always see themselves as authors, which they argue can lead to their simply copying and reproducing the textual material they have read. They found that the students who do not consider themselves 'players' in the academic world may feel little need to follow the rules, beyond the fear of being caught. In such cases, plagiarism can be seen as a morally tainted, though perhaps rational, response to the situation that students may find themselves in.

The relationship between the lack of voice and plagiarism is made explicit in the story Rose (1989) tells about Marita, the student accused of plagiarism. Marita was given an assignment that Rose felt she could not possibly understand and to write in a way that she had never learnt. '[S]he was still unsure as to how to weave quotations in with her own prose, how to mark the difference, how to cite whom she used, how to strike the proper balance between her writing and someone else's–how in short to position herself in an academic discussion' (180). As a result of her lack of sense of being an author, Rose argued that she could not negotiate the demands for using texts in the ways an experienced writer might; therefore, she simply copied texts word for word without the knowledge of the proper method of citation. Such strategies may have been 'successful' in the past, but that may no longer be as useful in the new writing contexts the student is struggling to understand.

This kind of response may be adequate for learning how to use quotation marks. However, by focusing only on plagiarism outside the context of the writing process, this approach seems to rely only on instilling a fear of making a costly mistake rather than on the rhetorical question of why the information is being cited. Abasi and Graves (2008) found that this fear of plagiarism dictated their use of texts rather than the pedagogical goal of creatively adding their own ideas to the existing body of knowledge.

Therefore, simply telling students not to copy or cite their sources may not be an adequate response to the problem of understanding the rhetorical purposes for textual borrowing. The result is that students may know where to place quotation marks but have no idea of the rhetorical purpose for which the citation was being used.

The role of being a perpetual outsider in predominantly English-speaking communities, as exemplified by Marita, can complicate the students' ability for understanding the norms that underlie common definitions of plagiarism (cf. Lillis & Carr, 2010). As Berkenkotter and Huckin (1993: 478) suggest, 'genre conventions signal a discourse community's norms, epistemology, ideology, and social ontology.' Wegner (1999) used the term 'community of practice' to describe the contexts in which learning is a collective and collaborative practice. In these contexts, plagiarism reflects the rules that have been established within the various discourse communities for using knowledge that has been written down and published.

A community is a group of individuals engaged in activities and discussions where they share information for a common goal. In academic communities, practitioners often share information through publication as well as other contexts such as conferences and private discussions. This information is shared by other practitioners in the pursuit of the common goal of knowledge creation. Rose's description of Marita highlights how a lack of understanding of this social context can cause trouble for a student who, as Rose put it, is an outsider to the academic community.

This understanding of the role of intertextuality in academic genres is something that sometimes even experienced college students must also learn. Despite the complexities of these contexts, students are usually held morally responsible for negotiating the constraints, regardless of whether they understand them, if they want to be accepted in their academic communities. The writing classroom is often one of the first places where they encounter these rules.

At the heart of the problem is the growing complexity of being literate, particularly as we expand our concept of what constitutes a genre or an academic literacy. Abasi and Graves (2008) cite one professor's explanation of the complexity that teachers must address:

You know one of the things we're trying to train you to do is research and an essential part of that ... is having at least a good sense of what's happening out there. What are people saying? What are the arguments? What are the theoretical foundations? What are the concepts? What are tangible issues? and ... sort of conveying to the reader of the paper, just as with the journal article, that you have surveyed the domain in sufficient detail in terms of publishing to make this paper publishable. (224)

Being able to effectively use intertextuality while avoiding plagiarism according to all the factors for using texts (e.g. Bazerman, 1988; Latour, 1988) can be difficult for any newcomer, perhaps more so for newcomers coming from different cultures. This professor is later cited as saying that the creative part of this process involves adding something new to this ongoing discussion, a sentiment popularized hundreds of years ago by Galileo in the expression 'standing on the shoulders of giants', highlighting the importance of intertextuality and collaboration in all forms of writing.

The problems in these cases with citing texts raise interesting perspectives on why the students may choose not to cite texts. This pedagogical problem is not a separate issue from that of culture and language development but can be seen as interconnected to both cultural and developmental factors. Nevertheless, this pedagogical problem has its own unique components. Sometimes, it reflects an attitude that students may have to the use of texts in their writing. While some students seem to feel bound to the text so they only repeat it with no explanations (Ivanic, 2008), others feel if they obscure the intertextuality of ideas in their own voice by not citing them, their papers will be judged more favorably.

A more problematic consequence of this confusion is how teaching pedagogies themselves can cause the student to plagiarize. Buranen (1999) argued that a pedagogy that makes strict levels of grammatical correctness the highest goal can lead students to plagiarize because of a fear that they will be penalized for grammatical errors. In his story about Marita, Rose argues that the nature of the assignment can make the student feel even more like an outsider to the academic community since they are asked to write on a topic about which they have little or no knowledge. In response to another story our students read about a high school student who intentionally plagiarized an assignment where she was not allowed to use any sources (Heaton, 2003), our students often feel that the high school student is morally responsible for her decision, although they can also sympathize with how the assignment, which forbade her for using any outside texts, could force her into a perhaps unnecessary position where a moral choice has to be made.

England (2008) argues that the assumptions underlying the advice that teachers and textbook writers give to students simply do not always capture the complexities of plagiarism, a situation further complicated by the potential of cultural misunderstandings. Plagiarism is not simply another problem for L2 writers; for them it can be far more complex. It may not only be a moral problem but may also be a developmental and cultural one. None of these issues can be separated.

The 'Game' Metaphor and Teaching about Writing

There has been a long tradition of attempting to deal with the problem of plagiarism at the institutional level, through honor codes (McCabe & Trevino, 1993; McCabe *et al.*, 1999), verbal instructions (Kerkvliet & Sigmund, 1999), the implementation of copy protection programs and multimodal presentations (see discussion below) in the same way that intellectual property has been governed by 'public officials in the government for public reasons and is enforced by public laws and by public judges' (Patry, 2009: 126). The effectiveness of these institutional approaches has varied; each has shown some reduction in the amount of plagiarism, but none have fully dealt with the problem. In countries such as the United States, however, where pedagogical decision making, particularly at the university level, is highly decentralized, it is an anomaly that policies regarding plagiarism, as are the laws regarding intellectual property, have been set primarily at the institutional level.

A more decentralized approach shifts the focus to the classroom where students do not need to be passive players. Lea and Street (2006) use the term 'academic literacies' to challenge teachers to engage students to become 'participants to the practices and texts which they encounter' (744). Within the framework of the 'game' metaphor, students need to understand the rules, learn strategies for dealing with the ambiguity of how plagiarism is viewed, connect the rules to the norms and values of academic writing and analyze some of the contradictions in how the university presents the issue of plagiarism. This approach shifts some of the burden to the teacher for ensuring that there is equilibrium in understanding plagiarism so that every student has the ability to negotiate the complexity of the problem. Such an equilibrium requires both an understanding about plagiarism and an increase in the level of writing skills so that the student can satisfy the goals for paraphrasing required to avoid charges of plagiarism.

The resulting pedagogy both resists simplifying discussions of plagiarism as being isolated from the other aspects of the writing process and incorporates a variety of approaches for helping students improve their writing ability. Instead of only relying on a fixed plagiarism policy succinctly stated at the beginning of the course, this approach places a greater responsibility on the teacher to initiate an ongoing conversation about plagiarism and give students a greater say in negotiating its meaning. This approach can, as Graff (2003) puts it, initiate students into an important academic discussion in the communities of practice they are entering, thus helping them begin to move toward the centers of these communities.

As the story by Mike Rose (1989) about Marita illustrates, students may not be aware that this discussion even exists. As a result, the equilibrium between these types of students and their teachers may be the most unbalanced. Research has indicated that the students least prepared for university, including both international and minority students, are often the most at risk for being caught plagiarizing (Dee & Jacob, 2010). It is perhaps inevitable that those students who have been educated the furthest outside of their academic learning communities are going to be the least prepared for understanding the values of these communities for the use of source texts. L2 writing teachers often find themselves caught in the double bind of wanting to value the norms, writing strategies and cultural heritage of what their students bring to the classroom and, at the same time, of wanting to help them become participating members of their academic and professional communities, regardless of the conflicting nature of these two goals.

One goal for the academic writing classroom is for students to best utilize intellectual property in their work while avoiding the pitfalls that seem to be constantly tripping them up. How do teachers situate a discussion of plagiarism within these institutional constraints? This problem of balancing what is taught inside the classroom with what is being taught outside the classroom is an old one in L2 writing theory, particularly in the area of English for Specific Purposes. For many years, teachers have struggled with how to balance their perceived views of the literacies practiced in various academic disciplines with their own best practices for teaching writing. There has been much research, such as the work of John Swales (1990) on genre, which challenges the traditional views of genres and which would later be developed into new pedagogical approaches (e.g. Swales & Feak, 2004). While not explicitly dealing with plagiarism, these approaches have provided the basis for integrating teaching about plagiarism into the genre pedagogy. Just as with the use of intellectual property, teachers may have to balance their resistance to those dominant institutional norms that contradict their pedagogical goals while still accommodating those rules they feel their students must understand to be accepted as members in the academic community.

The work of Swales (1990), Hyland (2000a), Tardy (2009) and others on genre in L2 writing classrooms has placed the attribution of texts at the center of various writing pedagogies. Intertextuality has important rhetorical consequences for fulfilling these goals. An understanding of how authors use texts, including how they incorporate the norms of their field into their use of intertextuality, can help students better understand how academic papers are situated within the process of knowledge creation. The dilemma for students, as Bazerman (2009b) notes, is that the use of citations must do two things at once: locate the writer's claims within the existing literature and distinguish those claims from the existing literature.

From this perspective, Bazerman (2009a) argues that there is a cognitive dimension to the use of source texts in that they can serve as a heuristic for generating new ideas as they force the writer to interact with them during the writing process. Bazerman (2009b) finds that the norms of the citation style, whether names or subscripted numbers, which are used to mark the citations, can affect the cognitive processes by which writers interact with these sources. There is a social dimension to the use of intertextuality as well, which reflects the 'communalism' of academic research (Merton, 1942). Citing texts provides readers with a 'map' of what the writer thinks is important so that the readers can better understand his or her perspective as well as an overview of additional texts for learning more about an issue. Citing other authors' claims, even those that might be considered common knowledge, can also demonstrate familiarity with the field. Understanding this *ethos* counters the misconception students often have that expressing the idea so it sounds like it is one's own is a better rhetorical strategy than citing the source, an approach that can easily lead to accusations of plagiarism. In this framework, citation is not simply a strategy for avoiding plagiarism but also a means for becoming an active participant in his or her discipline or community of practice and a better player in the writing game.

Latour (1988) has used the 'war' metaphor to describe how citations are used in constructing the rhetorical framework of a claim. Latour argues that one way academic writers use citations as 'allies' is to support their own claims. His metaphor, which may appear too violent or confrontational for some, is still useful for helping students go beyond the 'when in doubt, cite' approach that often dominates teaching about plagiarism. The metaphor captures the concept that not all allies are of equal value, and students need to discern which sources are more important than others.

The use of the 'ally' metaphor is also consistent with our use of the 'game' metaphor. One of the fallacies of the traditional approaches to the 'when in doubt, cite' advice for avoiding plagiarism is that such an approach does not attempt to account for the quality of the 'ally' or 'teammate'. Different texts have different degrees of quality, depending on a host of factors, including the age of the article, the fame of the author and the 'impact factor' of the journal in which the text is published. Writers must be able to assess the quality of an idea, not just its ownership. It is sometimes assumed that because an idea is found in a text, the author has ownership of that idea. However, as the debate over intellectual property has shown, this assumption cannot always be demonstrated. While the expression of the idea may belong to the author, the idea may have been published previously. This problem has become more complicated because of the growth of internet publishing. Thus, the problem is not with the citation but with the quality of the 'ally', a problem that cannot simply be solved by telling students to cite.

These factors affecting the use of citations can vary across different genres of texts and different academic communities. Latour has argued that even the acknowledgments of those who helped the author, which are sometimes included in an academic paper, can enhance its rhetorical strength. Swales' (1990) reference to the 'moves' a writer makes highlights how this sense of intertextuality is crucial in establishing the rationale for the research project the writer is reporting on. One approach we use in conjunction with discussing plagiarism, for example, is to ask students to examine the number of citations that an article contains, the dates of these citations and the various purposes (e.g. Bloch & Chi, 1995) as a way of focusing on the impact of these factors on the development of the claim.

By focusing on the nature of intertextuality, we are asking students to reflect on what it means to be an author. Such a focus cannot be separated from the lexical and syntactic decisions that emerge from this rhetorical context (Hopper, 1987). Research on grammatical forms, such as hedging (Hyland, 2000b) or the use of reporting verbs (Bloch, 2010; Hyland, 2002), illustrates how writers make choices in their use of citations that reflect their own identities as authors. Bawarshi and Rieff (2010) argue that understanding a genre involves the knowledge of its lexical-grammatical features and its social actions. An author is then a person who uses texts, not simply one who creates new ideas. This view contradicts the beliefs of students that citations are only a 'performance' demonstrating to the teacher that the assignment has been completed (Blum, 2009).

Understanding the norms underlying citations can, therefore, be a positive step for understanding the full range of rhetorical goals a writer needs to demonstrate in order to be considered a member of a community of practice. For students to enter into their chosen communities of practice, they must be able to reclaim that voice without violating the norms of that community. As Rose (1989: 180) argues, this ability to 'position [oneself] in an academic discussion' is a writing strategy not often taught to students, especially those struggling with learning English.

Student, Teacher and Administrative Attitudes toward Plagiarism and Intellectual Property

Much of this research on plagiarism has shown that students bring a variety of attitudes toward the use of intellectual property as they would toward any aspect of the writing process. Before involving students in the study of the usage of intellectual property, it is important to find out both the attitudes of the students and their teachers toward the various ways intellectual property can be used. Since one of the goals for the course was to involve our students in the ongoing debate and conversation about plagiarism (e.g. Graff, 2003), we first assessed their attitudes toward a variety of issues regarding plagiarism and intellectual property.

Student Attitudes toward Plagiarism

There have been a number of studies on student attitudes toward either intellectual property or plagiarism (e.g. Bennett, 2005; Bloch, 2001; Hayes & Introna, 2005; Introna *et al.*, 2003), but few to my knowledge integrate the study of both. Examining both the trait (e.g. ethical background) and state (e.g. fear of failing) backgrounds of lower-income UK students, Bennett found, for example, that students were more likely to plagiarize out of a fear of failure than because of a desire to succeed (cf. Blum, 2009). Much of my own research on student attitudes toward plagiarism and intellectual property has used qualitative methods such as by interviewing them (Bloch, 2001) or examining their discussion about plagiarism in response to blogging assignments (Bloch, 2007a, 2008c).

We quantitatively examined the attitudes that students had toward plagiarism and intellectual property. Because of the connections we have found between these two issues, we designed a survey to assess student attitudes toward both. The survey was administered to 237 incoming undergraduate and graduate students in our writing program. We were interested in particular where there were high and low areas of agreement among and between the students and the instructors of the classes. Understanding which issues had the lowest areas of agreement could help us in developing our pedagogy for discussing plagiarism since the results could indicate where the students were the most confused. Using an analysis of standard deviations, we identified those questions that had the greatest areas of agreement and disagreement among the students. Such disagreements could later be used as starting points for class discussions.

Low Levels of Agreement among Students

As has been discussed, students often receive vague and contradictory advice and, therefore, it would be expected that there would not be a high level of agreement as to the amount of copying that constituted plagiarism. In their study of UK and overseas students, Introna *et al.* (2003) found that there was a general agreement that copying a few sentences was a serious problem, although their students had a great deal of difficulty defining what constituted substantial plagiarism. We tried to distinguish between the consideration of the number of words and the importance of these words. These kinds of distinctions are the fundamental questions in such debates as to whether patchwriting should be considered a form of plagiarism or a form of language learning. In this particular question, we wanted to examine how many words students thought constituted plagiarism:

> You are a writing a paper and you copy a few words from another paper. Do you think this kind of copying is considered plagiarism? (n = number of responses)

(1) Copying even a few words is considered plagiarism. (n = 95)
(2) **Copying a few words is only plagiarism if the words are very important. (n = 61)**
(3) *Copying a few words doesn't matter. (n = 82)*[1]

Answers 1 and 3 drew a similar number of responses, mirroring the debate over whether copying a few words mattered when defining plagiarism. Answer 1, which the instructors considered the most problematic since it was inevitable that some words would always have to be copied, received the most answers from the students, perhaps reflecting a more strict interpretation of the definition of plagiarism than the teachers had. On the other hand, answer 2, which received the fewest number of responses, was the one the instructors stressed (boldfaced) since they wanted the students to be aware of how even sometimes a single word might need to be cited.

Another question that received a low level of agreement focused on collaboration and the citing of ideas they may have received orally rather than from texts. The growing importance of such collaboration, which can occur in group projects or within a peer review group, has also been considered a key issue in motivating changes in how plagiarism is defined (e.g. Howard, 1999). In the next question, we asked about citing ideas generated in a peer review group. The use of other people's ideas is another controversial area in the discussion of plagiarism since it expands on the concept of intellectual property in a collaborative context. What made this question most problematic was that these ideas were generated in oral discussions, but most intellectual property laws only cover materials placed in a fixed medium; therefore, ideas expressed orally are not considered to be intellectual property. However, many schools and universities require the appropriation of ideas, regardless of whether they are only orally expressed, to be cited in the same manner as texts, making the use of uncited ideas a form of plagiarism.

In a peer discussion group, you were asked to discuss your paper with your classmates before you started writing it. One of the members of your group gave you an interesting idea. Do you need to cite the idea in your paper just as you would cite a quotation from a published paper?

(1) *Yes, cite your group member's idea just as you would cite any other source. (n = 88)*
(2) No, you don't need to cite it since the idea was never published. (n = 59)
(3) **Put a footnote thanking your group member for the idea. (n = 90)**

Response 3 was favored by the instructors since it was felt that ideas need not be cited but should be acknowledged. This answer also received a slight majority from the students. Overall, the responses were almost equally split between citing the contribution (37%) and only acknowledging it (38%). If responses 1 and 3 were combined, 75% of the students felt that some form of acknowledgment to the members of their peer review group. A smaller number (25%) felt that no acknowledgment was necessary, which may not be considered to be an act of plagiarism but perhaps one of academic misconduct according to our university's policy on academic misconduct. Hayes and Introna (2003) similarly found a great deal of inconsistency between UK and overseas students in their judgment of the ethics of such collaboration, although their data indicate that few UK students admitted that they had collaborated in contradiction to course policies.

A key issues discussed throughout the course was how students accused of plagiarism should be treated, both by their teachers and the university. This question, which was based on a case that had been adjudicated by our university's Committee on Academic Misconduct, was intended to explore the students' attitudes toward punishment when the use of common knowledge and the amount of copying that the student did was involved.

> A student was accused of copying a paragraph from his textbook and including it in a much longer paper. He was sent to the Office of Academic Misconduct. What do you think should be the appropriate penalty?
>
> (1) *Since, the student copied without citing, he should be treated like any other plagiarist. (n = 95)*
> (2) **Since it was only a small amount, he should only be warned but not given a harsh penalty. (n = 107)**
> (3) Since what is in textbooks is usually common knowledge, the student did not commit plagiarism. (n = 36)

The number of students who felt this amount of copying of common knowledge did not warrant a strong penalty (47%) slightly exceeded the number (41%) who felt that this amount may warrant a harsher treatment. A smaller number (16%) agreed with the argument, which the student had made in front of the discipline committee, that common knowledge should not be cited. The results of this question are somewhat difficult to interpret because there are two issues here, the amount of copying and the nature of the text that had been copied. What defines whether knowledge is considered 'common' is a complex issue, so it was expected that there would be a high level of disagreement. However, the students seem to understand that even though the textbook contained common knowledge, it still could not be copied although there was a stronger disagreement over the seriousness of the act.

In the following question, we tried to examine more specifically the students' attitudes toward the attribution of common knowledge by asking them about when and why common knowledge might have to be cited.

> In your course, you are asked to write a research paper. You are new in the field, and much of what you know is from textbooks. This information is called common knowledge. How should you handle this kind of information in your paper?
>
> (1) **Cite it the same as it was any other kind of literature. (n = 98)**
> (2) **You don't need to cite it because it is common knowledge and belongs to everyone. (n = 59)**
> (3) *Cite it because it makes for a stronger argument in your paper. (n = 80)*

When eliminating the amount of copying as a factor, we found that a large percentage of students did feel that the citation of common knowledge was appropriate. Another 78% answered either 1 or 3, both of which referred to the need to cite common knowledge though for different reasons. The split seemed to focus more on the reasons for citing common knowledge rather than on whether it should be cited. Nevertheless, it was encouraging to see that a large number (n = 80) recognized that the citation of common knowledge could strengthen an argument, a principle that was the basis for much of our pedagogical approach.

Areas of High Agreement among Students

In order to make a more complete understanding of student attitudes, it was also important to find those areas where the students had high levels of agreement, although sometimes the basis for that agreement was very problematic. One of the highest degrees of common understanding was found in response to a question about purchasing papers.

You pay another student to write a research paper. What do you think about doing this?

(1) **Paying another student doesn't matter. Writing these papers isn't important to me. (n = 12)**

(2) *Since presidents and businessmen pay people to write for them, students can do it too. (n = 32)*

(3) **Handing in a paper you bought is the same as copying a paper – you are trying to deceive your teacher. (n = 193)**

While the overwhelming majority (81%) recognized that purchasing a paper is a form of plagiarism, or specifically copying, it might be surprising that 32 students (14%) found that buying a paper was acceptable since highly respected people, like politicians and businessmen, also 'outsource' their writing. This argument was included in the question since it is one that students often make to defend purchasing papers. A small number (5%) responded that they did not consider writing papers to be important; therefore, paying someone to write a paper for you is not a concern.

Both answers 1 and 2 have been central issues in the debate over plagiarism, reflecting disagreements over whether students lack a moral sense or whether they feel alienated from the academic culture in which they are supposed to be members. Students often readily admit that they both do this and it is justified. In an online discussion of plagiarism, one professor cited a student who had written that she felt no qualms about purchasing a paper since she was often too busy to write the paper or may not have understood the assignment. The proliferation of services that 'coach' students in preparing essays for college admission further blurs the distinctions between when a student is expected to do his or her own work.

Another high level of agreement was found in the responses to the question as to whether professors could appropriate what their students had written.

You suspect that one of your professors has taken something you wrote for a course. Is this considered plagiarism?

(1) **No, it's not considered plagiarism since you were a student in the class. (n = 167)**

(2) **Yes, it's considered plagiarism and you can report it to the Academic Misconduct Committee. (n = 26)**

(3) *It doesn't matter. It's considered plagiarism but you cannot do anything about it. (n = 43)*

Their response that it was not considered plagiarism did not reflect a key element of intellectual property law: that everything a student writes is copyrighted, which constrains the ability of their teachers to use their students' intellectual property. This problem has elsewhere been identified as a major concern, particularly of those graduate students who are doing research that is supported in some way by their professors. The results indicate the students did not recognize that they owned this intellectual property and, therefore, no one could use it without their permission. As with the other areas of low agreement, such findings indicated issues about the use of intellectual property that we needed to initiate in classroom discussions.

Some of the questions were designed focus on how intellectual property was to be used in our courses. One of the goals of our course, as will be discussed later, was to have the students become creators and perhaps publishers of intellectual property so that they would better understand these debates over digital intellectual property. We also wanted them to become involved in the creation of new forms of multimodal literacy, so we asked them to create what are called digital stories (Lambert, 2010), which are multimedia projects involving the use of the mages, as their photographs often downloaded from the internet. This assignment raised some complex intellectual property issues regarding the use of downloaded images and music, which complemented and extended the discussion of print texts as forms of intellectual property. Here, we asked whether students felt that they could appropriate images as well as texts.

Can you also plagiarize images as well as texts?

(1) **No, plagiarism refers only to copying texts, not anything else. (n = 164)**
(2) **Yes, if you use an image in a paper, you should cite it just like a text. (n = 49)**
(3) *Maybe, sometimes images are cited, but sometimes they don't need to be. (n = 26)*

Here again, the majority opinion did not reflect what is generally considered to be appropriate practice. Another 72% of the students felt that using images did not require citation in the way texts might, and another 11% felt that they were treated like texts only in certain cases. This result was important in helping us shape our assignment for digital stories. One of the focuses we would have with the digital story assignment was to make students aware of the need for citing every image they found on the internet. It has frequently been argued that one of the best ways to make students aware of the controversy regarding the use of intellectual property is to make them creators of intellectual property. Therefore, we asked them to determine how they could be used in the future, following the model developed by Creative Commons as discussed above.

While only a small amount of our survey data was presented here, it is clear that students have a wide variety of often conflicting attitudes toward intellectual property and plagiarism, a situation that is consistent with what can be found in the population of students as a whole. Such inconsistencies have provided us with a variety of issues that we could use in our writing classrooms for creating materials and assignments as well as discussion in class and online.

Staff Attitudes toward Plagiarism

Having collected opinions about plagiarism from our students, we next wanted to find out what our staff thought about some of these issues. We set up a focus group to discuss plagiarism with the full-time staff, each of whom had between 10 and 15 years' experience teaching in our program. The first topic we discussed was how instances of plagiarism in our department should be dealt with. As with the population of teachers in general, there had often been sharp divisions over the handling of plagiarism cases. Some teachers had been very aggressive in sending students to the Academic Misconduct Committee if there was any hint of plagiarism while others, perhaps the majority, would never send students to the Academic Misconduct Committee, preferring to handle the matter privately. One staff member discussed the division in this way:

> [T]he department was divided into two camps, the strict one and the lax one. The person I knew who reported the most cases, this was more than 10 years ago; they said we coddled our students too much and that it wasn't right that we baby the students and that was her rationale.

Sunderland-Smith (2008) likewise had found a variety of attitudes and approaches in her department. This lack of consensus could be seen as a microcosm of what the students would encounter throughout the university, which would increase the importance of sensitizing them to the different types of policies they may face in the university.

However, despite the past divisions, now there was a general consensus in our department that because this program was intended only for international students, special considerations need be taken, both in regard to defining plagiarism and creating policies for dealing with it, to create what could be called a 'safe haven' for students to develop their writing ability. One area where there was a strong consensus was with the argument that the teacher should consider whether an instance of plagiarism occurred on one of the early drafts, which was not graded, or on the final draft, which was graded. There was agreement that plagiarism on the early drafts should not be punished since it was felt that because the program focused on academic writing and that learning how to use sources was a primary focus of our pedagogy, students should not be penalized if they had not yet learned how to properly cite the sources. As this instructor put it:

> I'm not thinking of the punitive thing; I'm thinking of teaching. What does this student know; what does this student need to know to handle this thing correctly. If you have been in school long enough, it is difficult to carry out a conversation without citing sources.

As with most of the teachers, she did not want to punish the students by sending them to the Academic Misconduct Committee but wanted to take the students' background into consideration and, therefore, be able to make her own decisions about dealing with plagiarism.

In other cases, instructors felt that without a clear understanding of the motivation of the student for plagiarizing, it would be difficult to make a judgment that could have a major impact on that students' future. By allowing the individual instructor to make the decisions regarding how a case of plagiarism should be handled, many felt that they could best evaluate the nature of the problem.

The question is whether it is a linguistic issue or is it a problem of understanding citation conventions or was they [the students] too lazy and actually need to be corrected or trained. I don't know enough about the student to predict what was going on here.

However, being able to exercise control did not necessarily mean that the instructor would avoid giving a punishment. Even during the revision process, some instructors felt that some form of punishment must be given.

I would confront the student and require the student to redo it and then I would also mark down the grade, so there is a clear penalty associated with the plagiarism.

The differences between the departmental goals, and even the goals of individual teachers, highlight the importance of the local control of governance over plagiarism cases, just as has been discussed with intellectual property issues. Despite the different positions concerning how individual cases of plagiarism should be treated, there was a general consensus that the department should develop its own policies since there was a concern that the policies of the Committee on Academic Misconduct (COAM), which required teachers to report instances of plagiarism, did not reflect the concerns held in our department.

There is something in the COAM guidelines that encourages direct communication with the committee. I remember when that didn't serve the student very well because we are in a process writing context and it is possible that the instructor could send something up in the drafting process when in fact when we are supposed to be teaching this sort of thing.

Another instructor feared that COAM may be becoming stricter as a result of the highly publicized plagiarism scandals, particularly at the neighboring university where a number of international students had their degrees rescinded (e.g. Lederman, 2006).

Another controversial issue was the use of Turnitin.com, the so-called plagiarism detection program that has been at the center of a legal and ethical controversy over using such tools. The debate, however, was not simply about the legal and ethical issues, but about technical concerns over its implementation. The implementation of Turnitin.com had not been seamless with some of the other technologies used at the university, particularly the learning management system, which had already been implemented, so using the website required an extra effort for teachers although many still felt that it had been useful. As a result, few instructors in our department had used the program although some did use it to show their students instances of copying and then ask them to paraphrase and cite the texts without fear of punishment.

One of the key issues was over the privacy of students' work. The university had implemented a number of policies regarding sharing student information and work. Since all students had to submit their papers to Turnitin.com, there was a concern that the content of student papers would be exposed even though they had done nothing wrong. However, for a number of the instructors, the benefits still outweighed the limitations.

> The privacy issue doesn't seem to be a big thing. Of course we have to tell them up front we are going to use it. The privacy issue doesn't seem to bother them because they are the generation where everything is on the Web, but I'm sympathetic to graduate students because I wouldn't want my rough drafts out on the Web with the horrendous mistakes, but for undergraduates, it . . . seems to work great with the Web.

Another controversy centered on whether Turnitin.com violated the students' intellectual property rights since the program saved their papers and made money off their use. At the time, there was a court case brought by a group of high school students against Turnitin.com. However, other copy detection programs, such as Paper Rater (http://www.paperrater.com), claim they do not store papers and thus can avoid this problem. Although the court ruled that saving the papers was protected under the fair use provisions since its use was considered by the judge to be a transformative act and did not affect the value of the papers (Paul, 2009), some instructors still felt uneasy about using the program.

Overall, our instructors expressed a variety of often conflicting opinions that were also being debated throughout the academic community, although no one expressed the anger or even disappointment that was sometimes expressed in other venues toward students who plagiarize. They recognized the tension between their teaching goals and having to police for plagiarism, but most agreed that the nature of teaching second language writing necessitated creating policies that reflected the local context in which all of us were teaching. These attitudes raise an old question about second language writing pedagogy: To what extent should such pedagogies be influenced by the policies and practices of the institution? Nevertheless, most of our instructors wanted their own autonomy regarding dealing with plagiarism, both in terms of defining it and responding to apparent problems.

Graduate Teaching Assistants' Attitudes toward Plagiarism

To continue our study of attitudes toward plagiarism in our program, we conducted a second focus group with five graduate teaching assistants, two of whom were from China, one from Mexico, one from India and one American. Most of the teaching assistants had limited teaching experience in ESL programs in the United States. All the international assistants had taught English as a foreign language (EFL) in their home countries. The native English-speaking assistant had taught EFL in Vietnam.

Their EFL experiences gave us a different perspective on the role of plagiarism outside of the American university. Those who had taught EFL confirmed what we had often heard from our students: that plagiarism was rarely discussed in their home countries. The Indian teaching assistant related that 'particularly coming from India, we have never heard the word plagiarism.' Because of this lack of concern, she felt that Indian students would inevitably commit some act of copying that could be defined as plagiarism:

> Let me honestly tell you – every International student will plagiarize because there is no concept of plagiarism [in India]. ... If the university is so serious about plagiarism, then make it mandatory for all international students to take our courses, so we could educate them about plagiarism.

Similarly, the American teaching assistant had found that there was little interest in plagiarism when she was teaching in Vietnam. One Chinese TA also argued that plagiarism was not often addressed in China:

> Sometimes, they did [plagiarize]; I don't whether they using the Internet to copy information. But I remember that we did not address the issue of plagiarism when we teach; that was clear to me.

Not addressing the issue is the crucial issue here. The result can be a self-fulfilling cycle: No one addresses plagiarism; therefore, it will occur, but no one addresses it and so on. In fact, this teacher would later relate how she herself had once committed plagiarism as an undergraduate:

> Yes, I copied sentences. I think it helps me a lot. I don't have to use them in my writing, but knowing that the knowledge is there helps a lot.

A Chinese teacher in Sunderland-Smith's (2008) study likewise admitted to copying when she was a student and that such copying helped her develop her writing, which is similar to what Pecorari (2008) found. Although our teaching assistants admitted they were not familiar with the research on patchwriting, they were generally sympathetic to the argument that copying pieces of sentences could be a positive learning experience, perhaps because patchwriting had been part of their own language learning. The Chinese TA explained her attitudes in this way:

> Sometimes I do see it [copying] as a positive way; there are certain ways to end an essay and maybe there is a good sentence that would be appropriate to use in their essay and I think a good thing is for the student to copy it in her essay for her own purpose. I do think there are advantages there; I do see it as a learning process.

While their perspective on patchwriting did not differ greatly from that of the staff, their greater familiarity with the actual experience of patchwriting gave us a different perspective. One of the frequent complaints heard from teachers is that they keep working with students who still continue to 'plagiarize' regardless of the amount of instruction. Pecorari (2008) uses this occurrence as evidence that students are not intentionally violating the rules.

But why do they continually plagiarize? A possible answer can be found in Howard and her colleagues' 'The Citation Project', where they devised a complex coding scheme to determine whether a passage was copied, paraphrased or patchwritten. Students have to adopt their own personal coding schemes to determine whether their paraphrases are acceptable. Making such differentiations was shown to be difficult even for experienced writing teachers. From a cultural perspective, how do such schemes vary depends upon differences between what is considered original and what is imitation (Bloch, 2008b). A student may feel that his or her attempt was an appropriate paraphrase while their instructor was thinking it was copied or patchwritten. From a developmental perspective, the question is whether the student knows his or her work is patchwritten but feels that it cannot be improved or that he or she does not care to improve it. In all these cases, his or her decision making was influenced by a lack of information or a lack of skills, which often results in some degree of punishment.

One issue where there was a greater division was that of punishment. We began the discussion of punishment with a reading about the case at an American university (Duke) where the international students had appeared to receive harsher penalties for plagiarizing than their American counterparts (e.g. Redden, 2007). For some, it appeared that the differences in how the cases were handled resulted from differences in how readily the students took responsibility for their actions.

> I think it has to do with taking responsibility. The Americans students said that they apologized; they took responsibility for that. So the policy is that if you take responsibility for the wrong thing that you did, you will be excused.

The instructor here does not seem to show the same degree of sympathy that we had found when we gave this article to the students to summarize and discuss. As some of our examples of plagiarism, such as the two professors discussed by Li and Xiong (1996), illustrate, there may be cultural differences in the expected responses to such accusations. We have seen numerous examples of how a quick apology is what is expected of a person caught plagiarizing. When Maureen Dowd, a well-known columnist for *The New York Times* admitted plagiarizing a blog, she quickly issued an apology, claiming she had unknowingly used a quote from the blog that a friend had given her (Baram, 2009).

Our teachers sometimes find themselves mediating this kind of conflict. One teaching assistant told of a problem she was trying to resolve between an international student and an American professor:

> [T]here was miscommunication and academic misconduct and it is quite traumatic for her [the student]. Someone had asked for a definition and she took out a definition dictionary. I have wanted to talk to the professor and work something out.

Often the teaching assistants referred to their own lack of understanding of plagiarism and the problems that might have resulted from their lower English-language proficiency levels when trying to paraphrase. While many institutions attempt to create a common definition of plagiarism, it is often difficult to do so. As a result, the students may need a space to work through the possible different contexts they may have to face. During the discussion, they frequently used the term 'a safe window' or 'a safe place' to describe how they viewed the writing classroom, perhaps reflecting their own needs for this kind of instruction. However, even the American TA agreed that our classes should support the students' attempts to work out some of the problems they had with citing sources:

> Within this time we cannot expect them to have this full grasp and understanding of it [plagiarism], so 107 and 108 [two of our writing classes] is kind of a safe place for them to explore ... if they haven't really written in this style before.

At the same time, the assistants all expressed a concern, and sometimes a moral outrage, about plagiarism. As one TA, put it:

> I think what bothers me about plagiarism is that students are trying to claim other people's stuff as theirs.

She seems to be differentiating between how intentional and unintentional plagiarism should be treated. However, her sympathy does not seem to lie with the students who knew they were plagiarizing, expressing the same argument that Posner's (2007) incorporated into his 'fraud' metaphor. She felt that if she knew from whom the material had been taken, then she would not feel as bad when the students did not paraphrase the material accurately.

This TA was more specific about the minimum she wanted to see concerning references in a student's paper:

> I like to see a reference list and that is something we did [in India] as an undergrad. I did have a reference list even though I didn't actually cite the sources. We used the names of famous writers but we didn't have to write a page number and we didn't have to write a year. I just listed some books that I got this from. I would like to see from my own purpose of knowing which book I read.

There are some interesting differences here between citation practice in India and at our university, perhaps reflecting a different set of norms. Since she herself was not taught all the rules that she now needed to enforce, she may have felt that American universities are overly concerned with plagiarism.

> There is a lot of hype around it and it's getting more intense as the years go by. Now it is being more intense; now it is being transferred to

music. I just feel like it's too possessive of the property. If it is out there, it is supposed to be shared. That's the reason why it's out there.

She raises here a number of issues often associated with the connection between intellectual property, plagiarism and culture: that students often feel that information found on the internet is freely accessible and, therefore, can be used without attribution. As discussed earlier, this argument that information from the internet should be 'free' has emerged from the unique nature of internet culture. The argument has also been associated with the claims about cultural differences in understanding plagiarism, particularly among Asian students, as illustrated in the discussion in the Ohio State handbook for international students, which stated that international students may have different attitudes toward sharing information than do the American students.

Cultural differences in citation practices often arose in our discussion. One of the Chinese assistants expressed the concern that learning to write in English would negatively impact the Chinese students' writing style:

I think they will gradually lose their Chinese style of writing because in our style, one of the reasons we don't document is the assumption that readers should already know who is being cited.

Such examples of this practice of not citing those sources that are assumed to be easily recognizable seem to confirm arguments concerning the cultural impact on attribution. These citation practices can be seen in traditional forms of Chinese rhetoric dating back almost two millennia (Bloch & Chi, 1995). It is interesting to note that this practice still exists in some forms of Chinese writing although not in other forms since many aspects of citation practice have changed over the past 20 years. These changes also illustrate how cultural differences may spread unevenly through different communities or 'small' cultures within one 'big' culture.

Despite all the differences, it was agreed that it was necessary to teach the rules of attribution that students had to learn to follow. There was also a general agreement that the department should not have a policy requiring the teaching assistants to send students who plagiarized to the Academic Misconduct Committee. The assistants agreed that they should first focus on education and only consider punishment for the students if they plagiarized on later drafts:

I would probably check with other people in the department who were familiar with [the policies] because it would be the first time I would have encountered [plagiarism]. I wouldn't say I found you plagiarizing but start to talk to them about the paper and ask them more questions about it and how they knew about this and see how they respond when they are further questioned about this.

Unlike the teachers in Sunderland-Smith's (2008) study, none believed plagiarism was primarily intentional. However, as with our students and staff, the teaching assistants are caught between a variety of different forces related to the controversies over plagiarism: their own educational experiences, their lack of understanding of some of the complexities regarding citation practice and the contradictions that could arise between their desire to educate the students about plagiarism and the need to implement university policies toward academic misconduct. Pecorari and Shaw (2010) similarly found that there were often different attitudes toward among teachers, a situation that could portend difficulty for students in negotiating these various attitudes.

Administrative Attitudes toward Plagiarism

While our focus has been primarily on issues regarding plagiarism on the course and departmental level, others have suggested the primary importance should lie at the institutional level (e.g. McCabe et al., 2001). In comparing Australia and Sweden, Sunderland-Smith and Pecorari (2010) show how different countries have different policies for dealing with plagiarism. In the United States, each university has its own policies, most often administered by a committee. For the administrative perspective on these issues, we interviewed the head of the Committee on Academic Misconduct (http://oaa.osu.edu/coam.html). The committee was constituted by the university to adjudicate various kinds of academic misconduct and contains both faculty and students.

A number of issues arose during our discussions regarding institutional policies. One question was whether it was mandatory to report plagiarism cases to the committee; therefore, we first wanted to know what the university attitude was toward such local governance. Unlike the pressure found in Sweden (Sunderland-Smith & Pecorari, 2010), faculty and instructors are usually under little pressure to report instances of plagiarism. In our interview, the head of COAM told us that there was a policy requiring acts of plagiarism to be reported, but he admitted that only a small number of instructors reported such instances. He was especially critical of those instructors who do not report their cases, as was often the case in our department.

> [I]f we let faculty members avoid their responsibilities of education and that's a loss for the student. I've had students go through this and say this is the best thing that ever happened to them.

The charge that instructors do not take academic misconduct seriously has frequently been raised. Such instructors are often described as 'lazy' since filing charges at many universities requires a lot of time. However, these instructors may also underreport because they recognize the contradiction between being a policeman and being an educator, which both our staff and GTAs felt was appropriate.

On the other hand, he did remark, perhaps ironically, that underreporting could be fortunate since that if everybody did report all the cases, the committee would be overwhelmed. Nevertheless, he was still concerned with the implications of this underreporting on the integrity of the university:

> [A]s a sociologist I'm saying crime is being underreported in this city. What we do with that fact I don't know but I'm sure crime is underreported. Crime meaning plagiarism in this case. The second thing is what would we do if everybody systematically reported every case; we couldn't process 10,000 cases. As in all crimes, the norms dictate what will happen.

As has been discussed, the use of the 'crime' metaphor dominates his description of the situation at the university. However, he, like all of us, appears to be caught between his role of policing and judging such 'crimes' and his role as an educator:

> The view I've gotten from the university is that you are foremost an educator; you're not a policeman, but there is a grey area where you are the educator and you say this paper is terrible, you're getting a zero on this paper and the next time I am not going to bother to correct it and you are going to be sent up to academic misconduct.

From the committee's perspective, the contradiction may differ from the perspective of those who want to reform attitudes toward plagiarism at the classroom level.

Another issue that came up in our discussions was how COAM viewed international students. The head relates that the great number of international students, many of them enrolled in graduate school, sent to the Academic Misconduct Committee has aroused concern in the university:

> I see a disproportionate number of international students and many of them tell me that in their culture it was perfectly all right to do what they have done and in their defenses, they didn't know. When I was interviewing for the job as coordinator, the provost was particular that they wanted an educational mission, particularly for graduate students because what was happening was that graduate students would get suspended on the first response and so for these international students, all the expense and recruitment and here they show up ready to go and the next thing you know is that they were over here at COAM and were getting suspended, which means that if you had an international visa, you would be sent home because you couldn't be a student next quarter, so it was horrible.

The consequences of plagiarism by international students pose a particular problem for universities, given the effort the university goes through to recruit these students and the fact that a severe punishment could lead to them being expelled. Therefore, the head of COAM realized that education had to precede punishment, despite the 'criminal nature of the act':

> [S]o I intervened dramatically, if he were a green student, as coordinator I could step in and say you have done something that normally you would have been suspended for but you have only been here four weeks, so we have to deal with something and you have to get it straight. Or you will be suspended next time; let's not go the full route on this; let's have you explain what you were thinking, and we make a big effort for education so that they learn or otherwise they would look like they were getting harsher penalties because they were blindsided about how formal it is and that there is no recourse.

Another concern was the future of Turnitin.com in the university. While there had initially been great interest in using the website, the committee found that such sentiments were not widespread enough to continue the expense of a lease. The website had been implemented by the previous committee head, but the current head did not seem as enthusiastic, in part because of technical problems with integrating the website with other technologies used on campus. However, he also raised the same concerns as were discussed by members of our department about the possible contradictions between educating and policing that the use of the program had raised:

> It [Turnitin.com] is very mechanical, depending on your sense of education. Education means that you have a student and you show them your work and you show them the rule and then you have them talk about how this happened and they might tell you I have two jobs and this and that going on and I was late that night and I was out of time and I just did it and I feel rotten. That's the point you got to get to educate the student. You gotta get them to look at themselves. If you stay at the mechanical level, and say 17% from this paper is plagiarized; that's fine they know they did that but it doesn't get to what happened that made you do this.

As this discussion shows, administrators and teachers often feel caught between educating and making 'mechanical' decisions about what is a highly complex problem. Students were similarly caught between contradictory norms and values: the demands of the university, the problems of their own lives and the possible devastating consequences of their decisions.

Creating a Course for Discussing Plagiarism and Intellectual Property

I have discussed throughout this book the difficulties and failures of traditional approaches to teaching about plagiarism. These potential breakdowns in the educational process can place students in a position where plagiarism may be a logical, though highly problematical, decision. Dee and Jacob (2001) use the term 'rational ignorance' to describe the lack of understanding about plagiarism found in the university students they studied. Lea and Street (2006) refer to a problem as a gap in expectations among the different participants.

We have outlined a number of causes for this problem. Some result from an attempt to intentionally bypass the system, which may result from a lack of moral concern on the part of the student although other reasons may relate to the student's perceptions of the value of the academic system. Other reasons may be more directly connected to pedagogical issues: the disequilibrium between student and instructor possibly due to a lack of understanding of the goals of the writing assignments or the purpose of their assessment, the lack of understanding concerning the definition of plagiarism or the lack of adequate strategies to achieve the goals. Assignments, for example, where students do not have all the requisite background, cannot use sources to help them with what they do not know or have different assumptions about the goals of the assignment, can be invitations to plagiarize.

If plagiarism then simply resulted from moral decisions, then the only goal for a course would be to discuss maintaining the integrity of the institution, which could minimally be accomplished by reading a set of rules, sending the student to another website to read more rules or threatening them with the use of a copy detection program. Students would then be expected to adhere to the rules, whether they understood them or not, and receive appropriate punishments if they fail to follow them. However, in the framework presented here, part of the responsibility for understanding about the use of intellectual property shifts to the classroom to ensure that students share the same representation of the assignment as does the teacher.

While some teachers felt that such websites provided enough information for students to know how to cite their sources, others felt that this presence of such information may neither be sufficient nor guarantee that the student will understand it. The assumption of this approach is that by recommending the site, any form of ensuing plagiarism would be considered the student's fault and the teacher would be absolved of any responsibility, and the university would have fulfilled its obligations.

The writing classroom has often been thought to be where students should learn all these rules, and any failure to do so is often blamed on the teachers. However, the contradictions between the representations of the teacher and the student of the writing tasks can create a deficit model for both teachers and students that can affect not only the students' ability to learn but also the teacher's view of the student. In order to mediate this apparent contradiction, teachers can shift their pedagogical strategies away from having to take a purely moral perspective to creating a pedagogical approach that integrates teaching about plagiarism within the rhetorical context of the type or genre of writing being taught.

This approach, on the other hand, does not obviate the need for deterrents in dealing with plagiarism that raise the cost on intentional plagiarism. The 'game' metaphor reinforces the need for a set of such deterrents and punishments that recognize the importance of understanding the norms and values of the genre of writing being taught. In our context, we have the Academic Misconduct Committee, the possible use of copy protection programs and any local deterrents the individual teacher may use. However, all of the deterrents are used with the discretion of the teacher to support their own goals. This approach, therefore, allows teachers to position themselves in the debate according to their own values. As shown in the focus groups, our L2 writing teachers often want to create their own approaches for dealing with plagiarism, which may differ from the practices found in other classes in the university while making the students aware of rules they will encounter throughout their academic careers. This approach allows teachers to modify the rules to reflect the local context of their teaching, thus allowing for, though not determining, a framework for deconstructing the dominant rules regarding plagiarism that may conflict with other goals and values found in their writing pedagogies.

A Course about Plagiarism

Various attempts have been made to incorporate discussions of plagiarism into writing courses as a means of helping students understand the nature of authorship (Robillard, 2008). DeVoss and Rosati (2002) found that such discussions about plagiarism can encompass other discussions about what is appropriate research, what is good writing, what intellectual property rights mean and how changes in writing spaces, such as the growing importance of digital literacy, may affect concepts relating to plagiarizing both online and in print. Thus, perhaps no debate better fulfills Graff's (2003) goal of immersing students in the debates of the academy than does the one over plagiarism.

The main goal of the course is to integrate the teaching of academic writing with teaching about the controversies regarding plagiarism. The teacher's role is to create a context where the goals, rules and punishments can be understood by every participant so that they can engage in the debate on a level-playing field with the other actors – teachers, administrators, colleagues – who already are participating in this conversation. In their academic literacy framework, Lea and Street (2006) emphasize the importance of knowledge construction through reading and writing. Students begin this process by reading and writing about plagiarism, using a variety of different media: excerpts from books, newspaper articles and films. The students are expected to

- read and discuss a group of stories and movies about students who have been accused of committing plagiarism[2];
- read and discuss articles by writers such as by Stanley Fish (2010) on the moral aspects of plagiarism and cases of plagiarism such as those given by Mike Rose (1989);

- write a series of papers using a variety of source texts in which they discuss and argue about what plagiarism is and how it should be treated;
- publish and share their ideas about plagiarism on blogs[3];
- discuss paraphrasing, the rhetorical purposes of textual borrowing and attribution;
- discuss choosing appropriate reporting verbs, a variety of related lexical, syntactic and rhetorical issues relating to intertextuality and plagiarism; and
- create a multimodal digital story that interweaves texts and images together.

Both the print and digital assignments were designed to have students explore the relationships between their own voices and the voices found in other texts, in the process transforming these texts into new ones. The digital storytelling assignment (see Lambert, 2010) was of particular importance since it integrated a variety of issues regarding the authorship of a text; the relationship between texts and images and between print, visual and audio modalities; the use of visual intellectual property as source texts; and the nature of plagiarism in a digital context.

This approach attempts to encompass different aspects of the writing process – from immersing the students in the debate regarding plagiarism to discussing the rhetorical strategies for using both texts and images for developing academic arguments as well as for choosing the lexical and grammatical items related to the citation of texts, such as sentence structure and clausal forms, the choice of reporting verbs (e.g. Bloch, 2010) and the appropriate use of tenses, all of which are useful for expressing the writer's stance toward these texts (e.g. Hyland, 2000b).

Developing a Sense of Authorship in a Writing Course

In the framework we are using, teachers have a responsibility for structuring their class and creating assignments that do not place students in the position where plagiarizing is the most rational choice to make but rather should help students develop their sense of being an author. We wanted to create assignments that would ask students to think critically about their writing experiences, which could affect their decision-making strategies in ways that can minimize the possibilities for plagiarizing. As Abasi et al.'s (2006) research indicates, it is important to create assignments that can make students feel they have ownership of their texts.

The relationship between the students' sense of authorship and their decisions to plagiarize has been one of the major points of discussion in this book. Ivanic (1998) has made this relationship explicit in her discussion of voice and the social nature of literacy, raising the concern that students who feel they lack a voice are more likely to plagiarize. Mike Rose's (1989) story about the plagiarism accusations against a first-generation student illustrates how the writing assignment expected her to have knowledge of a topic about which she actually had no idea. No academic writer would ever take on a topic, as Marita had to, about which she knew as little as Marita did. We wanted our students to avoid falling into this bind. Therefore, it was imperative to make the students 'experts' in their topic, at least to the degree that was possible within a 10-week course.

Summarizing not only allowed us to have the students practice paraphrasing but also to help them focus on developing their own voices while writing. For each reading, students first summarized it, identifying what they felt to be the main issues regarding plagiarism, and then added their own evaluation of these issues they identified in the stories. One problem that Howard et al. (2010) have identified in students' summarizing strategies is that they focus too much on individual sentences and not on the larger issues in the texts. We emphasized beginning each summary with 1 to 2 descriptive sentences that focused on identifying these larger issues. The students were also expected to write a substantive evaluation of these issues, reflecting our concern with having the students develop a voice in regard to these issues.

In the second assignment, they synthesized the various opinions around these issues and then wrote an argumentative paper that both critiques the claims the writer disagrees with and uses the readings to support the writer's own claims. Our approach encourages students to 'self-plagiarize' by giving them a series of assignments that build upon each other, allowing the students to remix their previous texts while adding new ideas to develop new texts.

In all their assignments, the students are expected to integrate or 'weave' (e.g. Rose, 1989) the ideas from these texts with their own ideas, thus immersing them in the intertextuality between their own writing and the writing of their classmates. Following Graff's (2003) approach to immersing students in the controversial issues of the academy regarding plagiarism, the primary goal of this approach is to problematize each of the controversial issues (e.g. definition, punishment, the role of culture, intentionality). In this way, we hope the students can see the connection between the rules for plagiarism and the norms and values of the genres of writing they are learning. While helping students deconstruct what is meant by plagiarism, this approach does not necessarily reflect what is called a 'critical literacy' in a manner similar to that of Benesch (2001) or Pennycook (2001). The 'game' metaphor does not necessarily frame the problem of plagiarism as an act of resistance, just as it does not frame the problem in terms of morality, but primarily as a pedagogical problem that must be integrated with the other aspects of teaching writing.

This approach, moreover, acknowledges that certain forms of plagiarism, such as those that involve fraud, should be punished in the same way that reforms in intellectual property law, such as Creative Commons, do not support unlimited downloading and sharing music. More important, the approach warns them they may encounter different practices regarding plagiarism in other classrooms. By deconstructing these rules we believe the students will better understand the playing of the academic game, which can help create the equilibrium between teacher and student we are seeking.

Entering the Debate over Plagiarism in the Writing Classroom through Blogging

Concurrently throughout the course, we have attempted to develop our students' sense of authorship through the use of blogs where they could discuss the issues regarding plagiarism in a less formal way (Bloch, 2007, 2008c; Bloch & Crosby, 2006). Of all the new Web 2.0 technologies, blogging has emerged as a way to promote this sense of authorship (Shirky, 2008). Blogging allows writers to develop their own voices on a topic in a freer context without the pressure of classroom-based assignments or producing grammatically correct discourse that will be graded. Therefore, it was the preferred technology for allowing students to discuss plagiarism with their classmates. The students blogged weekly about their reactions to the articles they read as a way of generating ideas for their writing assignments on an ongoing basis in a more social context. The other students could read the blogs, comment upon the ideas and later cite them in their own texts. It was hoped that the use of blogs as texts could help the writers take greater ownership of their own texts knowing that they could be cited by their classmates and value their classmates' writing by engaging with them in a broader debate over plagiarism.

Thus, blogging was one approach that dealt directly with the question of student identity. Lea and Street (2006) stress the importance of identity in academic literacy, an approach that has traditionally been ignored. Throughout their blogs, the students explored various positions on plagiarism, incorporating different voices into this conversation, sometimes supporting and sometimes opposing the traditional viewpoints, which led to debates in the classroom and in the blogs over how different forms of plagiarism should be treated.

One of the key issues the students struggled with was the controversy over what constituted academic misconduct. We began this assignment with a discussion of their experiences with plagiarism. In this assignment, the students were asked to discuss whether they had plagiarized or knew someone who had plagiarized. In this blog, the student explores her own experiences plagiarizing and tries to explain why she did it:

> Yes, frankly I plagiarized so many times in my former school. . . . Sometimes, I plagiarized by cut and pasted the paper . . . and sometimes I listed the internet sources or magazines to my research paper. . . . Moreover, I just turned in somebody's paper to the professor by changing original name to my name. . . . I knew that was not good but I did not realize that it was against academic rule and it was a plagiarism. . . . I also did not get an education about plagiarism. And, sometimes when I did not have any idea about the paper or assignment and I did not have an enough time to finish of it, I plagiarized.

The readings about the students caught plagiarizing seem to trigger a personal response where the students could speak more freely than we had ever found in class discussions or other genres of their writing. Their responses could be later interwoven with the stories from the texts. In this way we felt that the blogging was contributing to their development of an authorial voice in their papers (Bloch, 2007a).

Perhaps because of the expressive nature of the blogs, the students often raised additional issues beyond what we had asked. This student also raises one of the central issues in the field of intercultural rhetoric: whether other cultures share the concern with plagiarism found in the West (Bloch, 2008a). Although he admits he knew what he did 'was not good', he argues that the reason he turned in someone else's paper was that he 'did not get an education about plagiarism', and, therefore, may not have known he was violating the rules. The student's final sentence raises a critical issue both in our discussions about plagiarism and in the course design: How should the university deal with students who have had no education about plagiarism? Was the warning given in the student handbook or at the beginning of the course sufficient? As the COAM administrator admitted, the university sometimes spent a lot of money recruiting international students and did not want to see them suspended soon after they arrived.

The student's concern about not knowing anything about the assignment echoed the concern Rose (1989) had about the lack of background knowledge students may bring to their assignments. However, many students did not admit to having plagiarized, but had heard stories about plagiarism either from friends or newspapers. Although sometimes international students are thought to be ignorant of the issues surrounding plagiarism, their blogs often showed a strong awareness of the issue. In this blog the student discusses news reports from Korea about the growth of plagiarism, the reasons students may plagiarize and her own opinions about plagiarism:

> As it is, I've never heard or saw someone ever been accused of plagiarism surrounding my work so far. However, I only read articles about Internet plagiarism in the Korea newspaper. According to the Korea Times, it is easier that many college students access Internet plagiarism for their assignments. ... If professor get to know students have plagiarized their report, they don't get to grade about report. ... In Korea, there are severe competitions among college students. If they don't get a good grade through their university life, they can't attend good company. Because student' grades are one of the most important company's requirements which they want to go. Students are always afraid of being what they get a bad grade from their professors. ... In my opinion, I think that plagiarism is unfair. Although it may easy and simple plagiarizing for their reports, I think that it is only a waste time. Plagiarism may stop their spirit growth and may interrupt to be a rich experience and intelligence in the University.

In this blog, the student uses many of the strategies that he or she could later use in their academic papers. The writer summarizes a key issue from a source, rather than only a single sentence, and uses that source to take a critical stand by arguing which forms of plagiarism should be taken seriously and which should not be.

The student's argument can be construed as being somewhat critical of the traditional institutional policies that do not differentiate between different types of plagiarism, exemplifying what Benesch (2001) argues to be critical to the development of academic literacy. At the same time, she expresses a strong moral concern for those who plagiarize. She argues that plagiarism undermines the moral and intellectual growth of the student since the student is demonstrating a lack of responsibility for the integrity of the society that both the individual and the community share.

As this argument illustrates, the students sometimes aligned their views with the official policies of the university and sometimes opposed them, reflecting a complex set of accommodation and resistance to the institutional constraints of the university. In this blog, the student discusses the relationship between the moral implications of plagiarism and the tools, such as the so-called plagiarism detection sites:

> As an honest student, I think that the students [who are] plagiarists must be found guilty; otherwise, the quality of the education and the work will decrease day by day. Many students begin to duplicate the other student's assignment and as a result of this there will be no improvement and no discovery in the academic life. Every student must make a huge and equal effort in order to deserve the degree they will get. If the students do not avoid plagiarism, we will have a plenty of unsuccessful adults all around the world in the future. When the students hear about the usage of a website to detect the plagiarism, they will realize that they can most probably get caught. Therefore, they will stop stealing ideas and try to form their own ideas and learn to show respect other people's ideas.

This writer also focuses on how plagiarism affects the moral development of the individual. He is sympathetic to the pressure that students can feel when a bad performance can dramatically affect their status in the university. However, this student believes that plagiarism can have a more general and personal impact on the moral and intellectual growth of the student. At the end of the blog, the student argues that plagiarism can negatively impact student growth and the nature of their experiences in the university, adding an additional moral dimension related to how plagiarizing in college can negatively impact the individual even after leaving the university, an argument similar to what was depicted in some of university library online websites dealing with plagiarism.

The writer, in fact, discusses many of the same issues regarding plagiarism in Korea that parallel the debates occurring in the West: the role of the internet and the stress for obtaining higher grades (e.g. Blum, 2009) as well as the concern that plagiarizing can retard a student's spiritual and intellectual growth. In fact, Dee and Jacob (2010) found a significant decrease in instances in plagiarism in courses that were pass/fail instead of graded, which illustrates the role of the pressure in plagarizing that Blum had found. Blum (2009) seemed to rarely find evidence of such moral responsibility, although this sentiment is frequently expressed by faculty concerned with academic integrity.[4] In fact, the writer seems to bring her own set of metaphors related to spiritual growth, unlike the dominant 'stealing' metaphor or the 'threat to academic integrity' metaphor often used in the West.

We have found over the years that their expression of voice was often more powerful in their blogs than it was in their other forms of academic writing. Lea and Street (2006) warn about dichotomizing these different forms of discourses. Since such a dichotomy would seem to undermine our goal to have the students express their identity in their writing, we attempted to bridge the gap between these different forms of literacy by having them cut and paste from their blog into the academic writing, often with some revisions to fit their organization. While the students often argued that a cut and paste strategy was at the heart of the plagiarism problem, we wanted them to see that it was the context of cut and pasting and not the act itself that could cause problems, particularly since they were owners of both pieces of intellectual property.

Debating the Institutional Response to Plagiarism

It might be expected that the issue that would most concern the students would be the institutional response to plagiarism, particularly in regard to punishment. Much like the academic community itself, the students here were deeply divided about what plagiarism was and how it should be dealt with by the institution. Despite their concern for how institutional policies toward how plagiarism could affect them, the students often connected their definitions of plagiarism with what penalties should be imposed.

Given the intense controversy regarding the use of Turnitin.com (e.g. Marsh, 2004; Purdy, 2005), it is interesting that few of the students were bothered by the method this teacher uses to 'nail plagiarists'. The strong moral sensibility often expressed toward plagiarism may explain that there has been little concern over the means used by the teachers to catch students plagiarizing. Few students, for example, have ever expressed concern over the use of Turnitin.com, even though in the case of the high school student, it was used surreptitiously by her teacher.

One issue that did concern them was the amount of material that needed to be copied to be considered plagiarism. In our survey discussed above, one of the lowest levels of agreement came from a question about how much copying constituted plagiarism. The students raised a number of issues related to the amount of text copied. In the stories they encountered in the course, the students who had been accused of plagiarism had copied a widely different amount of text. The high school student had copied 30% (Heaton, 2003), Marita had copied an entire section without the appropriate quotation marks (Rose, 1989) and,

Jamal, the fictional student in the movie *Finding Forrester* (2000), used one paragraph its author had given him to copy and then developed his own highly creative essay, which his literature teacher still considered to be plagiarized.

When asked in their blogs which of the students, if any, they would defend, the students had to struggle with this question of how the amount might affect the definition of plagiarism:

> I think, anybody don't want defend [the high school student]. To defend [the high school student] is harder than Jamal and Marita. If defended person is innocent, this situation may make easy work of defendant person. I prefer defended the Jamal, if I have to defend one of them. Because he is innocent about plagiarism, but the other persons, Marita and [the high school student], made plagiarism. [the high school student] made it purposely, but Marita made it unintentionally. To defend innocent person may be more easy than the others situations. Jamal come across misunderstand. He doesn't explain himself suitably to his literature teacher and school authorities. He misunderstands. If his teacher understood him truly, Jamal would be more creative student about literature. The literature teacher had to discovered Jamal's literature ability and contributed to improve it, but he made opposite of this.

Many of the students could identify with the stories of misunderstanding the rules of textual appropriation while taking a more critical perspective of those they felt should have already learnt about plagiarism, such as the high school student who had already been warned once. While the students had strong feelings about this problem, they, not unexpectedly, felt that educating students as well as themselves should be the primary institutional response.

Students were often explicit that intentionality was a critical factor in determining how instances of plagiarism should be dealt with. The relatively large amount copied by the high school student seemed to convince many that this particular act of plagiarism should be punished. As one student argued, '[the high school student] made it [committed plagiarism] purposely, but Marita made it unintentionally.' The amount seemed not to matter as much since Marita copied a larger percentage of her essay than did the high school student. In other cases, however, the students seemed to feel that the less the copying, the greater the sympathy the accused students should receive. Students responded to the more limited amount of copying by Jamal, along with the apparent 'brilliance' of the essay, with a great deal of sympathy with the ending of the film where he is exonerated of the charges of plagiarizing.

The alleged plagiarism by Jamal was considered by the students a more complicated case since it was not clear from the story itself whether he knew that copying just one paragraph in a longer essay would be considered plagiarism or that copying a paragraph from a published article could be easily discovered. Although fictional, this story illustrated well the combined issues of education, culture and creativity as they related to plagiarism. Jamal was seen as caught between conflicting institutional goals: the need of the school to uphold a strict definition of academic integrity, a sincere desire to foster the creative talents of the students and, since Jamal was an excellent basketball player along with being an excellent writer, an institutional desire to have him on the team in order to win a championship.

The inability to distinguish between intentional and unintentional plagiarizing has been a powerful argument for critiquing the 'stealing' metaphor since this metaphor does not consider the student's motivation or, as in the case of Jamal, the ability to transform a piece of text into a new creation, an issue that is central in intellectual property law. Pecorari (2008) argues that it is often obvious that some students were not attempting to deceive their readers when they copied a small amount of text, a point that Posner (2007) had stressed with his use of the 'fraud' metaphor, but rather were simply unable to successfully paraphrase the texts. On the other hand, the teacher in *Finding Forrester* who accuses Jamal of plagiarism argues forcefully that intentionality or creativity should not matter, a position held by many who feel that no exceptions should be made. For those holding this position, plagiarism is plagiarism regardless of the amount, intentionality or the background of the writer.

In this blog, a student attempts to sort out these complex issues regarding how prior education should affect the treatment of this 'unintentional' copying, such as that by Marita:

> [The student] copied and pasted the original text; at the second time, she paraphrased the sentences and mixed with her own ideas. However, she did not cite any. We can know that [the student] had no idea about academic writing. She even did not know citation is needed. In Marita's situation, she did know something about academic writing. She knew that it's necessary to cite reference, but she did not have the technique. These indicate that she did learn how to write in academic way, but she was not well trained. Who should take the responsibility? Did her high

school teacher know how to write academic articles? Why she did not be accused of plagiarism when she was in high school?

Although her reading of the text is somewhat problematic – the high school student had been warned about plagiarizing – the writer raises a critical question regarding the responsibility of the school to educate its students about plagiarism, which is the central argument for the use of the 'gaming' metaphor.

The students also showed great sympathy toward those whose alleged acts of plagiarism may have been influenced by cultural factors. As in the case of Marita (Rose, 1989), who was taught not to speak unless she was sure she had something to say, these cultural factors could upset the equilibrium between teacher and student. In this blog, the student defends the actions of Marita both on cultural and educational grounds:

I will prefer Marita to defend. The reason is Haley and Jamal knew what they were doing on the contrary Marita did not. Haley totally understood that plagiarism is wrong and risky. Furthermore, Haley has all the opportunities to learn about plagiarism but she kept doing it since she was irresponsible about her homework. In addition, Jamal said that he would not have turned in the paper if he had known the article was published in The New Yorker. It means that he was aware of plagiarism. ... On the other hand, the accusation was an unexpected event for Marita. She had no idea about why the assignment was considered as a plagiarized work. She used outside sources because of two reasons. First reason is her father's sayings about expressing ideas[5] and second reason is the lack of knowledge about academic work. She did cite but not all of them and she could not distinguish her work from the source. The event was a very good experience for her and she must have learned a lot. Since she was a very motivated student, she would not do it again for sure. I believe that she was on the right tack at least and by the help of the school she would be a perfect academician. Therefore, school's response to Marita was right.

The student develops a number of arguments to defend her choice of Marita as the one to defend. As was discussed above, an important theme in the students' blogs was that they did not learn about plagiarism before coming to the United States. Therefore, they often concluded, as this student did, that Marita's act was unintentional and that she should be exonerated. Moreover, the student uses the cultural argument, what she had learned from her father, as well as her own character, as part of the argument that, for students like Marita, accusations of plagiarism could be a learning experience.

Unlike these students, who did not seem to care about learning, the students mostly agreed with Rose (1989) that Marita demonstrated that, by consulting the encyclopedia when she did not understand the assignment, she was attempting to learn and not just finding an easy way to complete the assignment. As with Jamal, although he was a more experienced writer, Marita seemed to have a good and caring *ethos*, which many of the students considered a mitigating factor in the penalization process. As discussed earlier, the dilemma that Marita faced was often expressed by the students in their blogs, which could easily explain the greater empathy they had with her.

Throughout these blogs, the students discuss a variety of complex issues that go beyond the simplistic debate about plagiarism that sometimes occurs in an institutional setting. Their views both challenge and defend traditional definitions and practices, simultaneously negotiating attitudes toward language and institutional policies. Although their arguments may have little effect outside of our classroom, they are developing a strong voice and a variety of rhetorical strategies for supporting their arguments, which can be later transferred to their formal academic papers as a means of helping them avoid the trap of plagiarizing by knowing how to differentiate their voices from the voices of others.

Attitudes toward the Education versus Punishment Debate

The head of our Academic Misconduct Committee well expressed the dilemma that in an educational institution the first goal should be education, not punishment. We frequently hear this complaint from students that no one told them about the rules and that they did not understand what they had been taught. What constitutes appropriate punishment is a more compelling question that is often raised. The mother of the high school student felt that even probation was not enough to teach her daughter about plagiarism (personal communication). Her response expressed a minority position, defending the only student who many felt had clearly intentionally plagiarized. While many disagreed with the mother, at least one felt that the blame should be distributed among many parties. The student does not deny that plagiarism occurred but was more concerned with whether expulsion was appropriate for a young student:

> Comparing with two other cases which the punishments were not too hard, Marita had to write new assignment, while Jamal couldn't enter

the writing competition and had to write the apologized letter. However, I would not defend that [the high school student] was not guilty but my intention is I want us to look at this situation as it was a problem that needed to be concerned by everyone. What actually made [the high school student] plagiarize twice? How about the school responsibility in this case?

In the remainder of her blog, she works through the factors that should be considered in evaluating the significance of different forms of plagiarism. Here, the student considers different arguments regarding the punishment and then develops her response to them:

> On her first mistake, [the student] was on probation but did anyone told her what is the definition of plagiarism? And what would be the punishment, if she kept doing that? If the school taught her, she would not do it again. The expulsion was going to be really bad experience and also bad record in [the student]'s life. Moreover, doubting on school's decision by expelling the students without teaching them, the school would lose their reputation from angry parents. If the school gave [the student] a chance and taught her, not only [the student] would continue her student's life happily but also the school would be admired by the other.

Her word choice illustrates how the development of a writer's voice can be linked to her linguistic choices. The writer, for example, refers to the student's copying as a 'mistake' rather than as a 'crime' and then raises a number of questions that should be considered in deciding the punishment. The writer then implies that since it was the student's second offense, she may have known what she was doing and, therefore, may have intentionally plagiarized. Nevertheless, the writer still feels that the student should be given another chance, which the writer feels would have benefited both her and the school. This argument is an interesting rhetorical move for showing the relationship between individual and societal concerns, a strategy I have found in other Asian online writing (Bloch, 2001).

Other students similarly argued that punishments, such as expulsion, were too severe, particularly since the definitions of plagiarism used by the different institutions in the stories were often unclear. The finality of expulsion was hard for our students to accept even when it seemed clear that the accused student had intentionally copied a large amount of text.

Here, the student argues that even though the high school student understood what she had done, she still should not have been expelled:

> If I were asked to defend one of three students, I would help [the high school girl]. The reason that I choose to defend her is that in this situation not only *** but also the school would be helped. People may think that although *** knew that what she was going to do was plagiarism, she still did and also she did it twice. However, the expulsion was too severe.

No issue, in fact, touched the students more than this question of institutional sanctions. Students may not see themselves as potential targets of these sanctions, perhaps because they may not see themselves as potential plagiarists, a point Pecorari (2008) stresses in her study of plagiarism among graduate students. Such concerns can be considered as much a part of the cultural experience that many of these students bring to the L2 classroom as are some of the other considerations related to plagiarism.

Creating Academic Writing Assignments for a Discussion of Plagiarism

Much has been made about the importance of creating writing assignments that make it difficult or unnecessary to plagiarize. By giving the students enough information to make informative claims and by allowing them the time to develop their arguments, the students would not be placed in situations that could lead to plagiarizing. The students could develop their arguments first in their blogs, so they would feel more comfortable expressing them in their papers, even if by directly cutting and pasting. Moreover, by focusing only on one topic, the students could gain some expertise on the topic and more confidently express their own opinions. In subsequent classes, the pool of papers, with the authors' permission, could be used as an additional source of texts to borrow from. In this way, the students could better see themselves as authors, and we could give somewhat different assignments each course, again making it a little more difficult to copy from previously written papers.

The first assignment, a 10-sentence summary, was designed to directly address a number of key issues discussed so far. As mentioned earlier, students often feel that citing a claim as if it was one's own is a more powerful rhetorical strategy than simply citing it; therefore, the only reason for citation is to avoid plagiarizing. This problem is not limited to schools and universities but permeates all areas of academic writing even among the most advanced L2 writers (Flowerdew, 1999, 2001). As Lillis and Curry (2010) point out, some writers seem wedded to a vision of the scientific process that represses the writer's own voice. Therefore, the writer may feel it inappropriate to use this voice to advocate for his or her own claims. As a journal editor and a peer reviewer, I have found that the failure to cite the appropriate research causes even the advanced L2 writers to have their papers rejected, particularly those whose research is set on the 'periphery' of their research communities (cf. Lillis & Curry, 2010).

In order to respond to this problem, we began the course with an intensive unit on summary writing. Each summary assignment consists of one sentence that provides an overview of the text (descriptive), 3 to 4 sentences describing the main claims (informative) and 5 sentences expressing the writer's own opinions about the text (evaluative). In the first two parts, the primary goal was to have students practice citing the claims of other authors along with their stance toward these claims through the use of reporting verbs and other forms of hedging (Hyland, 2002), which could help students avoid unintentional plagiarism by including the proper attribution as well as by adding their own voice to the voices of the authors they were citing. The descriptive sentences were particularly useful in light of the concerns of Howard et al. (2010) that students only seem to focus on summarizing individual sentences and not the larger issues discussed in the text. In the evaluative part, we hoped that they would continue to develop their own voices and begin to see the differences between the sentences they had cited and those that belonged to them.

We did not ignore what Lea and Street (2006) somewhat derogatorily call 'study skills', but strove to integrate them with the epistemological issues they were discussing. Grammar teaching primarily focused on those syntactic forms related to the writer's stance or attitude, which included clauses, tenses and the use of reporting verbs (Bloch, 2010). Situating the discussion of grammar within the discussion of plagiarism afforded greater opportunities to discuss the connection between grammar, rhetoric and the content, as well as providing some specific rhetorical strategies for using texts to support the students' arguments. In practice, each time we discussed a problem that a student had with a particularly lexical or syntactic item, we were also reviewing some issue in the content of the student text related to plagiarism.

The choice of verb tense, for example, can be related to making decisions about the strength of a claim. With certain verbs the usage determines the tense. For example, a reporting verb such as 'find' is often used in the past tense since the claim was made during the research. Separate from the choice of tense of the reporting verb, the writer can choose a tense in the complementary clause depending on whether the writer feels the claim is still current. Similarly, a writer can choose to place a claim in either the past or present tense depending on whether the writer wants to generalize (present) or hedge by showing that the claim was true in a particular context, such as the research study being summarized, but may not be generalizable (past). In making such decisions, the writer can add news strategies for expressing his or her own voices to the already published texts of his or her community.

The discussion of reporting claims was similarly intended to integrate the syntactic and lexical issues surrounding paraphrasing with the rhetorical issues surrounding the degree of truth and certainty of the claim. Petric (2007) found that variations in how students cite their sources can affect the evaluation of their work. Part of this problem can be seen in their choice of reporting verbs. Students often randomly substitute one reporting verb for another, primarily to create a variation in their writing style rather than for rhetorical effect. Reporting verbs allow writers to reflect on the nature of the information they are citing (Sakita, 2002), a procedure that is important in helping to establish the identity of the writer in the paper. Choosing the appropriate reporting verb as part of paraphrasing a claim sometimes requires students to decide whether the claim was a fact or an opinion as well as how much the writer agrees or disagrees with the claim being cited (Bloch, 2010).

The evaluation section of the summary assignment was another way the writer could develop his or her voice while learning some of the rules for appropriating texts. One goal of having them write the evaluation section, therefore, was for the students to develop arguments that they could later use in their argumentative or research papers. One of the key strategies for avoiding plagiarism was to demonstrate how writers could distinguish between their own claims and the claims of other authors by using the name of the author and a reporting verb along with the appropriate complement. By placing the evaluation in a separate paragraph, the students could see the syntactic differences that occur when expressing their own opinions and those that occur when paraphrasing the opinions of others. Students could see that by dropping the reference and the reporting verb, the claim can be thought of as their own. In the later assignments, the students would interweave these various claims, so it was important to first distinguish whose arguments belonged to whom.

In this example, the student summarizes the story that Rose narrated about Marita:

In his writing, Mike Rose described the first writing assignment of a freshman named Marita. He explained that Marita had been accused of plagiarism because in her essay, she copied an old encyclopedia text.

The story starts with Marita, who was required to write essay agreeing or disagreeing the discussion about Jacob Bronowski. In that situation, Mike Rose felt that Bronowski's discussion was so hard to understand that Marita didn't know what to write in her paper. So she went to the library to find encyclopedias about creativities and sciences. However, Mike Rose believed that she copied the text from the encyclopedia, because he felt that the sentence that she wrote was very sophisticated for a freshman-writing. Nevertheless Mike Rose felt that Marita deserved her second chance, so she was excused of the accusation.

In my opinion, Marita deserved mercy since she was a freshman and it was her first writing assignment. Moreover she didn't understand the rules about academic misconducts especially plagiarism completely. She did cut and paste the texts from encyclopedia, but she also wrote the title of the encyclopedia in the back of her paper. So she tried her best to avoid plagiarism, didn't she? The action taken by Marita might be wrong but she deserved her second chance.

In this summary, the student identified some of the critical issues, including the nature of plagiarism, the possible reasons for the student's plagiarizing, the institutional response to plagiarism and the question of punishment. In her evaluation section, the writer begins to enter the conversation by giving her own opinions about what Marita did and how her alleged plagiarism should be treated, raising a central question about whether students should be held responsible for not following rules that they may not have understood.

Having established both the key issues in the discussion and their own positions, the students were then asked to synthesize these issues and develop their own opinions regarding them. Using Swales' (1990) research on the moves that open up a research space in the introduction of an academic paper, students wrote a short argumentative paper analyzing and arguing for their own opinions. This assignment was designed to introduce students to the genre of the academic paper as well as to continue to discuss the role of intertextuality and plagiarism. Based on the issues they had discussed in their summaries, the students were asked to pose a problem regarding plagiarism, argue about the different solutions presented in their readings and then develop their own solutions. Unlike the situation of Marita, our students had gained a certain 'expertise' about the topic before being asked for their opinion.

In this example of an introduction to the synthesis paper, the student follows the research of Swales (1990) and introduces the importance of the topic, the key articles she would discuss and the issues that would form the basis of her argument:

> Recently, plagiarism has become one of the most serious problems in society, especially at school. In fact, many students seem to have been thrown out from school because of committing plagiarism. For example, [the high school student], in the true story written by Neal Heaton (*Are Your Kids Cheating?* The Plain Dealer, Cleaveland.com. 04/27/03), was expelled from a high school because of plagiarism.It can be said that the students who have plagiarized do not really understand about plagiarism, so they seems to get confused about the definition of plagiarism. In other words, they seem to be confused with the amount of how much copy and paste is regarded as plagiarized.

One key issue was how to use citations to support a claim. In the introduction to her paper, the student discusses the seriousness of the problem using the story of the student expelled for plagiarizing to support this claim. The student focuses on two commonly discussed issues: whether students understood what plagiarism was and how should it be defined.

We have addressed this problem by creating assignments that called for the use of a variety of texts in these different ways. They could cite from their summaries and their blogs or their classmates' blogs to support or explain their claims. We encouraged them to think about their own texts, as well as their classmates' texts, as they would about any published text. In this paragraph from a critical review, the student uses her classmate's blog to support her own anecdotal evidence that universities in Korea are not overly concerned with plagiarism:

> One issue of plagiarism depends on student's background. Diverse backgrounds of can students cause students to plagiarize. In my case, my background was that my pre-university was not strict to plagiarism as I mentioned above. Miss Ahn thought Marita and *** who were accused of plagiarism committed academic misconduct because of their background. According to the story, Marita had come from the tough school which was not strict to plagiarism. Marita grew up with the strict father who had influence on her, and he educated his daughter 'Don't tell unless you know.' This education made Marita careful and prudent. Therefore she did not think she was creative person but she wanted to do homework better, so she copied prose from the encyclopedia. After that fact, she was accused of plagiarism. However, she did not think that it was plagiarism because she wrote the

references. I think that she did not mean to plagiarize because she just wanted to do her homework well. Miss Ahn said that she did not understand the rule of plagiarism because of her background. Cha said that Marita plagiarized because she did not understand how to cite other's ones appropriately. She did not learn about how to avoid plagiarism from her tough school.

In this paper, the student demonstrates a variety of rhetorical strategies for making her argument about Marita. She first argues for considering the student's cultural 'background' when discussing plagiarism, giving an example that she did not adhere to the strict standards regarding plagiarism. Many students considered culture as a factor that might limit their understanding of what was expected of them by their instructors. In a game, players must be able to anticipate the responses of other players. As Rose describes Marita, she does seem to be shocked at the accusation, and therefore, seem to lack an understanding of why her instructor had even accused her of plagiarism as well as an overall understanding of how this game about academic writing is played.

The writer then uses the citations from her classmates, 'Miss Ahn' and 'Cha' to make a stronger generalization to support her claim. In this approach, she seems to understand the purpose of using citations to support her claims by showing the agreement of others. More important, she demonstrates a rhetorical approach that students like Marita may not understand. Here the student connects her own ideas to those of her classmates. In this example, the student identifies intentionality as one of the critical issues she wants to discuss. She argues that Marita's plagiarism may have resulted because of her background, a claim which she also supports with her classmates' blogs. Unlike Marita, this student is able to intertwine her own ideas with those of others, thus achieving her rhetorical purpose by expressing her own identity in the text while integrating other texts as a means of support.

Citations, of course, are not always used in such overtly argumentative ways. They can also be used as background to lay out the research, which can help establish the *ethos* of the writer and provide readers with other materials to read (Bloch & Chi, 1995). In this example, the student lists a variety of solutions to the plagiarism problem simply by citing the blogs of his classmates:

There are several ways to prevent plagiarism before it occurs. According to Ahn, educating students about plagiarism can help them prevent performing this unethical act. Thus, she thinks that teachers must try to recognize how much of a problem plagiarism is. Some students do not know any idea about it. Ahn believes that these students need teacher's help. Cha also thinks that the students pay little attention their plagiarism so the education needs to make the students become aware of plagiarism.

This student can interweave her ideas with the ideas of those who wrote before her. In this way, the student is learning the conventions of academic writing as well as the norms for citation found in that genre, perhaps not in a way that is required of a formal academic paper but one that demonstrates an understanding of the complex issues that academic writers need to understand to write successfully.

It should be noted, however, that since the students came from a variety of majors, which often use different citation formats, we did not require them to use a particular citation format. Although this approach may be considered problematic, we found it justifiable because our main goal here was to focus on the rhetorical dimension of citation use. Proper attribution style could be learned later.

Teaching about Intellectual Property and Plagiarism in a Visual Context

As has been discussed, teaching about plagiarism cannot be divorced from teaching writing. The concept of academic literacies has greatly expanded the types of literacy that can be included in an academic writing classroom. New technologies, such as Facebook, Twitter and blogging, are continually expanding the list of new digital literacies (Ito & Hoerst, 2010). New approaches to thinking about what are academic literacies has framed new discussions about what types of discourse should be taught in writing classrooms? Multimodal forms of literacy integrate various modes of language – print, visual and aural – in ways where one form can expand the meanings of the other forms (Kress, 2003). Such an approach can provide students with alternative forms of discourse that may be more suitable for expressing their ideas (Hull & Nelson, 2005) or a means to explore the possible relationships between one form of discourse and another.

We elected to use digital storytelling as a way of exploring these new forms of multimodal texts (e.g. Lambert, 2010). The digital story project in our classroom was part of a larger project that was being developed in the university (Fields & Diaz, 2009). We wanted to develop various spaces where these stories could be shown outside the classroom, such as part of the university overseas recruitment process or part of staff development. As with other forms of online literacy, these forms can also change the nature of the audience, expanding it, sometimes dramatically. Their stories had the potential to be seen by an extensive audience, particularly if they elected to post their stories on an online site like YouTube.

Many of the aspects of this project had positive implications for expanding the pedagogy of the course. Each aspect of digital storytelling, however, raised questions about the use of different forms of intellectual property since the rules regarding classroom use may no longer apply in this new context. Images may not be ethically or legally treated in the same way as texts. An image used only as decoration on a webpage may be treated differently than when used in a more transformative usage for educational purposes (Herrington, 2010), as in digital stories. US law is particularly complicated about these issues. As seen in the Shepard Fairey case (Lessing, 2009b), what constitutes transformation can be very hard to define.

The nature of the audience can have an important affect as well. One of the important goals for using technologies that allow students to share their creations with others outside the classroom is to explore how such an expansion of audience affects their use of the technology. However, such pedagogical goals can be greatly constrained by intellectual property law. Using intellectual property for a small, closed audience, such as a class, may be treated differently in the law than when used for a larger audience, as found on YouTube (Herrington, 2010). Even in this case, it can be argued that the degree of transformation that the students add to the image by adding their stories gives them fair use rights to post it wherever they want.

These new literacy contexts are never static but are continually being 'created, sustained, negotiated, resisted, and transformed' (Gee, 2000: 191). This dynamic quality has important implications for the development of students as writers as well as users of intellectual property. As discussed previously, creativity in an online context has raised new tensions between maintaining traditional standards for the use of intellectual property and responding to the new ways it is used online. These tensions can frighten teachers away from the use of the internet. Fearful of possible violations of intellectual property law, some teachers restrict the use of online materials to those licensed by Creative Commons or those available in the public domain. By doing so, however, students are not confronting the issues raised by downloading intellectual property.

Regardless of one's position on all of these issues, they provide important points of discussion for helping students become users of digital intellectual property. It is the internet, after all, which has been continually blamed for the 'plagiarism epidemic'; therefore, the students may not understand the ramifications of using intellectual property in a digital context. Therefore, it is crucial to immerse them in understanding the role of the internet, as one might immerse them in the study of any aspect of a genre (e.g. Bazerman, 1988; Tardy, 2009).

The Use of Digital Storytelling in the Discussion of Intellectual Property

Digital storytelling is a product of some of the radically new approaches to creativity that have often been discussed in the reform of intellectual property law (e.g. Lessing, 2005, 2009a). Digital stories require their creators to 'remix' or 'mash up' various forms of intellectual property. A personal story is interwoven with related images and music. Digital storytelling involves students both in the discussion of fair use for transformative purposes and in traditional concerns for the user of copyrighted information as well as in the creation of a new form of digital literacy.

Although the creators of digital stories can use their own images and music to go with their stories, they often have to find the most appropriate ones on the internet, which involves the students in many of the controversial issues regarding the use of technology and intellectual property. For example, is their use of images downloaded from the internet supported by fair use? It can be argued that their usage is primarily for illustration, which should be considered fair use although there may be concern if too many images are taken from the same source ('Code of Best Practices', 2011). As the Center for Social Media's handbook on the use of intellectual property puts it:

> Because media literacy education cannot thrive unless learners them-
> selves have the opportunity to learn about how media functions at the
> most practical level, educators using concepts and techniques of media
> literacy should be free to enable learners to incorporate, modify, and
> re-present existing media objects in their own classroom work. Media
> production can foster and deepen awareness of the constructed nature
> of all media, one of the key concepts of media literacy. ('Code of Best
> Practices', para 42)

These arguments are, of course, relevant for the use of intellectual property since what they call 'the constructed nature of literacy' involves these rules for the use of media, as do any genre. We attempted to utilize some of the 'best practices' suggested by the Center to help students understand the issues surrounding the creation and distribution of their stories. The students produced stories about their transitions to university and new cultures, their perceived cultural differences, their families, their experiences travelling, their interests and hobbies, their future careers and occasionally their love lives. In doing so, they had to write, speak, listen, edit and choose images to complement their stories. In doing all of these actions, they were transforming the intellectual property they were using.

Becoming an intellectual property creator and not just a consumer could itself give students a new perspective on the nature of intellectual property, particularly if they allow their stories to be shown outside the classroom. Moreover, because of this increase in potential audience, we first asked the students to give us permission for the use of their stories. Students could choose who they wanted to view their stories. They could upload them to YouTube, allow them to be discussed in future classes or be shown to other teachers or be kept private. Each choice reflects the different questions about the use of intellectual property that have been discussed here. What does educational use mean? What rights do you have to your own work? What are the implications of publishing on YouTube? What are the rules for downloading and attributing online images? What does a 'take down notice' mean? As it becomes easier and easier to publish on the internet, students may face these questions both inside and outside the classroom.

Second we wanted them to attribute all the images and music they used. There are differences with the attribution of the intellectual property they had downloaded from what they were accustomed to with print texts. Instead of being incorporated both inside the text and in a reference list, their attributions are placed only in the ending credits, thus allowing students to acknowledge where the images they had downloaded came from. Finally, we asked them to copyright their own work by going to the Creative Commons website, filling out their form and incorporating the Creative Commons copyright logo into the credits of their story. They had to understand the cultural constraints placed on creating or remixing their digital stories imposed by intellectual property law and then decide how to copyright their own work, a process that can help them better understand the social context of being a creator of multimodal texts. Thus, their stories, as are all such forms of intellectual property, are automatically copyrighted by US law. By going through the Creative Commons process, the students could make their own decisions about how they wanted their stories to be used, which could give them a better understanding of their own use of intellectual property.

As with all of these assignments, digital story telling was designed to be the opposite of the kind of assignments that Blum (2009) and others have described that seem to only want students to simply regurgitate information with little understanding of why they need to attribute that information. More important, this approach could decentralize the control over how plagiarism is defined and treated by giving greater autonomy to the teachers. Benkler (2006) argues that highly centralized intellectual property laws and policies limit the autonomy individuals have, which in turn undermines some of the basic concepts of democracy, an argument that can equally apply to discussions of plagiarism.

Designing Additional Materials for a Course on Plagiarism

The internet has allowed for the easy creation and distribution of teaching materials, which can be accessed on the Web 24 hours a day, 7 days a week, what has been called the 'just enough, just in-time' web. Examples of such websites, some of which were mentioned in Chapter 1, often focus on a single topic, such as on explaining plagiarism, and can be accessed whenever necessary. Wiley (2001) has used the term 'learning objects' to frame the design of these kinds of narrowly defined online artifacts.

Since websites dealing with the nature of plagiarism are often designed by the institutions, they obviously will reflect the traditional institutional concerns. The Colby, Bates and Bowdoin (http://abacus.bates.edu/cbb), for instance, provides a tutorial asking them a series of questions regarding their attitudes toward plagiarism. Dee and Jacob (2010) found that using this site could reduce the amount of plagiarism. The website's approach to teaching, however, is often limited to prescriptive rules about avoiding plagiarism. In their self-test, the students are required to click on what they consider the 'correct' answer or they are forced to redo the question until they click on the correct one, regardless of whether they actually read the answer. Their explanations often ignore the rhetorical dimension of citation. For example, the program discusses whether it is necessary to cite common knowledge in the same way as any other form of text:

As a general rule well-known or basic facts do not need to be documented; however, interpretations of such facts do.

If something is not common knowledge, or if you are not certain whether it is or not, cite the source. During the course of your studies, you will need to be able to distinguish between different kinds of common knowledge: common knowledge for the general public versus common knowledge for a specialized audience. (http://abacus.bates. edu/cbb/quiz/intro/common.html)

While this definition is true, the underlying message is that the only reason to cite a source is to acknowledge its ownership, an approach that ignores the rhetorical dimension of intertextuality. This point is again emphasized by focusing only on appropriate citation style, again ignoring the importance of using citations to support your claims regardless of whether the claims are proprietary or common knowledge.

In order to reflect our own experiences and approaches to teaching about plagiarism, we designed two learning objects, one on plagiarism (http://esl.osu.edu/staff/bloch/plagiarism) and one on the uses of reporting verbs (http://eslcomposition.osu.edu; Bloch, 2009). These sites were designed to better reflect our own approaches to thinking about plagiarism. The plagiarism site contains a short tutorial to introduce the student to various issues concerning plagiarism and intellectual property (Figure 6.1). Although the site could be used by students outside our program, its design

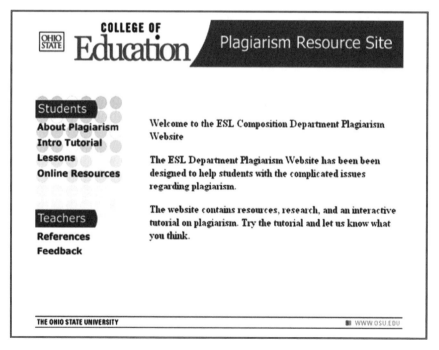

Figure 6.1 Plagiarism Resource Site (esl.osu.edu/staff/bloch/plagiarism)

often reflects local issues that have arisen in our courses. Many of the questions were based on incidents that had been reported by our instructors, some of which would later be used in the questionnaire discussed above. In this question, for example, we asked about a particular assignment we gave in the class:

> In your 106G course, you were asked to write a definition paper. When you entered 107G, you found that you had the same assignment, but the paper was a little longer. If you add a little to your old paper and hand it in, are you plagiarizing from yourself. What should you do?

(1) *Ask your 107G teacher whether you can rewrite the paper,*
(2) *Simply rewrite the paper to make it fit the 107G assignment,*
(3) *Choose another topic and write a different paper.*

The topic of this question was self-plagiarism, an issue that both our graduate and undergraduate students are frequently confronted with. Ohio State's misconduct code does not call this action 'plagiarism' but a violation of class rules. Although there were a relatively small number of such cases, around 25 per academic year, adjudicated by our committee on academic misconduct, 'self-plagiarism' was still an important concept linking plagiarism and intellectual property law. The question reminded students that although they owned the papers they wrote, they could not do whatever they choose with them.

Our approach contextualized the teaching within the goals of our course and issues such as those discussed above could be discussed in class. We did not always provide one 'correct' answer to these questions, at least according to what is generally believed in an institutional context. With each question, we provided three possible answers, none of which were necessarily identified as the 'correct' one although we did sometimes imply which is a 'better' answer. For example if the student clicked on the first answer about asking the teacher, they were given the following response: This way is the safest choice because you have permission from the teacher. If they choose the second answer, they would receive the following message: Even though the paper belongs to you and you can't 'steal' it from yourself, you take the risk of being accused of 'self-plagiarism'. In addition, we included in our design some additional related information. In this answer, they receive a short discussion of intellectual property as well as a warning about how the Academic Misconduct Committee may treat such cases.

In the second question, we asked about the attribution of common knowledge, another issue that had been frequently discussed in class:

> In your 108 course [our advanced writing course], you are asked to write a research paper. You are new in the field, and much of what you know is from textbooks. This information is called common knowledge, and you don't know if you are supposed to cite it.

This question, which was earlier discussed, was derived from an actual incident. In our gloss on the answer, we point out that writers should consider how simply citing sources, regardless of whether it is necessary, could help them avoid accusations of plagiarism as well as strengthen the rhetorical impact of their claim. We wanted here to give the students some possible suggestions for citing common knowledge. The first answer, which was identified as the safest choice, was simply to cite common knowledge in the same manner as they cited any other type of knowledge:

> Common knowledge is the same as any other type of knowledge, and so it must be cited. If you found it in the textbook, then you have to cite the textbook the same way as you would cite anything else you read.

The second possible answer reflects the strategy the aforementioned student used:

> You can use the ideas without citing them if you think they are common knowledge.

In the commentary they received with this answer, we reminded the student of the risk of this strategy. The third possible answer, which is the one we favored, focuses on the rhetorical importance of citation:

> Cite the information if you think it is useful to your research. This strategy is also useful if you are new to a field and are not sure if something is common knowledge.

In one response to the question, we point out that such a strategy can illustrate the rhetorical importance of the citation for demonstrating support for the writer's own claims or for demonstrating the writer's own familiarity with a topic.

A companion learning object was designed to support the students' use of reporting verbs (Figure 6.2). As discussed above, the complexity of

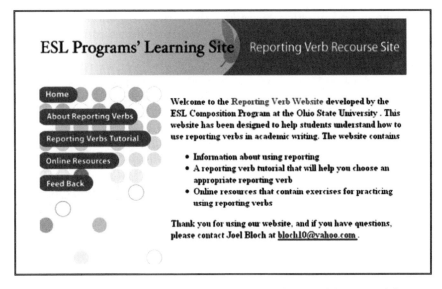

Figure 6.2 Reporting Verb Resource Site (eslcomposition.osu.edu)

using reporting verbs can make it difficult to understand the implications of making such decisions, which can often require making subtle distinctions in the choice of reporting verbs. Dictionaries, which many students rely on in choosing lexical items, do not always help because they do not always give the nuanced distinctions that can be exploited for clearly expressing a stance (e.g. Hyland, 2000b). As with the design of our learning object about plagiarism, there is not always one correct choice for the use of a reporting verb; rather the choice often emerges from its rhetorical context.

To develop materials to discuss the choice of reporting verbs, I designed a concordancing website based on a corpus of academic papers and found which reporting verbs were most frequently used (Bloch, 2009). Concordancing is one approach that has been used to explore grammatical choice in a way that requires the students to reflect on the decisions being made, what Johns (1994) calls 'data-driven learning'. As with any use of 'data-driven learning', this approach does not guarantee a correct answer but rather requires the user to decide whether the examples are relevant.

The website guides students through a variety of decisions necessary for choosing an appropriate reporting verb, which include choosing the form of the citation, the attitude of the writer toward the claim and the strength of the attitude. On the basis of their choices, the users were given a series of sample sentences to illustrate which reporting verbs matched their decisions, as well as a gloss related to the use of the reporting verb in the sample sentence, such as the reason for the choice of tense.

Conclusion

Our approach was designed to give students the opportunity to participate in the debate through their papers and their blogs. Through this process, students could better understand the issues regarding plagiarism and, as Benkler (2006) has noted, participate in discussions about the institutional control over intellectual property that are occurring throughout the world today.

However, implementing this approach has not meant that the problems with plagiarism have been completely avoided. We still have had cases where students either intentionally or unintentionally plagiarize, sometimes reflecting the same situations they discussed in class. In one case, a student plagiarized because he admitted he felt stressed out. In another case, a student plagiarized a paragraph from a text we had given him to summarize, seemingly without knowing we would easily recognize the copying. However, it was still hoped that even these students would become aware of why this strategy may not be appropriate and how they could have avoided the problems these actions could cause.

The approach has not always been well received by students who sometimes write on their evaluations that spending the entire course on plagiarism was 'boring'. Teachers may also not find this approach possible or even useful; however, there are aspects of these courses that can be useful in helping students not only 'play the game' of academic writing but also develop a better awareness of the controversies both inside and outside the classroom. Students can become better writers and better citizens in a world where plagiarism is becoming a more serious issue and intellectual property law is becoming more important for both teachers and students.

Notes

(1) N refers to raw number of respondents; the boldfaced answers were the one preferred by the course's three teachers.
(2) We began with two articles: 'Are the Kids Cheating,' by Neil Heaton (2003) and an excerpt from Rose (1989), pages 179–181, and the movie *Finding Forrester* (2000) directed by Gus van Zant. We later added additional stories about the case at Duke

University where a group of international students received heavier penalties for academic misconduct than did their American counterparts (Redden, 2007), and another case about a group of graduate students at a nearby university whose dissertations and theses were found to have been plagiarized (Lederman, 2006). An additional article contained a 'letter' a professor wrote to a student he had caught plagiarizing (Couser, 2009), as well as the one discussed earlier about the instructor who publicized the names of a group of Hispanic students he caught plagiarizing and was later fired (Jascik, 2008). In addition, we used some theoretical discussions by Stanley Fish (2010) and by Susan Blum (2009) as well as comments that had been posted online in response. For more examples of articles we have used, see http://www.scoopoit/t/plagiarism.

(3) For an example of a class blog for discussing plagiarism, see http://www.chere paha2.blogspot.com

(4) For example, see the short film 'What Is So Important about Academic Integrity' (http://www.clemson.edu/curp/flash/08cairesponses.htm) produced by the Center for Academic Integrity (http://www.academicintegrity.org). For additional films we have developed, see http://plagiarismstories.tumblr.com

(5) Her father had told her not to say anything unless she was sure she knew what she was talking about.

7 Conclusion

The only time I have been accused of plagiarism was when I was a university freshman in an introductory literature class. During the first half of the class, we discussed poetry, a topic I hated and wrote badly about. During the second half, we discussed short stories, a topic about which my writing dramatically improved. After handing in my first assignment on a short story, my instructor called me aside and politely asked if I had plagiarized. I told him this somewhat incredulous reason for the dramatic improvement, which he perhaps reluctantly accepted, given that he had no other evidence.

Many years later, the issues of plagiarism for me have become even more complex. I began this book with a quote from Rene Clair that I remember reading 35 years ago. I chose the quote not just because it well reflects the dilemma many feel about the use of intellectual property but also to exemplify the problem of how the appropriate citation practices can constrain the creative process. Although I cannot remember where I read the quote, I still wanted to use it. Is it appropriate to use a quote without proper attribution, particularly in the context of an academic book on plagiarism and intellectual property law? How do the constraints of these practices constrain the creative process I employed in writing the book?

This connection between intellectual property and plagiarism has great importance in understanding how plagiarism is seen in the changing contexts our students find themselves. Such changes have greatly impacted the teaching of writing. One of the main themes that run throughout Jim Berlin's (1984) history of writing teaching in the United States is that as the type of student entering the American university changed, the writing pedagogy had to change as well. For Berlin, one factor was the growing number of immigrant students whose futures depended primarily on how well they did in university. Changes in the British system in the 1990s similarly impacted the teaching of writing (Lea & Street, 2006). Today we have a growing number of immigrant and international students entering the university as well as an expanding number of English classes being taught in non–English-speaking countries. Perhaps the greatest change has been the impact of the internet on the spread of literacies as well as the even newer changes with the increased use of mobile devices. I have heard so many times how this attitude toward intellectual property on the internet is the cause of plagiarism in both high schools and colleges, often without attribution or supporting research, that the claim can be considered an example of 'common knowledge'.

The introduction of new forms of literacy has further complicated this process, as new technologies have always complicated how we view literacy and creativity. Lessing (2009a) and others have pointed out that we are often awestruck by how the web has transformed millions of people into creators and authors. As the controversial term 'digital natives' has come to represent (Palfrey & Gasser, 2008), many of our students embody the attitudes that many fear. Many clearly believe that information on the internet is 'free' and can be used in any way that furthers their creative and innovative goals. Of course, many adults also believe that the information on the internet is, or at least should be, free as witnessed by the difficulty that content providers, such as newspapers and magazines, have had in realizing profits from their online editions. However, the problems of teenagers seem to always represent a greater threat to the integrity of our society than the 'crimes' their parents commit.

Much of this creativity we see in places like YouTube is arguably worthless, but still it can inspire the creativity in others, with probably the overwhelming majority lacking the background or support to know what is considered appropriate or legal. I was recently helping my daughter with a book report on a popular novel called *The Hunger Games*. She had found a number of faked 'trailers' for an imaginary movie of the book that had been posted to YouTube. These trailers often contained pages with a short summary of the plot interwoven with clips from completely unrelated movies that were intended to illustrate the story. In this way, they transformed the traditional 'book report' while raising a whole new set of issues related to intellectual property.

Although some might feel that these teenage girls (I assume most of them were teenagers) were violating various aspects of intellectual property law, an application of the standards of fair use, at least under US law, could be used to show that the transformative nature of their work, its educational value, the short nature of the clips and that there was no monetary value gained or lost may have made these short movies, in fact, 'legal'. In many ways, these clips encapsulate the dilemma and the potential that the interrelationship between these two issues reflects, particularly as they illustrate how groups, in this case young girls, can find a voice on the web they previously did not have.

As a writing teacher, I could bemoan the fact that few of these films bothered to include credits that acknowledge where the clips came from, something we insist our students do in their digital stories, or to inform a nonteenager like myself from what movies these clips were used. However, at the same time, this approach is not new. We can see the same remixing in thousands of years of Chinese writing. In fact, all of these new technological literacies are going to bring with them challenges to traditional ways of citation in the same way that the growing internationalization of teaching English has done. As with the Chinese rhetors 1600 years ago (Bloch & Chi, 1996), these teenagers seem to assume that their audience is immersed in the culture enough to know where these citations came from without the author having to mention the source.

These connections between intellectual property law and plagiarism have made research in this area one of the most interesting topics in the field of teaching writing. There is little doubt that their relationships are changing, not necessarily by moral suasion or the fear of legal retribution, but more likely because of the same social, technological and economic changes that were faced in the 17th century by Great Britain and even today by many countries who not only produce content but also recognize that if they want their research to be taken seriously they have to play by the same rules of the communities to which they want to contribute. The result is that we must greatly expand our field of studies in order to understand how these changes are affecting the kinds of literacies we are teaching and our students are bringing into the classroom.

Nowhere is this any truer than in China where dramatic economic changes have been accompanied by changes in attitudes toward plagiarism. The blogosphere in China has become an important space for discussing plagiarism cases among Chinese academics. For example, the plagiarism case of Wang Hui, a highly controversial academic, has raised a number of issues regarding traditional Chinese culture, current economic theory and the nature of Chinese academic life (Custer, 2010). Growing economic opportunities and resources has greatly increased the pressure for testing in China as more and more students want to enter the university, which has also impacted the controversies surrounding plagiarism (Wong, 2009). This new attention undoubtedly will change the nature of the equilibrium as a greater understanding of the issues is required, and as Nash's theory would predict.

The focus of this book has been on how should we deal with change? Stanley Fish's provocative title 'Plagiarism Is Not a Big Moral Deal' has challenged academics to rethink how they consider whether at least some problems with citation, perhaps such as leaving off quotation marks, should be considered plagiarism at all. However, it also raised many accusations that Fish had dropped the moral ball. At the heart of this debate remains a moral dilemma, which still differentiates plagiarism from most other pedagogical issues. Any apparent attempt to relegate the moral nature of plagiarism is often met with scorn and derision. Changing the rules will always bring objections about standards. When the American professional football league changed the rules to reduce injuries, many fans and players objected that these changes were changing the character of the game for the worse. The importance that the issues surrounding plagiarism has in the overall discussion of academic integrity have already brought out similar sentiments. For many inside and outside the academy, plagiarism, regardless of the form it takes, undermines the integrity of the institution and cannot be dismissed by arguments about the decline of authorship or the consequences of pedagogical changes. Questions about the necessity of traditional 'standards' and the moral integrity of the university underlie the challenges to the reformers.

The school or university may respond to this challenge by either increasing the deterrents, for instance, by employing copy detection programs, honor codes or academic misconduct committees or by increasing the value of the learning, such as, by modifying assignments, reducing the pressure to achieve high grades or, in our case, directly teaching about textual borrowing. Our students are increasingly caught up in this debate. Lessing (2009a) ends his book on the social and economic importance of remixing with a call for legislatures to decriminalize being a teenager, a reference to the proliferation of lawsuits as well as moral censure addressed primarily at teenagers for sharing music across the internet. Can we raise the same question about 'decriminalizing' student plagiarism? As mentioned earlier, Lessing himself does not seem to think so. Moreover, the concern for plagiarism has not been limited to students. Although many 'adult' plagiarizers have not suffered any diminution of the reputations when caught plagiarizing, some have seen their careers derailed as a result.

In a similar way, second-language-writing teachers have seen the 'criminalization of nonnative English speakers' long before the internet became a factor in our literacies. It has been assumed that the 'differences' or 'otherness' of these students might be a mitigating factor in how their acts of plagiarism should be treated, but there is far less discussion of whether the attitudes they bring to the classroom should impact how plagiarism is viewed. The ongoing controversies over the role of culture and the notion of language development have questioned whether NNES, like their teenage counterparts, are being forced into a potentially dangerous context by doing what they normally do.

How teachers respond to this problem is an integral part of our view of writing classrooms within the larger institutional context of the school, university or society as a whole. As Post (2009: 117) argues, the fundamental question is 'how do we build "republican" institutions–institutions that respect the equal worth of all individuals and their right to participate in the formation of the rules under which they live.' It is, therefore, crucial that both teachers and students participate in this discussion. In a speech to educators, Lessing offers these educators 'a certificate of entitlement' from 'a Harvard law professor' that states:

The bearer of this certificate, an educator, or one trained in the field of science, is hereby officially entitled to question whether copyright law as currently crafted makes sense for education or science. (http://blip.tv/ lessig/it-is-about-time-getting-our-values-around-copyright-2847688).

This participation is what is meant by the term 'equilibrium', but it is also what is meant by the term 'democracy'.

My approach acknowledges the seriousness of some forms of plagiarism but with the recognition that it must be understood in different ways. As Post (2009) argues, we will pay a price down the road in creativity for imposing too strict a law today; therefore, careful consideration must be paid to each new law, or rule, that we apply. The same principle can be applied to plagiarism: the more restrictions we place, the more we can choke off creativity. Students may need to acknowledge who created all those ideas, more for the rhetorical importance of building their arguments than for acknowledging who first spoke them, something that is often hard to sort out in the first place. Post calls this problem of balancing the 'Goldilocks Principle': the rules should not be too strong so creativity will not be suppressed or become too weak that there is no incentive or acknowledgment of rhetorical intent. As I have argued, creating this balance is the goal of every game maker, including the writing teacher.

Another point of view is the appropriate response to plagiarism; that is, how to value writing in such a way that the student's 'best response' is to follow the appropriate rules for textual borrowing. The perception that students have about the purpose of their writing assignments is closely related to the perception of how their writing will be assessed. Such a perception can be tied to the artificiality of most classroom assignments. There has been much discussion on designing assignments to avoid plagiarism. Colorado State's website for writing teachers has a page entitled 'Making Plagiarism-Proof Assignments' (http://writing.colostate.edu/guides/ teaching/plagiarism/assignments.cfm). Oxford Brookes University has also published a guidebook for teachers for designing assignments as well as for discussing plagiarism with students and creating an atmosphere for promoting what they consider to be ethical conduct (Carroll & Appleton, 2001). Assignments can be judged on whether they foster learning or encourage students to 'regurgitate' information. The design of assignments, as well as their assessment, then, can be critical factors in determining the student representation of the assignment. The relationship between assessment and writing context presents various obstacles to be negotiated in deciding on an ethical approach. In a group assignment, does the instructor want to assess each student individually or the project as a whole?

Understanding the intent of the assessment is an important consideration for understanding the ethical concerns of the different contexts in which writing is taught. Collaboration in one class, for example, may be valued differently than collaboration in another class. A similar distinction can be applied to the workplace. The heart of this deeply emotional debate over plagiarism is how such variations should be considered in judging the ethical nature of the work? The intensity of the debate illustrates how there may never be a clear-cut answer to this dilemma. The equilibrium by which all stakeholders in the academic 'game'–teachers, students and administrators–have an equal understanding of these issues has been especially disrupted by technological changes in how information is produced in the same way that it may have been disrupted long ago, and as Plato found out, by the practice of literacy itself.

By attempting to achieve an equilibrium between teacher and student, I hope that both will think of the writing process as a cooperative game, where students can better understand the goals for attributing texts and teachers can better understand the strategies their students are using when incorporating the greater variety of texts they now have access to. As one student put it in a blog about what he learned about plagiarism in our class:

> I learned a lot of things about plagiarism. I learned that regardless how much you copy if you do not cite correctly you committing plagiarism. I did not know that before. ... That was exciting thing I learned from plagiarism. I am big fan of using my idea, but in the world of business teaches you that you are required to use your idea and someone else ideas. If I use someone else idea I will cite the work correctly.

As with this student, teachers too have a great deal to learn about both plagiarism and the use of intellectual property. Teachers have an increasingly complex role to play in facilitating their students' understanding of these challenges. Teachers have their own interests to consider as well. In response to this challenge, teachers will have to cross over into a variety of new areas of study. The pedagogical approach to teaching about plagiarism as part of an overall approach to the teaching of writing is based on a synthesis of research from a variety of fields. Doing the research presented here necessitated drawing upon research from a variety of fields, including historical, contemporary and intercultural rhetoric, linguistics, second language acquisition, technology and intellectual property law. I hope this book has provided a framework for continuing such a study.

References

2600 News (2000, April 23). *A holiday message from Disney chief. Retrieved July 6, 2011, from* http://www.2600.com/news/view/article/326

Abasi, A.R., Akbari, N. & Graves, B. (2006). Discourse appropriation, construction of identities, and the complex issue of plagiarism: ESL students writing in graduate school. *Journal of Second Language Writing, 15*, 102–117.

Alford, W.P. (1995). *To steal a book is elegant: Intellectual property law in Chinese civilization.* Stanford, CA: Stanford University Press.

Allen, K. (2008, April 9). Plagiarism at UNI: An open letter to students from English teacher Suzanne Linder. Retrieved April 22, 2008, from http://www.uni.uiuc.edu/og/news/2008/04/plagiarism-uni-open-letter-students-e

Anderson, C. (2006). *The long tail: Why the future of business is selling less of more.* New York: Hyperion.

Angélil-Carter, S. (2000). *Stolen language? Plagiarism in writing.* Harlow, UK: Longman.

Ardalan, F., Arfaei, H., Mansouri, R., Balalimood, M., Farhud, D. & Malekzadeh, R. (2009). Iran's scientists condemn instances of plagiarism. *Nature, 462*(7275), 847.

Artflaw. (2010, February 26). *Sculptor Frank Gaylord wins copyright infringement appeal vs. US.* Retrieved October 10, 2010, from http://www.artflaw.com/art/scultpor-frank-gaylord-successfully-appeals-copyright-infringment-suit-against-us

Atkinson, D. (2003). Writing and culture in the post-process era. *Journal of Second Language Writing, 12*, 49–63.

Aufderheide, P. (2011, August 2). Myths about fair use. *Inside Higher Education.* Retrieved August 2, 2011, from http://www.insidehighered.com/views/2011/08/02/essay_calls_on_academics_to_use_their_fair_use_rights

Baram, M. (2009, May 17). Maureen Dowd admits inadvertently lifting line from TPM's Josh Marshall. *Huffpost Media.* Retrieved June 22, 2011, from http://www.huffingtonpost.com/2009/05/17/maureen-dowd-admits-inadv_n_204418.html

Barlow, J.P. (1994). *The economy of ideas.* Retrieved December 20, 2011 from http://www.wired.com/wired/archive/2.03/economy.ideas.html

Barthes, R. (1967). *Death of the author.* Retrieved June 15, 2011, from http://www.deathoftheauthor.com

Barthes, R. (1972). *Mythologies* (A. Lavers, trans). New York: Farrar, Straus and Giroux.

Bawarshi, A.S. & Reiff, M.J. (2008). *Genre: An introduction to history, theory, research, and pedagogy.* West Lafayette, IN: Parlor Press.

Bazerman, C. (1988). *Shaping written knowledge: The genre and activity of the experimental article in science.* Madison: The University of Wisconsin Press.

Bazerman, C. (2009a). Genre and cognitive development: Beyond writing to learn. In C. Bazerman, A. Bonini & D. Figueiredo (Eds.), *Genre in a changing world* (pp. 279–294). Fort Collins, CO: WAC Clearinghouse.

Bazerman, C. (2009b). How does science come to speak in the courts? Citations, intertexts, expert witnesses, consequential facts, and reasoning. *Law & Contemporary Problems, 72*, 91–120. Retrieved June 4, 2011, from http://www.law.duke.edu/journals/lcp/lcptoc72winter2009

Bazin, A. (1967/1971). *What is cinema?* (Vol. 1 & 2, Hugh Gray, Trans. & Ed.). Berkeley: University of California Press.

Bell, T.W. (1998). Fair use versus fared use: The impact of automated rights management on copyright's fair use doctrine. *North Carolina Law Review, 76,* 557–619.

Benesch, S. (2001). *Critical English for academic purposes: Theory, politics, and practice.* Mahwah, NJ: Lawrence Erlbaum Associates.

Benjamin, W. (1936/1968). The work of art in the age of mechanical reproduction. In H. Arendt (Ed.), *I lluminations: Essays and reflections* (pp. 217–252). New York: Harcourt, Brace & World.

Benkler, Y. (2006). *The wealth of networks: How social production transforms markets and freedom.* New Haven, CT: Yale University Press.

Bennett, R. (2005). Factors associated with student plagiarism in a post-1992 university. *Assessment & Evaluation in Higher Education, 30,* 137–162.

Berkenkotter, C. & Huckin, T. (1993). Rethinking genre from a sociological perspective. *Written Communication, 10,* 475–509.

Berkenkotter, C. & Huckin, T. (1995). *Genre knowledge in disciplinary communication: Cognition/culture/power.* Hillsdale, NJ: Lawrence Erlbaum Associates.

Berlin, J.A. (1984). *Writing Instruction in nineteenth-century American colleges.* Carbondale: Southern Illinois University Press.

Berne Convention for the Protection of Literary and Artistic Works (Paris Text 1971). Retrieved December 20, 2011 from http://www.law.cornell.edu/treaties/berne/overview.html

Berners-Lee, T. (1999). *Weaving the Web: The original design and ultimate destiny of the World Wide Web.* New York: Harper Collins.

Biagioli, M. (2003). Rights or rewards?: Changing frameworks of scientific authorship. In P. Galison & M. Biagioli (Eds.), *Scientific authorship: Credit and intellectual property in sciences* (pp. 253–279). New York: Routledge.

Binmore, K.G. (1992a). Foundations of game theory. In J.J. Lafont (Ed.), *Advances in economic theory: Sixth world congress* (pp. 1–31). Cambridge: Cambridge University Press.

Binmore, K.G. (1992b). *Fun and games: A text on game theory.* Lexington, MA: D.C. Heath.

Bledstein, B.J. (1978). *The culture of professionalism: The middle class and the development of higher education in America.* New York: Norton.

Bloch, J. (2001). Plagiarism and the ESL student: From printed to electronic texts. In D. Belcher & A. Hirvela (Eds.), *Linking literacies: Perspectives on L2 reading-writing connections* (pp. 209–228). Ann Arbor: University of Michigan Press.

Bloch, J. (2007a). Abdullah's blogging: A generation 1.5 student enters the blogosphere. *Language, Learning and Technology, 11,* 128–141.

Bloch, J. (2007b). *Technology in the L2 composition classroom.* Ann Arbor: University of Michigan Press.

Bloch, J. (2008a). Plagiarism in a contrastive rhetoric context: How is it evolving? In U. Connor & E. Nagelhout (Eds.), *Contrastive to intercultural rhetoric: Proceedings of the first annual ICIC conference on written discourse and contrastive rhetoric* (pp. 257–274). Amsterdam: John Benjamins Publishing Company.

Bloch, J. (2008b). Plagiarism across cultures: Is there a difference? in C. Eisner & M. Vicinus (Eds.), *Originality, imitation, and plagiarism: Teaching writing in the digital age* (pp. 219–230). Ann Arbor: The University of Michigan Press.

Bloch, J. (2008c). Blogging as a bridge between multiple forms of literacy: The use of blogs in an academic writing class. In D. Belcher & A. Hirvela (Eds.), *Oral/written connections* (pp. 288–309). Ann Arbor: University of Michigan Press.

Bloch, J. (2009). The design of an online concordancing program for teaching about reporting verbs. *Language, Learning, & Technology, 13,* 59–78.

Bloch, J. (2010). A concordance-based study of the use of reporting verbs as rhetorical devices in academic papers. *Journal of Writing Research, 2*, 219–244.

Bloch, J.G. & Chi, L. (1995). A Comparison of the use of citations in Chinese and English academic discourse. In D. Belcher & G. Braine (Eds.), *Academic writing in a second language* (pp. 231–274). Norwood, NJ: Ablex.

Bloch, J. & Crosby, C. (2006). Creating a space for virtual democracy. *Essential Teacher, 3*(3), 38–41.

Blum, S.D. (2009). *My word!: Plagiarism and college culture*. Ithaca, NY: Cornell University Press.

Bolter, J.D. (2001). *Writing space: Computers, hypertext, and the remediation of print* (2nd ed.). Mahwah, NJ: Lawrence Erlbaum Associates.

Boon, M. (2010). *In praise of copying*. Cambridge, MA: Harvard University Press.

Boyle, J. (1996). *Shaman, software, and spleens: Law and the construction of the information society*. Cambridge, MA: Harvard University Press.

Boyle, J. (2010). *The public domain: Enclosing the commons of the mind*. New Haven, CT: Yale University Press.

Brandt, D. (2004). 'Who's the president?': Ghostwriting and shifting values in literacy. *College English, 69*, 549–557.

Brereton, J. (1995). *The origins of composition studies in the American college, 1875–1925: A documentary history*. Pittsburgh, PA: The University of Pittsburgh Press.

Breyer, S. (1970). The uneasy case for copyright: A study of copyright in books. *Harvard Law Review, 84*, 281–355.

Brutt-Griffler, J. (2002). *World English: A study of its development*. Clevedon, UK: Multilingual Matters Press.

Buranen, L. (1999). But I *wasn't* cheating. Plagiarism and the cross-cultural myth. In L. Buranen & A. Roy (Eds.), *Perspectives on plagiarism and intellectual property in a postmodern world* (pp. 63–74). Albany: State University of New York Press.

Caden, M.L. & Lucas, S.E. (1996). Accidents on the information superhighway: On-line liability and regulation. *The Richmond Journal of Law & Technology, 2*. Retrieved from http://law.richmond.edu/jolt/v2i1/caden_lucas.html

Carpenter, D. (n.d.). *Hoovering to Byzantium*. Retrieved January 20, 2010 from http://www.dccarpenter.com/hoovering.htm

Carroll, J. & Appleton J. (2001). *Plagiarism: A good practice guide*. Retrieved June 14, 2011, from http://www.jisc.ac.uk/uploaded_documents/brookes.pdf

Casanave, C.P. (2002). *Writing games: Multicultural case studies of academic literacy practices in higher education*. Mahwah, NJ: Lawrence Erlbaum Associates.

Chandrasoma, R., Thompson, C.M. & Pennycook, A. (2004). Beyond plagiarizing: Transgressive and nontransgressive intertextuality. *Journal of Language, Identity, and Education, 3*, 171–193.

Cheating case hit Asian students hardest. (2007, May 22). *Diverse*. Retrieved July 3, 2008, from http://www.diverseeducation.com/artman/publish/article_7363.shtml

Code of best practices for online video. Center for Social Media. Retrieved June 14, 2011 at http://www.centerforsocialmedia.org/fair-use/related-materials/codes/code-best-practices-fair-use-online-video.

Cohen, J.E. (1998). Lochner in Cyberspace: The new economic orthodoxy of 'rights management'. *Michigan Law Review, 97*. Retrieved February 21, 2011, from http://www.law.georgetown.edu/faculty/jec/lochner.pdf

Coleman, R. & Curry, T. (2010). *Committee on Academic Misconduct (COAM) annual report summer quarter, 2009 – Spring Quarter, 2010*. Retrieved December 20, 2011 at http://oaa.osu.edu/assets/files/coam/annual-report-2010-2011.pdf.

Collins, P.S. (1998). Who's the plagiarist here? Using the Web to reciprocate source disclosure. *ACE Journal, 1*, 46–55.

Connor, U. (2004). Intercultural rhetoric research: Beyond texts. *Journal of English for Academic Purposes, 3*, 291–304.

Couser, G.T. (2009, July 2). Dear plagiarist. *Inside Higher Education*. Retrieved February 19, 2011, from http://www.insidehighered.com/views/2009/07/02/couser

Couzin-Frankel, J. & Grom, J. (2009. May 22). Plagiarism sleuths. *Science, 32*, 1004–1007.

Crane, D. (1972). *Invisible colleges. Diffusion of knowledge in scientific communities*. Chicago: The University of Chicago Press.

Crews, K.D. (2001). The law of fair use and the illusion of fair-use guidelines. *Ohio State Law Journal, 62*, 599–702.

Critical Art Ensemble. *Utopian plagiarism, hypertextuality, and electronic cultural production*. Retrieved July 5, 2011, from http://college.cengage.com/english/amore/demo/ch5_r4.html

Custer, C. (2010, April 13). Wang Hui and plagiarism in Chinese academia. *China Geeks*. Retrieved December 21, 2011, from http://chinageeks.org/2010/04/wang-hui-plagiarism-chinese-academia

Dante, E. (2010, November 12). The shadow scholar. *The Chronicle of Higher Education*. Retrieved December 21, 2011 from http://chinageeks.org/2010/04/wang-hui-plagiarism-chinese-academia/.

Davis, M.D. (1983). *Game theory: A nontechnical introduction*. New York: Basic Books.

Dawkins, R. (1976). *The selfish gene*. Oxford: Oxford University Press.

Deckert, G.D. (1993). Perspectives on plagiarism from ESL students in Hong Kong. *Journal of Second Language Writing, 2*, 131–48.

Dee, T.S. & Jacob, B.A. (2010). *Rational ignorance in education: A field experiment in student plagiarism* (Working Paper 15672). Cambridge, MA: National Bureau of Economic Research. Retrieved January 26, 2010, from http://www.swarthmore.edu/Documents/academics/economics/Dee/w15672.pdf

DeVoss, D.N. & Porter, J.E. (2006). Why Napster matters to writing: Filesharing as a new ethic of digital delivery. *Computers and Composition, 23*, 178–210.

DeVoss, D.N. & Rosati, A.C. (2002). 'It wasn't me, was it?' Plagiarism and the web. *Computers and Composition, 19*, 191–203.

Donahue, C. (2008). When copying is not copying: Plagiarism and French composition scholarship. In C. Eisner & M.V. Vicinus (Eds.), *Originality, imitation, and plagiarism: Teaching writing in the digital age* (pp. 90–103). Ann Arbor: The University of Michigan Press.

Eisenstein, E. (1979). *The printing press as an agent of change: Communications and cultural transformations in early modern Europe*. Cambridge: Cambridge University Press.

Elkin-Noren, N. (1998). Public/private and copyright reform in Cyberspace. *Journal of Computer-Mediated Communication, 2*. Retrieved December 21, 2011 from http://jcmc.indiana.edu/vol2/issue2/elkin.html.

Elliot, N. (2005). On a scale: A social history of writing assessment in America. New York: Peter Lang.

Etter (2008). Message posted to http://www.insidehighered.com/news/2007/05/24/cheating#comment-332226653

Fair use. (2009). *Library of Congress*. Retrieved June 15, 2011, from http://www.copyright. gov/fls/fl102.html

Fearn, H. (2011, January 20). Plagiarism software can be beaten by simple tech tricks. *Times Higher Education*. Retrieved January 23, 2011, from http://www.timeshigher education.co.uk/story.asp?sectioncode = 26&storycode = 414881&c = 1

Feather, J. (1994). From rights to copies to copyright: The recognition of authors' rights in English law and practice in the sixteenth and seventeenth centuries. In M. Woodmansee & P. Jaszi (Eds.), *The Construction of authorship: Textual appropriation in law and literature* (pp.191–208). Durham, NC: Duke University Press.

Fields, A. & Diaz, K. (2008). *Fostering community through digital storytelling : A guide for academic libraries*. Westport, CT: Libraries Unlimited.

Fish, S. *(2010, August 10). Plagiarism is not a big moral deal*. The New York Times. *Retrieved August 10, 2010, from http://opinionator.blogs.nytimes.com/2010/08/09/plagiarism-is-not-a-big-moral-deal*

Fisher, W.W. (1998). *Property and contract on the Internet*. Retrieved February 23, 2011, from http://cyber.law.harvard.edu/propertycourse/resources/98fish.html

Fisher, W.W. (1999). The growth of intellectual property: A history of the ownership of ideas in the United States. In H. Siegrist & D. Sugarman (Eds.), *Eigentum im internationalen Vergleic* (pp. 265–29). Gottesberg, Germany: Vandenhoeck & Ruprecht. Retrieved February 21, 2011, from http://www.lawFread.harvard.edu/Academic_ Affairs/coursepages/tfisher/iphistory.htm

Fisher, W. (2001). Theories of intellectual property. In S. Munzer (Ed.), *New essays in the legal and political theory of property* (pp. 168–200). Cambridge: Cambridge University Press. Retrieved January 20, 2010, from http://cyber.law.harvard.edu/people/tfisher/ iptheory.pdf

Flower, L. (1981). *Problem-Solving strategies for writing*. New York: Harcourt Brace Jovanovich.

Flower, L. & Hayes, D. (1980). The cognition of discovery: Defining a rhetorical problem. *College Composition and Communication*, 31, 21–32.

Flowerdew, J. (1999). Writing for scholarly publication in English: The case of Hong Kong. *Journal of Second Language Writing*, 8, 243–264.

Flowerdew, J. (2001). Attitude of journal editors to nonnative speaker contributions. *TESOL Quarterly, 35*, 121–150.

Foucault, M. (1980) 'What is an author!?.' In D.F. Bouchard & S. Simon Ithaca (Eds.), *Language, counter-memory, practice* (pp. 113–138). New York: Cornell University Press.

Fox, H. (1994). *Listening to the world: Cultural issues in academic writing*. Urbana, IL: NCTE.

Freadman, A. (1994). Anyone for tennis. In P. Medway & A. Freedman (Eds.), *Genre and the new rhetoric* (pp. 43–66). London: Taylor and Francis.

Freiberger, P. & Swaine, M. (2000). *Fire in the valley: The making of the personal computer* (2nd ed.). New York: McGraw-Hill.

Geanakopolis, J. (1993). *Common knowledge*. New Haven, CT: Cowles Foundation.

Gee, J. (2000). The new literacy studies and the social turn. In D. Barton, M. Hamilton & R. Ivanic (Eds.), *Situated literacies: Reading and writing in context* (pp. 180–196). New York: Routledge. Retrieved July 10, 2011, from http://www.schools.ash.org.au/ litweb/page300.html.

Geist, M. (2008). *Eight tech law issues to watch in 2008*. Retrieved February 22, 2011, from http://www.michaelgeist.ca/content/view/2541/135.

Geist, M. (2010, December 15). *Clearing up the copyright confusion: Fair dealing and bill C-32.* Retrieved February 22, 2011, from http://www.michaelgeist.ca/content/view/ 5519/125.

Gere, A.R. (1994). Common properties of pleasure: Texts in the nineteenth century women's clubs. In M. Woodmansee & P. Jaszi (Eds.), *The construction of authorship: Textual appropriation in law and literature* (pp. 382–399). Durham, NC: Duke University Press.

Gladwell, M. (2004, November 22). Something borrowed. *New Yorker.* Retrieved July 6, 2011, from http://www.gladwell.com/2004/2004_11_25_a_borrowed.html.

Gold, D. (2008). *Rhetoric at the margins: Revising the history of writing instruction in American colleges, 1873–1947.* Carbondale: Southern Illinois University Press.

Goldstein, L. (2006). Feedback and revision in second language writing: Contextual, teacher, and student variables. In K. Hyland & F. Hyland (Eds.), *Feedback in second language writing: Contexts and issues* (pp. 185–205). Cambridge: Cambridge University Press.

Graff, H. (1987). *Legacies of literacy: Continuities and contradictions in western culture and society.* Bloomington: Indiana University Press.

Graff, G. (2003). *Clueless in academe: How schooling obscures the life of the mind.* New Haven, CT: Yale University Press.

Green, S.P. (2002). Plagiarism, norms, and the limits of theft law: Some observations on the use of criminal sanctions in enforcing intellectual property rights. *Hastings Law Journal, 54,* 167–242.

Greenberg, D. (2008, August 25). The write stuff? Why Biden's plagiarism shouldn't be forgotten. *Slate.* Retrieved December 21, 2011, http://www.slate.com/articles/ news_and_politics/history_lesson/2008/08/the_write_stuff.html.

Gross, A.G. (2006). *Starring the text: The place of rhetoric in science studies.* Carbondale: Southern Illinois University Press.

Gu, Q. & Brooks, J. (2008). Beyond the accusation of plagiarism. *System, 36,* 337–352.

Haas, H. (2009). *Stop plagiarism.* Retrieved December 9, 2009, from http://www.haas-consulting.com/plagiarism.html

Hall, J. (2005). Plagiarism across the curriculum: How academic communities can meet the challenge of the undocumented writer. *Across the Discipline, 2.* Retrieved September 25, 2005, from http://wac.colostate.edu/atd/articles/hall2005.cfm.

Hallak, J. & Poisson, M. (2007). *Corrupt schools, corrupt universities: What can be done?* Paris: International Institute for Educational Planning. Retrieved November 19, 2007, from unpan1.un.org/intradoc/groups/public/documents/UNESCO/UNPAN025403.pdf.

Halpern, S.W. (2001). The digital threat to the normative role of copyright law. *Ohio State Law Journal, 62,* 569–598.

Hardin, G. (1968). The tragedy of the commons. *Science, 162,* 1243–1248.

Hardy, I.W. (1996). The ancient doctrine of trespass to web sites. *Journal of Online Law, art. 7.* Retrieved Dec 13, 2011 from http://scholarship.law.wm.edu/cgi/viewcontent.cgi? article=2224&context=facpubs.

Harold, C. (2007). *OurSpace: Resisting the corporate control of culture.* Minneapolis: University of Minnesota Press.

Hayes, D.L. (2000). Internet copyright: Advanced copyright issues on the Internet. *Computer Law & Security Report, 16,* 363–377.

Hayes, N. & Introna, L. (2005a). Cultural values, plagiarism, and fairness: When plagiarism gets in the way of learning. *Ethics & Behavior, 15*(3), 213–231.

Hayes, N. &. Introna L.D. (2005b). Plagiarism gets in the way of learning. *Ethics & Behavior, 15*(3), 213–231.

Heaton, N. (2003, April 27). Are your kids cheating? *Cleveland Plain Dealer Sunday Magazine*, 10–15.
Helft, M. (2009, March 24). YouTube blocked in China, Google says. *New York Times*. Retrieved May 30, 2011, from http://www.nytimes.com/2009/03/25/technology/internet/25youtube.html.
Helprin, M. (2009). *Digital barbarism*. New York: Harpers.
Herrington, T.K. (2010). *Intellectual property on campus: Students' rights and responsibilities*. Carbondale: Southern Illinois University Press.
Hess, C. & Ostrum, E. (2006). Introduction: An overview of the knowledge commons. In C. Hess & E. Ostrum (Eds.), *Understanding knowledge as a commons* (pp. 3–26). Cambridge: MIT Press.
Hopper, P. (1987). Emergent grammar. *Berkeley Linguistics Society, 13*, 139–157.
Howard, R.M. (1999a). *Standing in the shadow of giants: Plagiarists, authors, collaborators*. Stamford, CT: Ablex.
Howard, R.M. (1999b). The new abolitionism comes to plagiarism. In L. Buranen & A.M. Roy (Eds.), *Perspectives on plagiarism and intellectual property in a postmodern world* (pp. 87–95). Albany: State University of New York.
Howard, R.M. (2001, November 16). Forget about policing plagiarism. Just teach. *The Chronicle of Higher Education*. Retrieved October 6, 2010, from http://chronicle.com/article/Forget-About-Policing-Plagi/2792.
Howard, R.M. (2007). Understanding 'Internet plagiarism'. *Computers and Composition, 24*, 3–15.
Howard, R.M., Serviss, T. & Rodrigue, T.K. (2010). Writing from sources, writing from sentences. *Writing and Pedagogy*, 177–192.
Hull, G.A. & Nelson, M.E. (2005). Locating the semiotic power of multimodality. *Written Communication, 22*, 224–261.
Hull, G. & Rose, M. (1989). Rethinking remediation: Toward a social-cognitive understanding of problematic reading and writing. *Written Communication, 6*, 139–154.
Hyde, L. (2010). *Common as air: Revolution, art, and ownership*. New York: Farrar, Straus and Giroux.
Hyland, K. (2000a). *Disciplinary discourses: Social interactions in academic writing*. Harlow, UK: Longman.
Hyland, K. (2000b). Boosting, hedging, and the negotiation of academic knowledge. *Language Awareness, 9*, 179–197.
Hyland, K. (2002). Activity and evaluation: Reporting practices in academic writing. In J. Flowerdew (Ed.), *Academic discourse* (pp. 115–130). Harlow, UK: Longman.
Hyland, K. (2008). As can be seen: Lexical bundles and disciplinary variation. *English for Specific Purposes, 1*, 4–21.
Hyland, K. & Hyland, F. (2006). Interpersonal aspects of response: Constructing and interpreting teacher written feedback. In K. Hyland & F. Hyland (Eds.), *Contexts in second language writing: Contexts and issues* (pp. 206–224). Cambridge: Cambridge University Press.
Introna, L., Hayes, N., Blair, L. & Wood, E. (2003). *Cultural attitudes towards plagiarism: Developing a better understanding of the needs of students from diverse cultural backgrounds relating to issues of plagiarism*. Retrieved September 4, 2010, from http://sites.google.com/site/lucasintrona/home/reports.
Ito, M. & Horst, H.A. (2010). *Hanging out, messing around, and geeking out: Kids living and learning with new media*. Cambridge: MIT Press.

Ivanic, R. (1998). *Writing and identity: The discoursal construction of identity in academic writing.* Amsterdam: John Benjamins.

Jaquith, W. (2009). Chris Anderson's free contains apparent plagiarism. *Virginia Quarterly Review.* Retrieved June 28, 2009, from http://www.vqronline.org/blog/2009/06/23/chris-anderson-free.

Jascik, S. (2008, November 13). Vigilante justice on plagiarism. *Inside Higher Education.* Retrieved November 20, 2008, from http://www.insidehighered.com/news/2008/11/13/tamiu

Jascik, S. (2009, February 3). It's culture, not morality. *Inside Higher Education.* Retrieved February 22, 2011, from http://www.insidehighered.com/news/2009/02/03/myword.

Jaszi, P. (1994). On the author effect: Contemporary copyright and collective creativity. In M. Woodmansee & P. Jaszi (Eds.), *The construction of authorship: Textual appropriation in law and literature* (pp. 29–56). Durham, NC: Duke University Press.

Jaszi, P. & Woodmansee, M. (1994). Introduction. In M. Woodmansee & P. Jaszi (Eds.), *The construction of authorship: Textual appropriation in law and literature* (pp. 1–13). Durham, NC: Duke University Press.

Jellife, R. (1956). *Faulkner at Nagano.* Tokyo: Kenkyusha.

Johns, T. (1994). From printout to handout: Grammar and vocabulary teaching in the context of data-driven learning. In T. Odlin (Ed.), *Perspectives of pedagogical grammar* (pp. 293–313). Cambridge: Cambridge University Press.

Johns, A. (1998). *The nature of the book: Print and knowledge in the making.* Chicago: The University of Chicago Press.

Johns, A. (2010). *Piracy: The intellectual property wars from Gutenberg to Gates.* Chicago: University Of Chicago Press.

Johnson-Eilola, J. & Selber, S.A. (2007) Plagiarism, originality, assemblage. *Computers and Composition, 24,* 275–403.

Kaplan, R.B. (1966). Cultural thought patterns in intercultural education. *Language Learning, 16,* 1–20.

Keen, A. (2010, May 26). Hunger artists. *BarnesandNoblereview.com.* Retrieved May 17, 2011, from http://bnreview.barnesandnoble.com/t5/Public-and-Private/Hunger-Artists/ba-p/2680.

Kerkvliet, J. & Sigmund, C.L. (1999). Can we control cheating in the classroom? *Journal of Economic Education, 4,* 331–343.

Koch, A. & Peden, W. (1944). *The life and selected letters of Thomas Jefferson.* New York: Random House.

Kolko, B.E. (1998). Intellectual property in synchronic and collaborative virtual space. *Computers and Composition, 15,* 163–183.

Kolowich, S. (2009, October 6). Course hero or course villain? *Inside Higher Education.* Retrieved October 5, 2009, from http://www.insidehighered.com/news/2009/10/06/coursehero.

Kolowich, S. (2010, February 15). frustration over 'framing'. *Inside Higher Education.* Retrieved February 21, 2011, from http://www.insidehighered.com/news/2010/02/15/framing.

Kopleson, K. (2008). Diary. *London Review of Books, 30*(10), 30–31. Retrieved December 9, 2009, from http://www.lrb.co.uk/v30/n10/kevin-kopelson/diaryhttp://www.lrb.co.uk/v30/n10/kevin-kopelson/diary

Kress, G. (2003). *Literacy in the new media age.* London: Routledge.

Kubota, R. (1998). An investigation of L1–L2 transfer in writing among Japanese university students: Implications for contrastive rhetoric. *Journal of Second Language Writing, 7,* 69–100.

LaFollette, M.C. (1992). *Stealing into print: Fraud, plagiarism, and misconduct in scientific publishing.* Los Angeles: University of California Press.

Lakoff, G. (2004). *Don't think of an elephant: Know your values and frame the debate.* White River Junction, VT: Chelsea Green Publishing.

Lakoff, G. & Johnson, M. (1980). *Metaphors we live by.* Chicago: The University of Chicago Press.

Lambert, J. (2010). *Digital storytelling: Capturing lives, creating community* (3rd ed.). Berkeley, CA: Center for the Study of Digital Storytelling.

Latour, B. (1988). *Science in action.* Cambridge, MA: Harvard University Press.

Lea, M. & Street, B.V. (1998). Student writing and staff feedback in higher education: An academic literacies approach. *Studies in Higher Education, 23,* 157–172.

Lea, M. & Street, B.V. (2006). The 'academic literacies' model: Theory and applications. *Theory into Practice, 45,* 368–377.

Lederman, D. (2006, June 1). Student plagiarism, faculty responsibility. *Inside Higher Education.* Retrieved January 16, 2006, from http://www.insidehighered.com/news/2006/06/01/plagiarism.

Leight, D. (1999). Plagiarism as metaphor. In L. Buranen & A. Roy (Eds.), *Perspectives on plagiarism and intellectual property in a postmodern world* (pp. 221–229). Albany: State University of New York Press.

Lemley, M.A. (1995). Rights of attribution and integrity in online communications. *Journal of Online Law, art. 2.* Retrieved December 21, 2011 from http://web.archive.org/web/20060911004958/http://www.wm.edu/law/publications/jol/95_96/lemley.html.

Lessing, L. (2002). *The future of ideas: The fate of the commons in a connected world.* New York: Vintage Books.

Lessing, L. (2004). *Free culture: How big media uses technology and the law to lock down culture and control creativity.* New York: Penguin.

Lessing, L. (2009a). *Remix: Making art and commerce thrive in the hybrid economy.* New York: Penguin.

Lessing, L. (2009b, February 26). *Remix: Steven Johnson, Lawrence Lessing and Shepard Fairey.* New York: New York Public Library. Retrieved October 18, 2010, from *http://fora.tv/2009/02/26/Remix_Steven_Johnson_Lawrence_Lessig_and_Shepard_Fairey#fullprogram.*

Lethem, J. (2007, February). The ecstasy of influence: A plagiarism. *Harper's,* 59–71. Retrieved February 22, 2011, from http://www.harpers.org/archive/2007/02/0081387.

Levine, (2001). What we are learning about academic integrity. *About Campus, 6*(1), 9–16.

Li, X. & Xiong, L. (1996). Chinese researchers debate rash of plagiarism cases. *Science, 274,* 337–338.

Lillis, T. & Curry, M.J. (2010). *Academic writing in a global context: The politics and practices of publishing in English.* London: Routledge.

Limitations on exclusive rights: Fair use. Ithaca, NY: Cornell University Law School. Retrieved February 23, 2011, from http://www.law.cornell.edu/uscode/17/107.html.

Link, P. (1981). *Mandarin ducks and butterflies: Popular fiction in early twentieth-century Chinese cities.* Berkeley: The University of California Press.

Litman, J. (2001). *Digital copyright.* Amherst, NY: Prometheus Books.

Litman, J. (2008). Choosing metaphors. In C. Eisner & M.V. Vicinius (Eds.), *Originality, imitation, and plagiarism: Teaching writing in the digital age* (pp. 13–26). Ann Arbor: The University of Michigan Press.

Lodhi, A. (2010, April 18). Country suffering from absence of research culture. *Daily Times.* Retrieved February 24, 2011, from http://www.dailytimes.com.pk/default.asp?page = 2010%5C04%5C18%5Cstory_18-4-2010_pg13_6.

Long, T.C., Errami, E., George, A.C., Sun, Z. & Garner, H.R. (2009, March 6). Responding to possible plagiarism, *Science, 323*(1293). Retrieved March 16, 2009, from www.sciencemag.org/cgi/content/full/323/5919/1293/DC1.

Lukács, G. (1983). *The historical novel* (H. Mitchell & S. Mitchell, Trans.) Lincoln: University of Nebraska Press.

Lunsford, A.A. & Ede, L. (1994). Collaborative authorship and the teaching of writing. In M. Woodmansee & P. Jaszi (Eds.), *The construction of authorship: Textual appropriation in law and literature* (pp. 417–438). Durham, NC: Duke University Press.

Mallon, T. (1989). *Stolen words*. New York: Penguin Books.

Marsden, H., Carroll, M. & Neill, J.T. (2005). Who cheats at university? A self-report study of dishonest academic behaviour in a sample of Australian university students. *Australian Journal of Psychology, 57*, 1–10.

Marsh, B. (2004). Turnitin.com and the scriptural enterprise of plagiarism detection. *Computers and Composition, 21*, 427–438.

Marsh, B. (2007). *Plagiarism: Alchemy and remedy in higher education*. Albany: SUNY Press.

Matalene, C. (1985). Contrastive rhetoric: An American writing teacher in China. *College English, 47*, 789–808.

McCabe, D.L. (1999). Academic dishonesty among high school students. *Adolescence, 34*, 681–689.

McCabe, D.L., Treviño, L.K. & Butterfield, K.D. (2001). Cheating in academic institutions: A decade of research. *Ethics and Behavior, 11*, 219–232.

Merges, R.P., Menell, P.S., Lemley, M.A. & Jorde, T.M. (1997). *Intellectual property in the new technological age*. Rockwell, MD: Aspen Publishing.

Merton, R.K. (1973). The normative structure of science. In N.W. Storer (Ed.), *The sociology of science: Theoretical and empirical investigations* (pp. 267–280). Chicago: University of Chicago Press.

Metz, C. (1974). *Film language: A semiotics of the cinema* (M.W. Taylor, Trans.). Chicago: University of Chicago Press.

Miller, C.R. (1984). Genre as social action. *Quarterly Journal of Speech, 70 ,* 151–167.

New London Group. (1996). A pedagogy of multiliteracies: Designing social futures. *Harvard Educational Review, 66*, 60–93.

Nimmer, J. (2003). 'Fairest of them all' and other fairy tales of fair use. *Law & Contemporary Problems, 66*, 263–287.

Okediji, R. (2001). Givers, takers and other kinds of users: A fair use doctrine for Cyberspace. *Florida Law Review, 53*, 107–182.

Ong, W.J. (1982). *Orality and literacy: The technologizing of the word*. London: Methuen.

Oppenheim, C. (1996, December 21). Copyright battles: The Shetlands. *Ariadne*. Retrieved May 13, 2011, from http://www.ariadne.ac.uk/issue6/copyright.

Ostrum, E. (1990). *Governing the commons: The evolution of institutions for collective action*. New York: Cambridge University Press.

Palfrey, J. & Gasser, U. (2008). *Born digital: Understanding the first generation of digital natives*. New York: Basic Books.

Parry, M. (2011, July 21). NYU Prof vows never to probe cheating again – and faces a backlash. *The Chronicle of Higher Education*. Retrieved July 24, 2011, from http://chronicle.com/blogs/wiredcampus/nyu-prof-vows-never-to-probe-cheating-again%E2%80%94and-faces-a-backlash/32351?sid = at#comment-260289457

Patry, J. (2009). *Moral panic and the copyright wars*. New York: Oxford University Press.

Paul, R.A. (2009). A.V. V. IPARADIGMS, LLC. *The Judicial Review.* Retrieved September 3, 2010, from http://www.judicialview.com/Law-Review/Copyright/A.V.-v.-iParadigms-LLC/562-F.3D-630-4th-Cir.-2009/55/8537.

Pecorari, D. (2001). Plagiarism and international students: How the English-speaking University responds. In D. Belcher & A. Hirvela (Eds.), *Linking literacies: Perspectives on L2 reading-writing connections* (pp. 229–245). Ann Arbor: The University of Michigan Press.

Pecorari, D. (2003). Good and original: Plagiarism and patchwriting in academic second-language writing. *Journal of Second Language Writing, 12* , 317–345.

Pecorari, D. (2008). *Academic writing and plagiarism: A linguistic analysis.* London: Continuum.

Pecorari, D. & Shaw, P. (2010). *University teachers discussing plagiarism: Divided perspectives on teaching writing and shaping a culture of honesty.* Paper presented at the 4th International Conference, Newcastle. Retrieved June 12, 2011, from http://www.plagiarismadvice.org/documents/conference2010/papers/4IPC_0032_final.pdf.

Pennycook, A. (1996). Borrowing others' words: Text, ownership, memory, and plagiarism. *TESOL Quarterly, 30,* 201–230.

Pennycook, A. (2001). *Critical applied linguistics: A critical introduction.* Mahwah, NJ: Lawrence Erlbaum Associates.

Peterson, J.D. & Gregor, J.L. (2011). Copycat: Plagiarism, copyright infringement, & lawyers. *Wisconsin Lawyer, 84.* Retrieved June 20, 2011, from http://www.wisbar.org/AM/Template.cfm?Section = Wisconsin_Lawyer&template = /CM/ContentDisplay.cfm&contentid = 102960.

Petric, B. (2007). Rhetorical functions of citations in high- and low-rated master's theses. *Journal of English for Academic Purposes, 6,* 238–253.

Phillipson, R. (1992). *Linguistic imperialism.* Oxford: Oxford University Press.

Posner R.A. (2007). *The little book of plagiarism.* New York: Pantheon Books.

Post, D.G. (2009). *In search of Jefferson's moose: Notes on the state of Cyberspace.* Oxford: Oxford University Press.

Prensky, M. (2001). Digital natives, digital immigrants, Part 1. *On the Horizon, 9,* 1–6.

Price, M. (2002). Beyond 'Gotcha!' Situating plagiarism in policy and pedagogy. *College Composition and Communication, 54,* 88–115.

Price, M.E. & Pollack, M. (1994). The author in copyright: Notes for the literary critic. In M. Woodmansee & P. Jaszi (Eds.), *The construction of authorship: Textual appropriation in law and literature* (pp. 439–456). Durham, NC: Duke University Press.

Prior, P. (2005). Moving multimodality beyond the binaries: A response to Gunther Kress' 'Gains and Losses'. *Computers and Composition, 22,* 23–30.

Purdy, J.P. (2005). Calling off the hounds: Technology and the visibility of plagiarism *pedagogy, 5,* 275–296.

Ralli, T. (2005). Software strives to spot plagiarism before publication. *New York Times.* Retrieved December 6, 2009, from http://www.nytimes.com/2005/09/05/technology/05plagiarism.html?scp = 5&sq = John + Barrie&st = nyt.

Rampell, C. (2008, April 25). Journals may soon use anti-plagiarism software on their authors. *The Chronicle of Higher Education, 54* (33), A17.

Raymond, E. (1998). *The cathedral & the bazaar: Musings on Linux and Open Source by an accidental revolutionary.* Retrieved May 14, 2011, from http://www.redhat.com/support/wpapers/community/cathedral/whitepaper_cathedral.html.

Read, B. (2008, February 29). Anti-cheating crusader vexes some professors. *The Chronicle of Higher Education, 54* (25), A1. Retrieved July 3, 2008, from http://chronicle.com/weekly/v54/i25/25a00101.htm.

Redden, E. (2007, May 24). Cheating across cultures. *Inside Higher Education.* Retrieved June 25, 2007, from http://www.insidehighered.com/news/2007/05/24/cheating.

Reyman J. (2010). *The rhetoric of intellectual property: Copyright law and the regulation of digital culture.* New York: Routledge.

Ritter, K. (2005). The economics of authorship: Online paper mills, student writers, and first-year composition. *College Composition and Communication, 56,* 601–631.

Robillard, A.E. (2008). Situating plagiarism as a form of authorship: The politics of writing in a first-year writing course. In R. Howard & A. Robillard (Eds.), *Pluralizing plagiarism: Identities, contexts, pedagogies* (pp. 27–42). Portsmouth, UK: Boynton/Cook.

Roig, M. (2001). Plagiarism and paraphrasing criteria of college and university professors. *Ethics and Behavior, 11,* 307–323.

Rose, M. (1983). Remedial writing courses: A critique and a proposal. *College English, 45,* 109–128.

Rose, M. (1989). *Lives on the boundary: A moving account of the struggles and achievements of America's educational underclass.* New York: Penguin Books.

Rose. M. (1993). *Authors and owners: The invention of copyright.* Cambridge, MA: Harvard University Press.

Rose, M. (1994). The author in court: *Pope vs. Curl.* In M. Woodmansee & P. Jaszi (Eds.), *The construction of authorship: Textual appropriation in law and literature* (211–230). Durham, NC: Duke University Press.

Rosenthal, J. (2011). *No such thing as a free sample? Media Berkman.* Retrieved May 4, 2011, from http://blogs.law.harvard.edu/mediaberkman/2011/04/25/radio-berkman-180-no-such-thing-as-a-free-sample-rethinking-music-vi.

Roy, A. (1999). Whose words there are I think I know: Plagiarism, the postmodern, and faculty attitudes. In L. Buranen & A.M. Roy (Eds.), *Perspectives on plagiarism and intellectual property in a postmodern world* (pp. 55–62). Albany: State University of New York.

Russell, D.R. (1991). *Writing in the academic disciplines, 1870–1990.* Carbondale, IL: Southern University Press.

Sakita, T.I. (2002). *Reporting discourse, tense, and cognition.* Amsterdam: Elsevier.

Samuelson, P. (1999). Intellectual property and the digital economy: Why the anti-circumvention regulations need to be revised. *Berkeley Technology Law Journal, 14,* 519–566. Retrieved August 16, 2010, from http://people.ischool.berkeley.edu/~pam/papers/Samuelson_IP_dig_eco_htm.htm

Sapp, D.A. (2002). Towards an international and intercultural understanding of plagiarism and dishonesty in composition: Reflections from the People's Republic of China. *Issues in Writing, 13,* 58–79.

Scanlon, P.M. (2007). Song from myself: An anatomy of self-plagiarism. *Plagiary, 2,* 1–11. Retrieved December 21, 2011, from http://quod.lib.umich.edu/p/plag/5240451.0002.007?rgn=main;view=fulltext.

Schrimsher, R.H., Northrup, L.A. & Alverson, S.P. (2011). A survey of Stamford University students regarding plagiarism and academic misconduct. *International Journal for Educational Integrity, 7,* 3–17. Retrieved July 4, 2011, from http://www.ojs.unisa.edu.au/index.php/IJEI/article/viewFile/740/552.

Schuetze, C.F. (2011, April 24). *The whiff of plagiarism again hits German elite*. Retrieved December 21, 2011, from http://www.nytimes.com/2011/04/25/education/25iht-educside.html.

Scollon, R. (1995). Plagiarism and ideology: Identity in intercultural discourse. *Language and Society, 24*, 16–28.

Selwyn, N. (2008). 'Not necessarily a bad thing …': A study of online plagiarism amongst undergraduate student. *Assessment & Evaluation in Higher Education, 33*, 465–479.

SEPLAN '09 Workshop. (2009). *Uncovering plagiarism, authorship, and social software misuse*. Retrieved December 4, 2009, from http://www.webis.de/pan-09/competition.php

Shea, D. (2010, April 13). Gerald Posner resigns from Daily Beast over plagiarism scandal. *Huffington Post*. Retrieved February 22, 2011, from http://www.huffingtonpost.com/2010/02/11/gerald-posner-resigns-fro_n_458169.html.

Shi, L. (2004). Textual borrowing in second-language writing. *Written Communication, 21*, 171–200.

Shi, L. (2006). Cultural backgrounds and textual appropriation. *Language Awareness, 15*, 264–282.

Shirky, C. (2008). *Here comes everybody: The power of organizing without organizations*. New York: Penguin.

Sinor, J. (2008, August 8). When a syllabus is not your own. *The Chronicle of Higher Education*. Retrieved December 27, 2008, from http://chronicle.com/jobs/news/2008/08/2008080801c.htm.

Stanley, K. (2002). Perspectives on plagiarism in the ESL/EFL classroom. *TESL-EJ, 6*. Retrieved August 15, 2004, from http://www-writing.berkeley.edu/TESL-EJ/ej23/f1.html.

Street. B. (1996). Academic literacies. In D. Baer, C. Fox & J. Clay (Eds.), *Challenging ways of knowing in maths, science, and English* (pp. 101–134). London: Falmer Press.

Sugden, J. (2008, October 31). Half of Cambridge students admit cheating, *Times Online*. Retrieved July 4, 2011, from http://www.timesonline.co.uk/tol/life_and_style/education/student/article5054310.ece

Sunderland-Smith, W. (2008). *Plagiarism, the Internet and student learning: Improving academic integrity*. New York: Routledge.

Sunderland-Smith, W. & Pecorari, D. (2010). *Policy and practice in two academic settings: How the administrative structures of Australian and Swedish universities serve a culture of honesty?* Paper presented at the 4th International Conference, Newcastle. Retrieved June 12, 2011, from http://www.plagiarismadvice.org/documents/conference2010/papers/4IPC_0037_final.pdf.

Surowiecki, J. (2005). *The wisdom of crowds*. New York: Anchor.

Swales, J. (1990). *Genre analysis: English in academic and research settings*. Cambridge: Cambridge University Press.

Swales, J.M. & Feak, C.B. (2004). *Academic writing for graduate students* (2nd ed.). Ann Arbor: University of Michigan Press.

Szabo, A. & Underwood, J. (2004). Cybercheats: Is information and communication technology fuelling academic dishonest? *Active Learning in Higher Education, 5*, 180–199.

Tardy, C.M. (2009). *Building genre knowledge*. Anderson, SC: Parlor Press.

The electronic disturbance. (n.d.) *Critical Art Ensemble*. Retrieved July 20, 2011, from http://www.spunk.org/library/pubs/autonomd/sp000914.txt.

The ethics of American youth. (2008). Josephson Institute. Retrieved July 4, 2011, from http://charactercounts.org/programs/reportcard/

The Free Network homepage. Retrieved February 23, 2011, from http://freenet.sourceforge.net.

The Working Group on Intellectual Property Rights. (1994). *Intellectual property and the national information infrastructure.* Retrieved January 20, 2010, from http://www.uspto.gov/web/offices/com/doc/ipnii/lawcopy.pdf.

Tong, Q.S. (2008). Between knowledge and 'plagiarism', or how the Chinese language was studied in the West. *System, 30,* 499–511.

Uniform requirements for manuscripts submitted to biomedical journals: Writing and editing for biomedical publication. (2010). *The International Committee of Medical Journal Editors.* Retrieved January 27, 2010, from http://www.icmje.org/urm_full.pdf.

Vaidhyanathan, S. (2001). *Copyrights and copywrongs: The rise of intellectual property and how it threatens creativity.* New York: New York University Press.

van Sant, G. (Director). (2000). *Finding Forrester* [Motion picture]. Los Angeles: Columbia/Tri-Star.

Veysey, L.R. (1965). *The emergence of the American university.* Chicago: The University of Chicago Press.

Volokh, E. (2011). Judge copies most of his decision from a party's briefs – why is that wrong? *Volokh Conspiracy.* Retrieved June 14, 2011, from http://volokh.com/2011/04/15/judge-copies-most-of-his-decision-from-a-partys-briefs-why-is-that-wrong

von Neumann, J. (1953). *Theory of games and economic behavior.* Princeton, NJ: Princeton University Press.

Weber-Wulff, D. (2008, May 1). If you go looking, you will find. *Copy, shake, and paste: A blog about plagiarism from a German professor.* Retrieved December 9, 2009, from http://copy-shake-paste.blogspot.com/2008/05/if-you-go-looking-you-will-find.html

Weber-Wulff, D. (2010, January 7). Results of the plagiarism detection software test 2010. *Copy, Shake, and Paste: A blog about plagiarism from a German professor.* Retrieved December 21, 2011, from http://plagiat.htw-berlin.de/software-en/2010-2.

Weber-Wulff, D. (2011, May 8). *Zu Guttenberg plagiarized on purpose.* Retrieved December 21, 2011, from http://copy-shake-paste.blogspot.com/2011/05/zu-guttenberg-plagiarized-on-purpose.html.

Wegner, E. (1999). *Communities of practice: Learning, meaning and identity.* Cambridge: Cambridge University Press.

Weinberger, D. (2003). *Small pieces loosely joined: A unified theory of the web.* Cambridge, MA: Perseus Books Group.

Wesch, M. (2007). A vision of students today [motion picture]. *You Tube.* Retrieved February 19, 2011, from http://www.youtube.com/watch?v=dGCJ46vyR9o.

'What is Copyleft?' (1999). Retrieved February 24, 2011, from http://www.gnu.org/copyleft.

White paper: The effectiveness of Turnitin.com. (2010). Oakland, CA: Iparadigms. Retrieved January 25, 2011, from https://api.turnitin.com/static/resources/documentation/turnitin/company/Turnitin_Whitepaper_on_Effectiveness_hires.pdf.

Wiley, D. (2001). Connecting learning objects to instructional design theory: A definition, a metaphor, and a taxonomy. In D. Wiley (Ed.), *The instructional uses of learning objects* (online version). Retrieved December 2, 2008, from http://reusability.org/read.

Williams, S. (2002). *Free as in freedom: Richard Stallman's crusade for free software.* North Sebastopol, CA: O'Reilly.

Wong, S. (2009, August 22). No stopping China's cheaters. *Asia Times*. Retrieved February 22, 2011, from http://www.atimes.com/atimes/China/KH22Ad01.html.

Woodmansee, M. (1984). The genius and the copyright: Economic and legal conditions of the emergence of the author. *Eighteenth-Century Studies, 17*, 425–448.

Woodmansee, M. (1994). On the author effect: Recovering collectivity. In M. Woodmansee & P. Jaszi (Eds.), *The construction of authorship: Textual appropriation in law and literature* (pp. 15–28). Durham, NC: Duke University Press.

Woodmansee, M. & Jaszi, P. (1995). The law of texts: Copyright in the academy. *College English, 57*, 769–778.

Wueste, D. (2008, March 31). Response to UTSA honor code controversy: Letter to *USA Today*. *Center for Academic Integrity*. Retrieved June 7, 2011, from http://www.academicintegrity.org/news_and_notes/USA_LtrToEd.php.

Young, J.R. (2011, June 11). Academic publisher steps up efforts to stop piracy of its online products. *The Chronicle of Higher Education*. Retrieved June 27, 2011, from http://chronicle.com/article/Academic-Publisher-Steps-Up/128031/?sid = at&utm_source = at&utm_medium = en

Zittrain, J. (2008). *The future of the Internet – and how to stop it*. New Haven, CT: Yale University Press.